Miss Kobayashi's
Dragon Maid
Kanna's Daily Life

story & art by
Mitsuhiro Kimura

original story by
Coolkyousinnjya

Miss Kobayashi's
Dragon maid
Kanna's Daily Life

KANNA'S MORNING

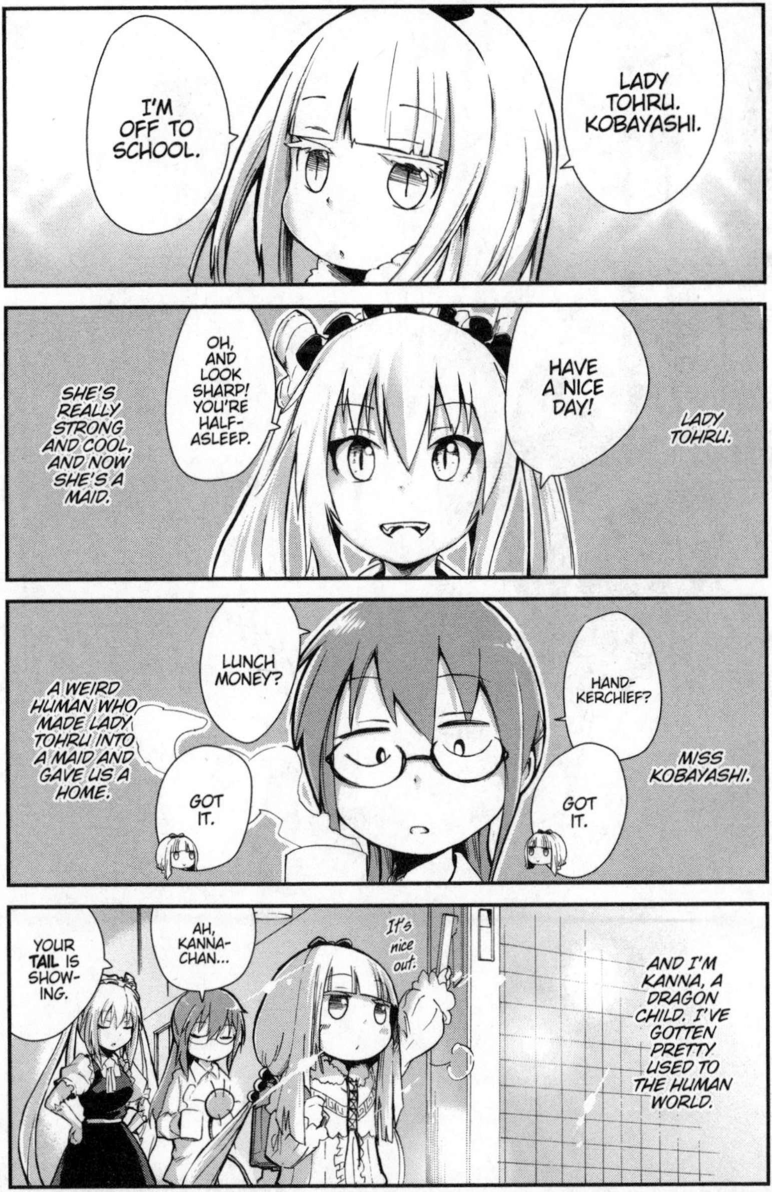
LADY TOHRU. KOBAYASHI.
I'M OFF TO SCHOOL.
LADY TOHRU.
HAVE A NICE DAY!
OH, AND LOOK SHARP! YOU'RE HALF-ASLEEP.
SHE'S REALLY STRONG AND COOL, AND NOW SHE'S A MAID.
MISS KOBAYASHI.
HAND-KERCHIEF?
GOT IT.
LUNCH MONEY?
GOT IT.
A WEIRD HUMAN WHO MADE LADY TOHRU INTO A MAID AND GAVE US A HOME.
AND I'M KANNA, A DRAGON CHILD. I'VE GOTTEN PRETTY USED TO THE HUMAN WORLD.
It's nice out.
AH, KANNA-CHAN...
YOUR TAIL IS SHOWING.

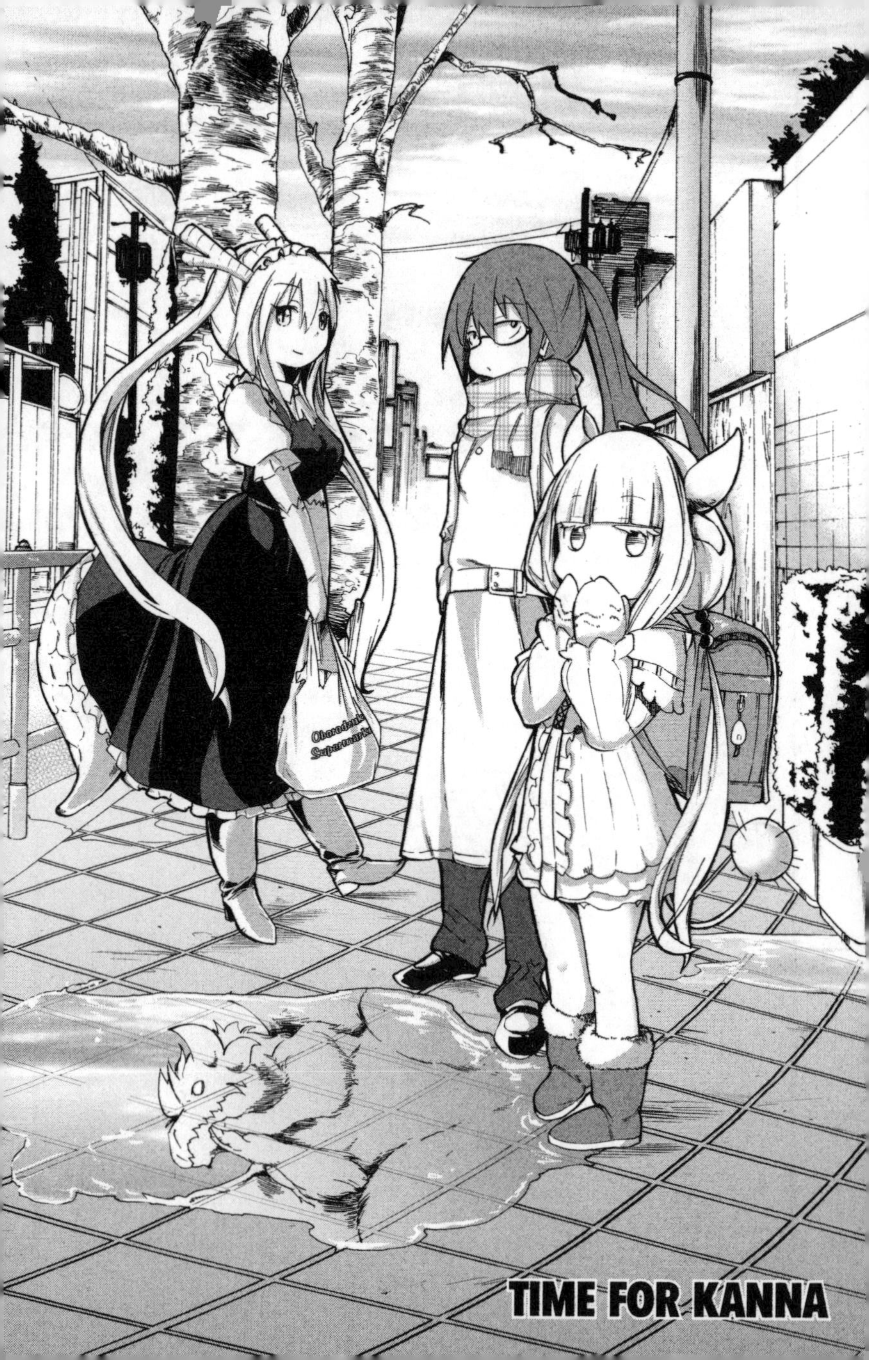

TIME FOR KANNA

KANNA AND SAIKAWA

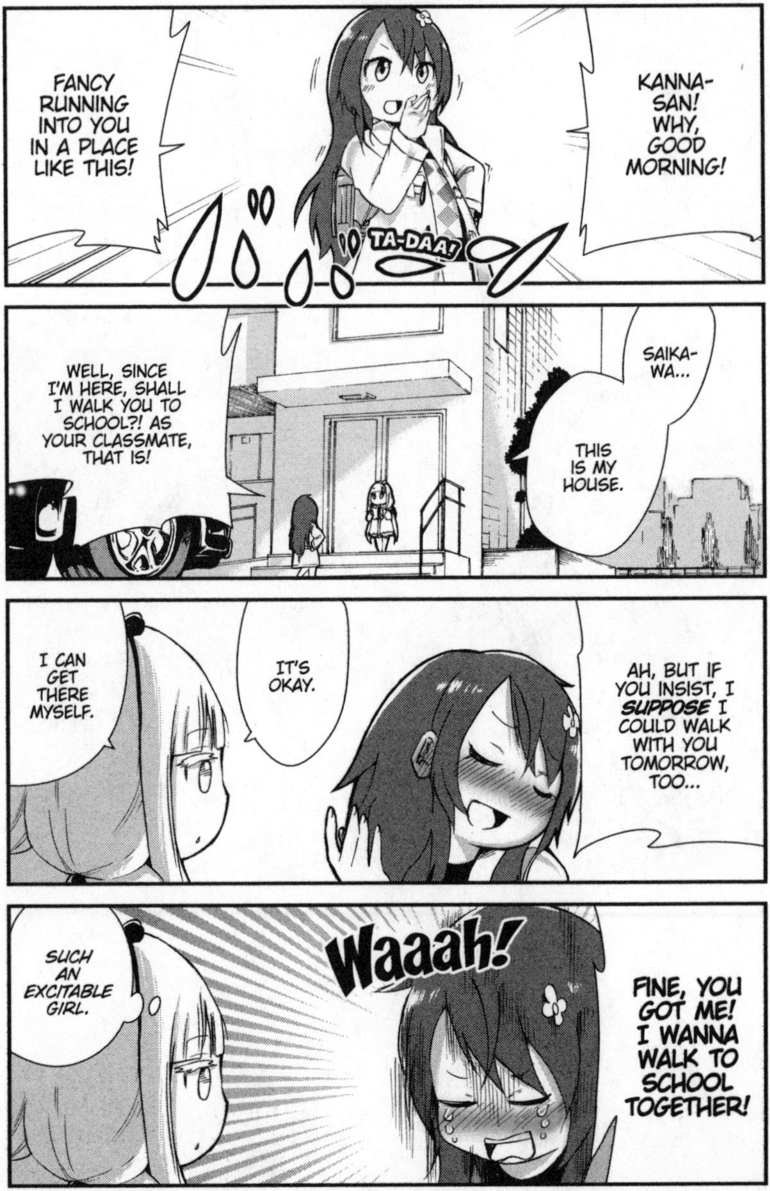
KANNA-SAN! WHY, GOOD MORNING!
TA-DAA!
FANCY RUNNING INTO YOU IN A PLACE LIKE THIS!
SAIKAWA...
THIS IS MY HOUSE.
WELL, SINCE I'M HERE, SHALL I WALK YOU TO SCHOOL?! AS YOUR CLASSMATE, THAT IS!
AH, BUT IF YOU INSIST, I *SUPPOSE* I COULD WALK WITH YOU TOMORROW, TOO...
IT'S OKAY.
I CAN GET THERE MYSELF.
FINE, YOU GOT ME! I WANNA WALK TO SCHOOL TOGETHER!
Waaah!
SUCH AN EXCITABLE GIRL.

KANNA-CHAN DOESN'T GET EXCITED

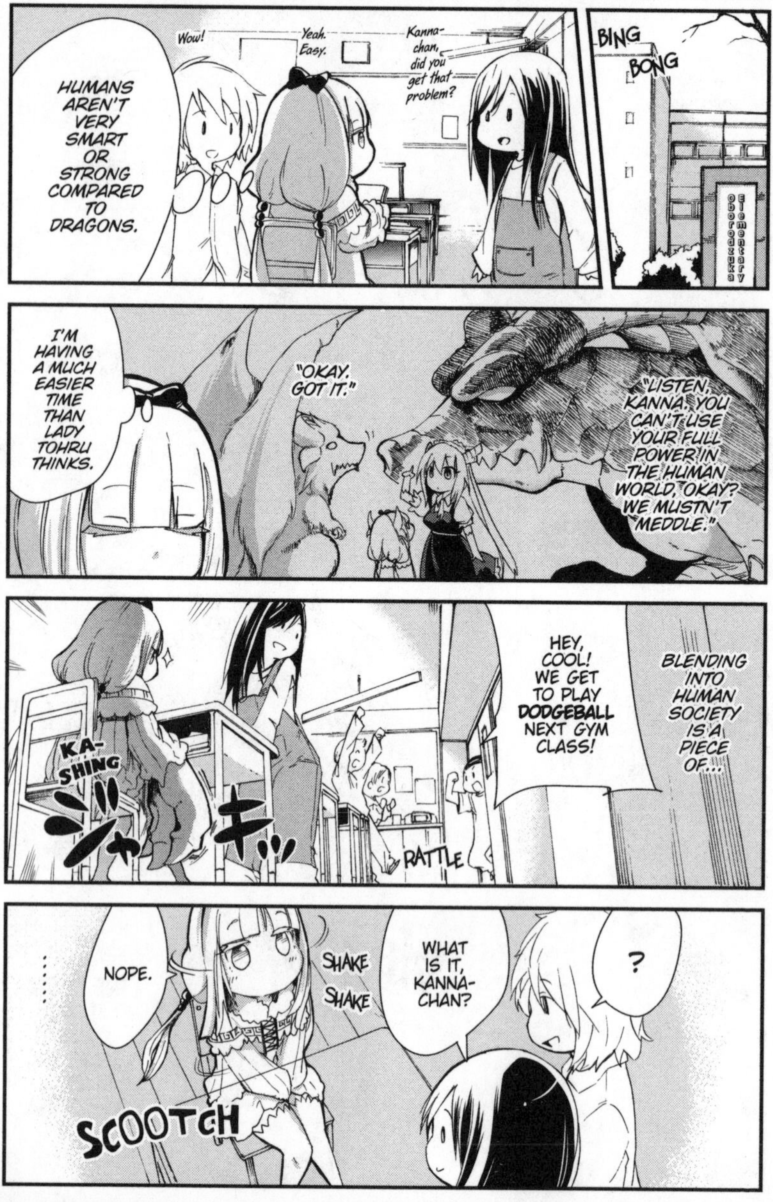
BING
BONG
oborodzuka Elementary
Kanna-chan, did you get that problem?
Yeah. Easy.
Wow!
HUMANS AREN'T VERY SMART OR STRONG COMPARED TO DRAGONS.
"LISTEN, KANNA. YOU CAN'T USE YOUR FULL POWER IN THE HUMAN WORLD, OKAY? WE MUSTN'T MEDDLE."
"OKAY. GOT IT."
I'M HAVING A MUCH EASIER TIME THAN LADY TOHRU THINKS.
BLENDING INTO HUMAN SOCIETY IS A PIECE OF...
HEY, COOL! WE GET TO PLAY **DODGEBALL** NEXT GYM CLASS!
RATTLE
KA-SHING
?
WHAT IS IT, KANNA-CHAN?
SHAKE
SHAKE
NOPE.
......
SCOOTCH

CLASS PET

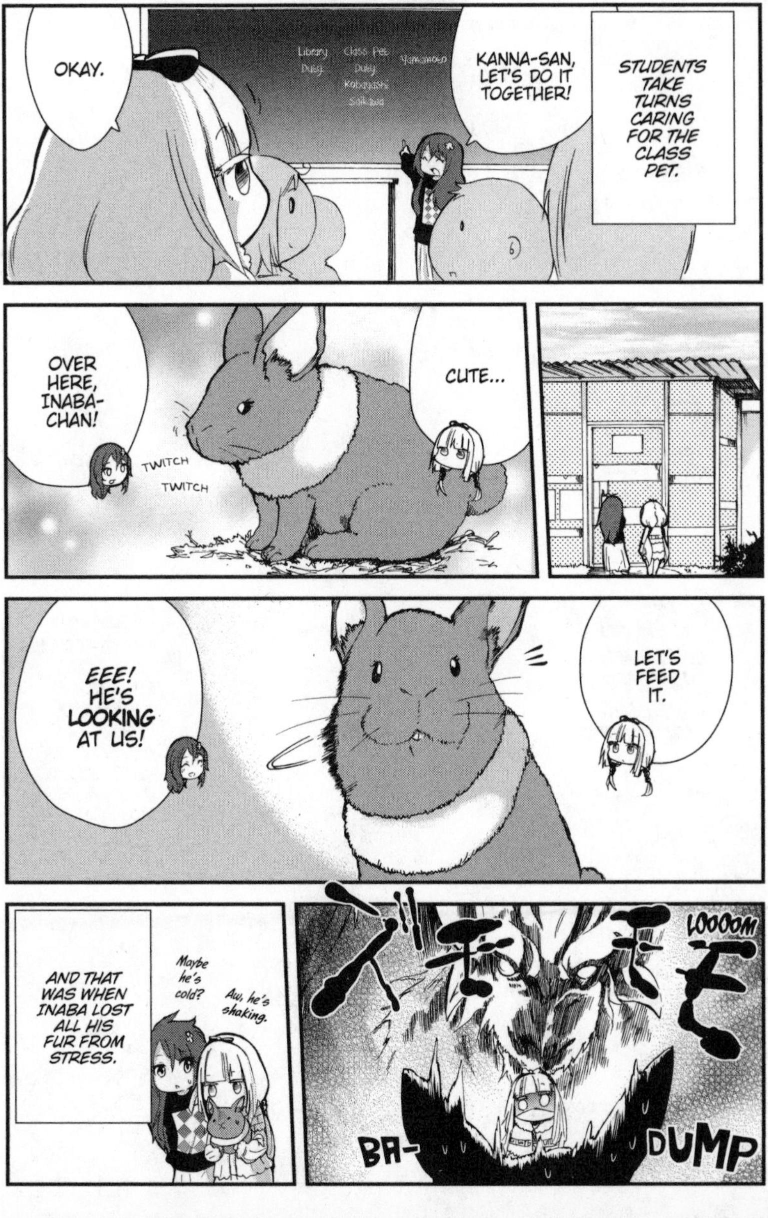
STUDENTS TAKE TURNS CARING FOR THE CLASS PET.
KANNA-SAN, LET'S DO IT TOGETHER!
Library Duty
Class Pet Duty
Kobayashi
Saikawa
Yamamoto
OKAY.
CUTE...
OVER HERE, INABA-CHAN!
TWITCH
TWITCH
LET'S FEED IT.
EEE! HE'S LOOKING AT US!
LOOOOM
BA-
DUMP
Aw, he's shaking.
Maybe he's cold?
AND THAT WAS WHEN INABA LOST ALL HIS FUR FROM STRESS.

RABBIT'S REVENGE

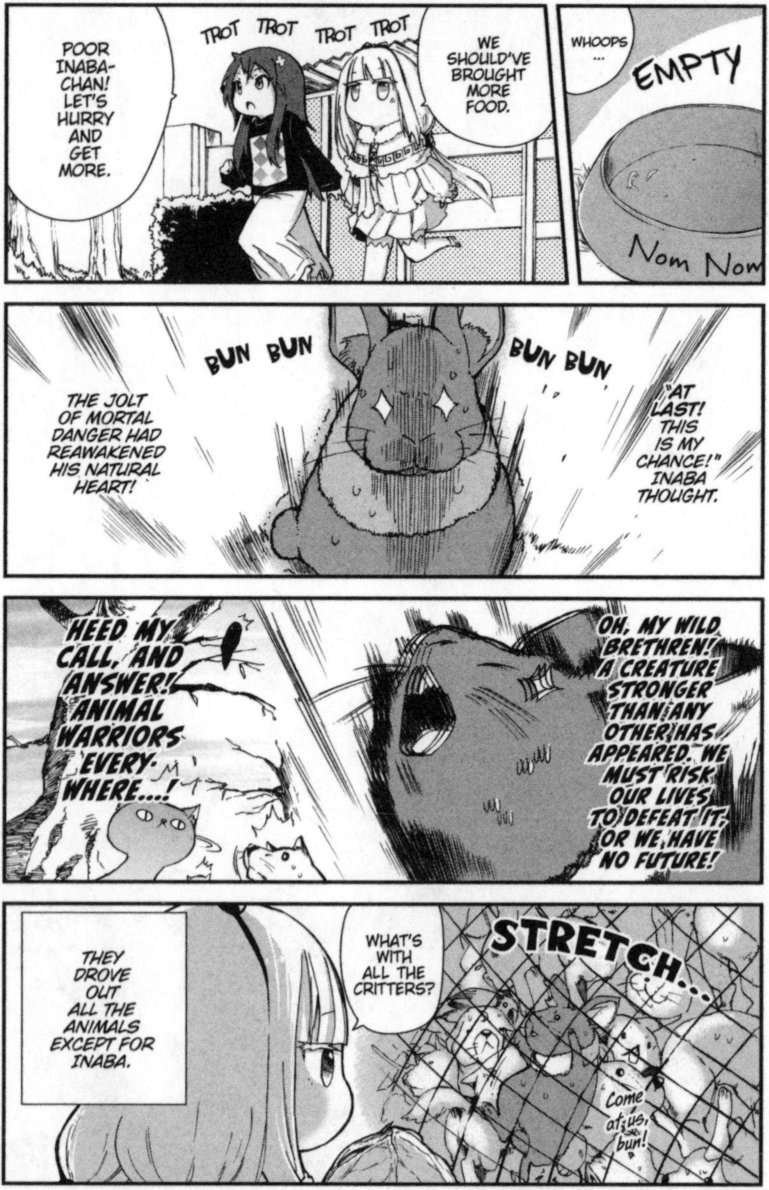

WHOOPS...
EMPTY
Nom Nom
WE SHOULD'VE BROUGHT MORE FOOD.
TROT TROT TROT TROT
POOR INABA-CHAN! LET'S HURRY AND GET MORE.
"AT LAST! THIS IS MY CHANCE!" INABA THOUGHT.
BUN BUN
BUN BUN
THE JOLT OF MORTAL DANGER HAD REAWAKENED HIS NATURAL HEART!
OH, MY WILD BRETHREN! A CREATURE STRONGER THAN ANY OTHER HAS APPEARED. WE MUST RISK OUR LIVES TO DEFEAT IT, OR WE HAVE NO FUTURE!
HEED MY CALL, AND ANSWER! ANIMAL WARRIORS EVERY-WHERE...!
STRETCH...
Come at us, bun!
WHAT'S WITH ALL THE CRITTERS?
THEY DROVE OUT ALL THE ANIMALS EXCEPT FOR INABA.

MASTERFUL

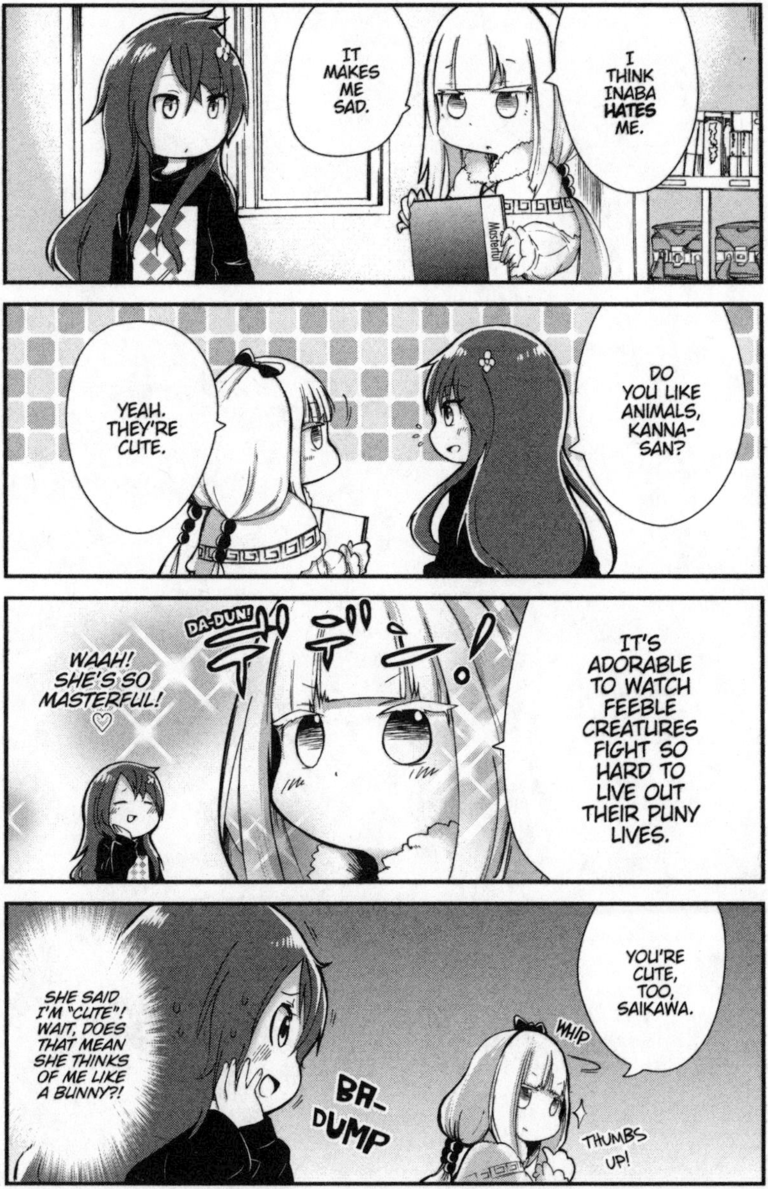

I THINK INABA HATES ME.
IT MAKES ME SAD.
Masterful
DO YOU LIKE ANIMALS, KANNA-SAN?
YEAH. THEY'RE CUTE.
IT'S ADORABLE TO WATCH FEEBLE CREATURES FIGHT SO HARD TO LIVE OUT THEIR PUNY LIVES.
DA-DUN!
WAAH! SHE'S SO MASTERFUL!
YOU'RE CUTE, TOO, SAIKAWA.
WHIP
THUMBS UP!
BA-DUMP
SHE SAID I'M "CUTE"! WAIT, DOES THAT MEAN SHE THINKS OF ME LIKE A BUNNY?!

ALL FOR LOVE

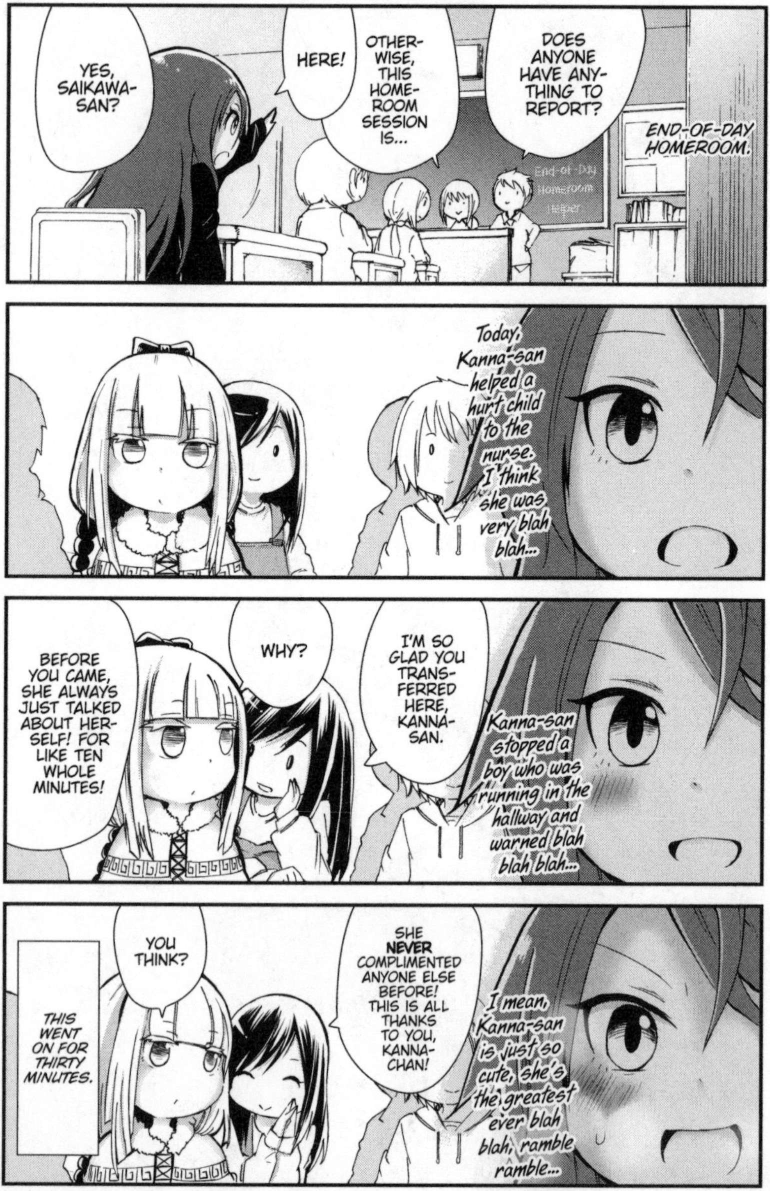
END-OF-DAY HOMEROOM.
DOES ANYONE HAVE ANYTHING TO REPORT?
End-of-Day Homeroom Helper
OTHERWISE, THIS HOMEROOM SESSION IS...
HERE!
YES, SAIKAWA-SAN?
Today, Kanna-san helped a hurt child to the nurse. I think she was very blah blah...
Kanna-san stopped a boy who was running in the hallway and warned blah blah blah...
I'M SO GLAD YOU TRANSFERRED HERE, KANNA-SAN.
WHY?
BEFORE YOU CAME, SHE ALWAYS JUST TALKED ABOUT HERSELF! FOR LIKE TEN WHOLE MINUTES!
I mean, Kanna-san is just so cute, she's the greatest ever blah blah, ramble ramble...
SHE **NEVER** COMPLIMENTED ANYONE ELSE BEFORE! THIS IS ALL THANKS TO YOU, KANNA-CHAN!
YOU THINK?
THIS WENT ON FOR THIRTY MINUTES.

STICKING POINT

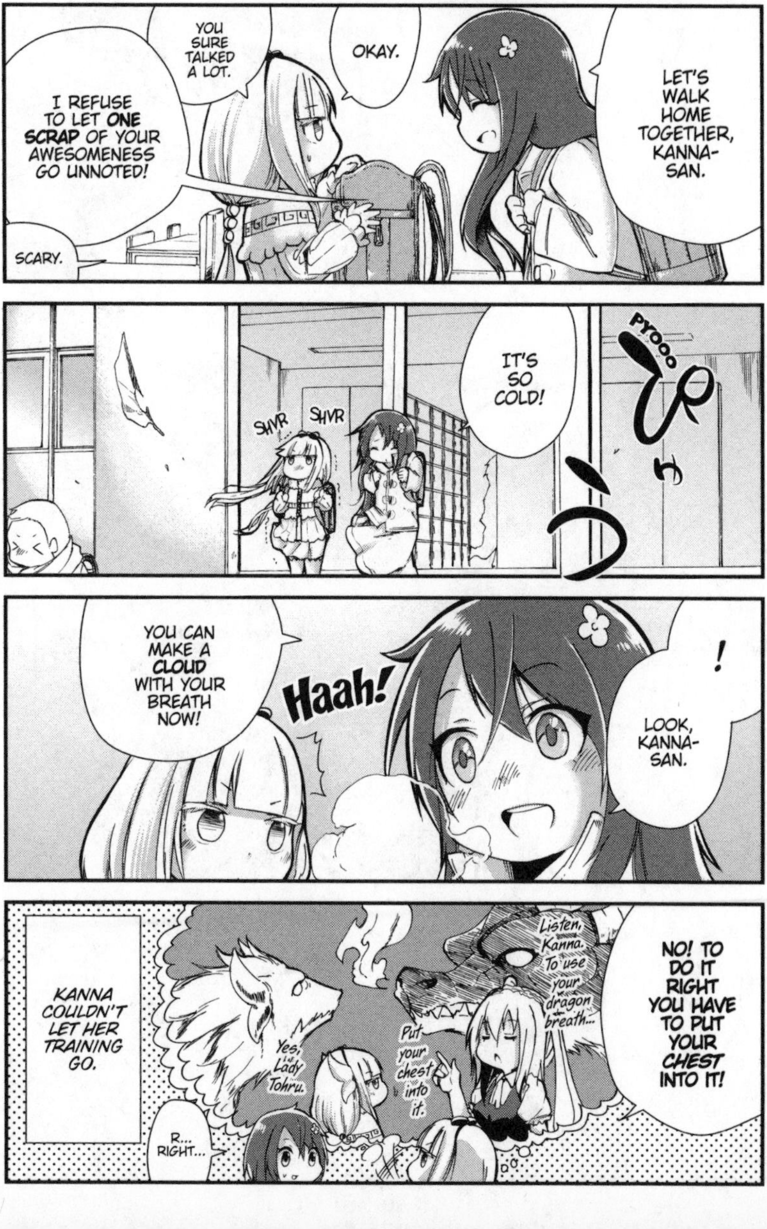
LET'S WALK HOME TOGETHER, KANNA-SAN.
OKAY.
YOU SURE TALKED A LOT.
I REFUSE TO LET **ONE SCRAP** OF YOUR AWESOMENESS GO UNNOTED!
SCARY.
PYOOO
IT'S SO COLD!
SHVR
SHVR
!
LOOK, KANNA-SAN.
Haah!
YOU CAN MAKE A **CLOUD** WITH YOUR BREATH NOW!
NO! TO DO IT RIGHT YOU HAVE TO PUT YOUR **CHEST** INTO IT!
Listen, Kanna. To use your dragon breath...
Put your chest into it.
Yes, Lady Tohru.
R... RIGHT...
KANNA COULDN'T LET HER TRAINING GO.

IT'S GONNA BE BAD! REAL BAD!

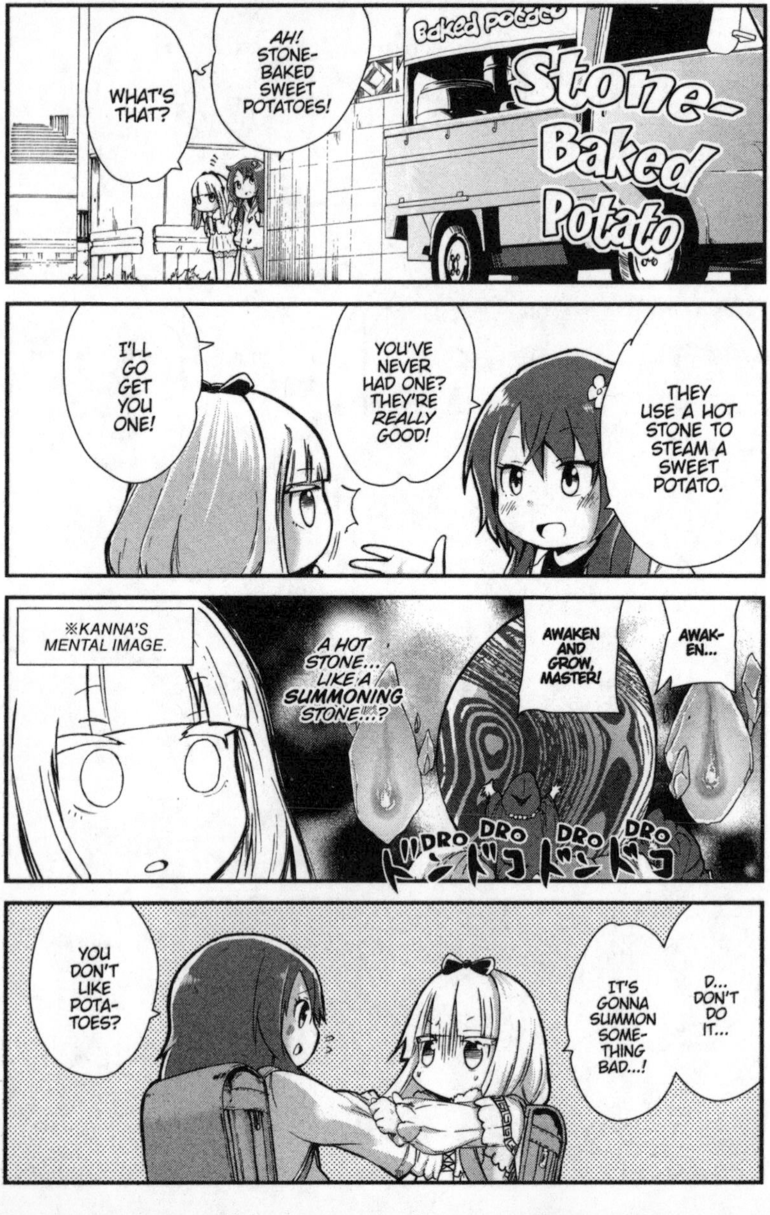
Baked potato
Stone-Baked Potato
AH! STONE-BAKED SWEET POTATOES!
WHAT'S THAT?
THEY USE A HOT STONE TO STEAM A SWEET POTATO.
YOU'VE NEVER HAD ONE? THEY'RE *REALLY* GOOD!
I'LL GO GET YOU ONE!
AWAK-EN...
AWAKEN AND GROW, MASTER!
A HOT STONE... LIKE A SUMMONING STONE...?
※KANNA'S MENTAL IMAGE.
DRO DRO DRO DRO
D... DON'T DO IT...
IT'S GONNA SUMMON SOME-THING BAD...!
YOU DON'T LIKE POTA-TOES?

INEVITABLE (1)

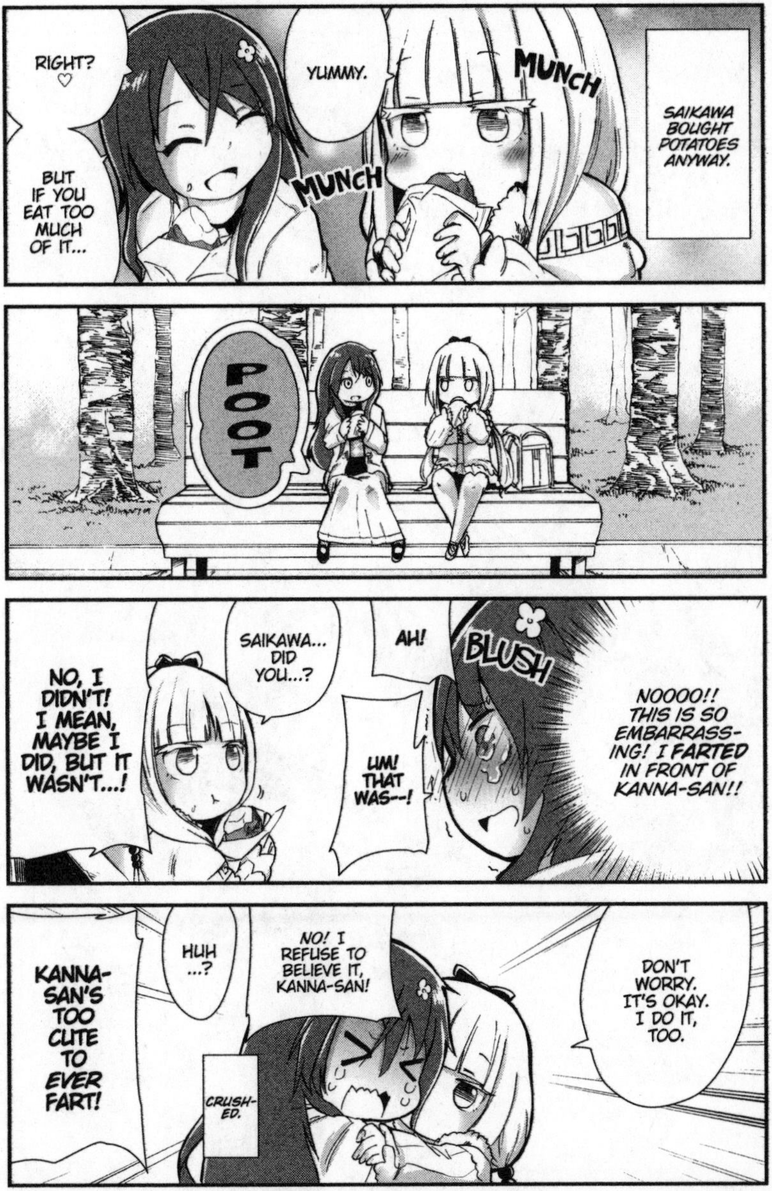
SAIKAWA BOUGHT POTATOES ANYWAY.
MUNCH
YUMMY.
RIGHT? ♡
MUNCH
BUT IF YOU EAT TOO MUCH OF IT...
POOT
AH!
BLUSH
NOOOO!! THIS IS SO EMBARRASS-ING! I FARTED IN FRONT OF KANNA-SAN!!
SAIKAWA... DID YOU...?
UM! THAT WAS--!
NO, I DIDN'T! I MEAN, MAYBE I DID, BUT IT WASN'T...!
DON'T WORRY. IT'S OKAY. I DO IT, TOO.
NO! I REFUSE TO BELIEVE IT, KANNA-SAN!
HUH ...?
KANNA-SAN'S TOO CUTE TO EVER FART!
CRUSH-ED.

INEVITABLE (2)

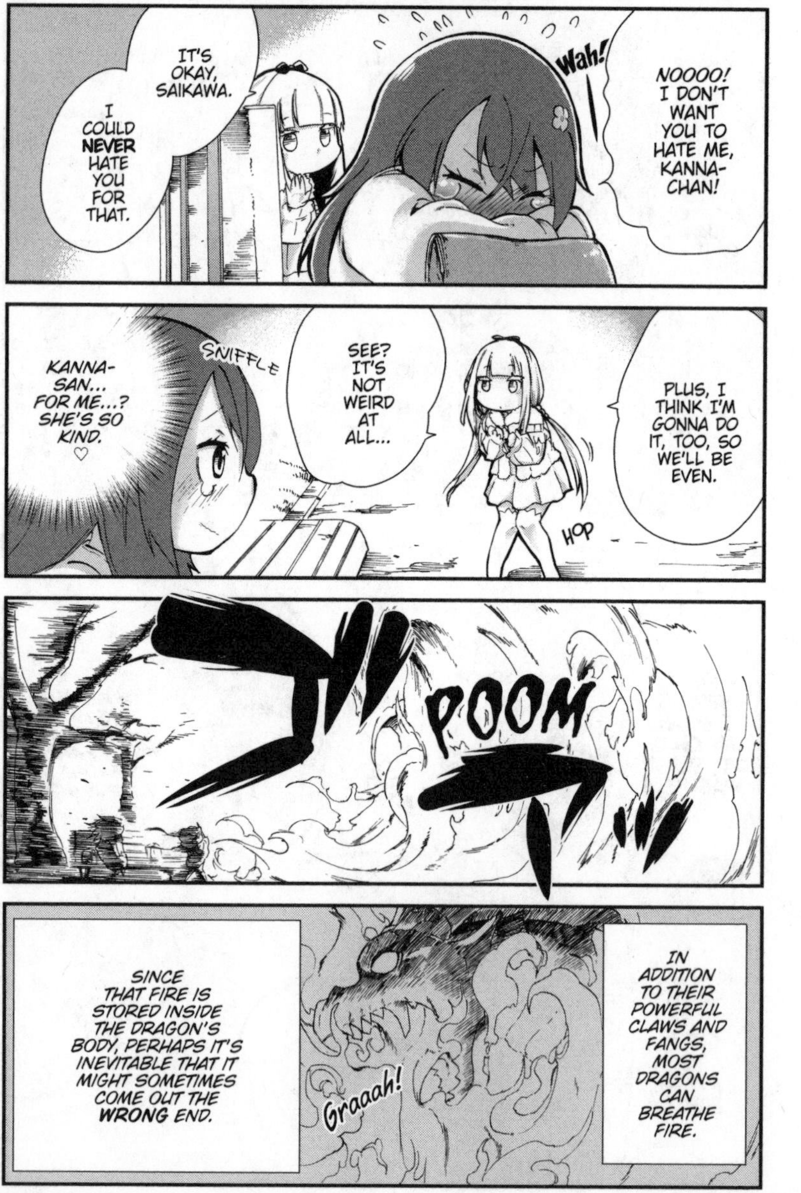
NOOOO! I DON'T WANT YOU TO HATE ME, KANNA-CHAN!
Wah!
IT'S OKAY, SAIKAWA.
I COULD **NEVER** HATE YOU FOR THAT.
PLUS, I THINK I'M GONNA DO IT, TOO, SO WE'LL BE EVEN.
SEE? IT'S NOT WEIRD AT ALL...
SNIFFLE
KANNA-SAN... FOR ME...? SHE'S SO KIND. ♡
HOP
POOM
IN ADDITION TO THEIR POWERFUL CLAWS AND FANGS, MOST DRAGONS CAN BREATHE FIRE.
Graaah!
SINCE THAT FIRE IS STORED INSIDE THE DRAGON'S BODY, PERHAPS IT'S INEVITABLE THAT IT MIGHT SOMETIMES COME OUT THE **WRONG** END.

KANNA-CHAN AND SHOUTA-KUN'S CLOSE CALL

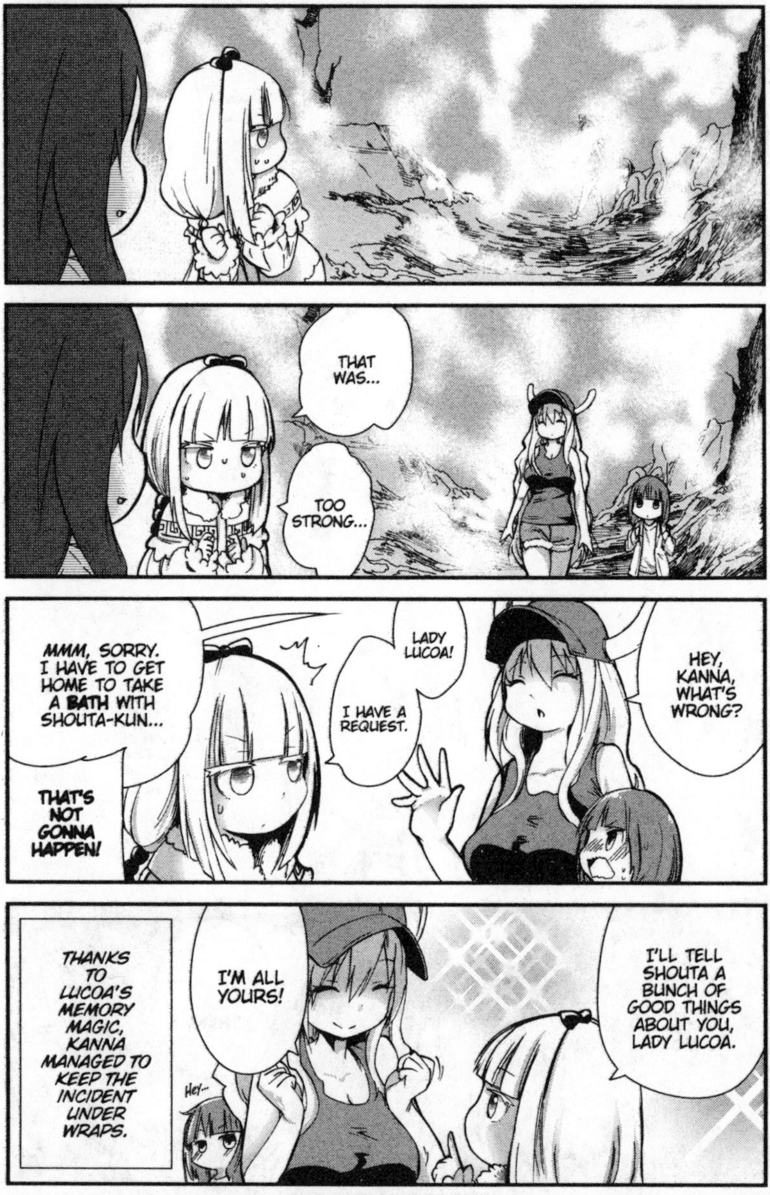
THAT WAS...
TOO STRONG...
HEY, KANNA, WHAT'S WRONG?
LADY LUCOA!
I HAVE A REQUEST.
MMM, SORRY. I HAVE TO GET HOME TO TAKE A BATH WITH SHOUTA-KUN...
THAT'S NOT GONNA HAPPEN!
I'LL TELL SHOUTA A BUNCH OF GOOD THINGS ABOUT YOU, LADY LUCOA.
I'M ALL YOURS!
Hey...
THANKS TO LUCOA'S MEMORY MAGIC, KANNA MANAGED TO KEEP THE INCIDENT UNDER WRAPS.

HARMONY

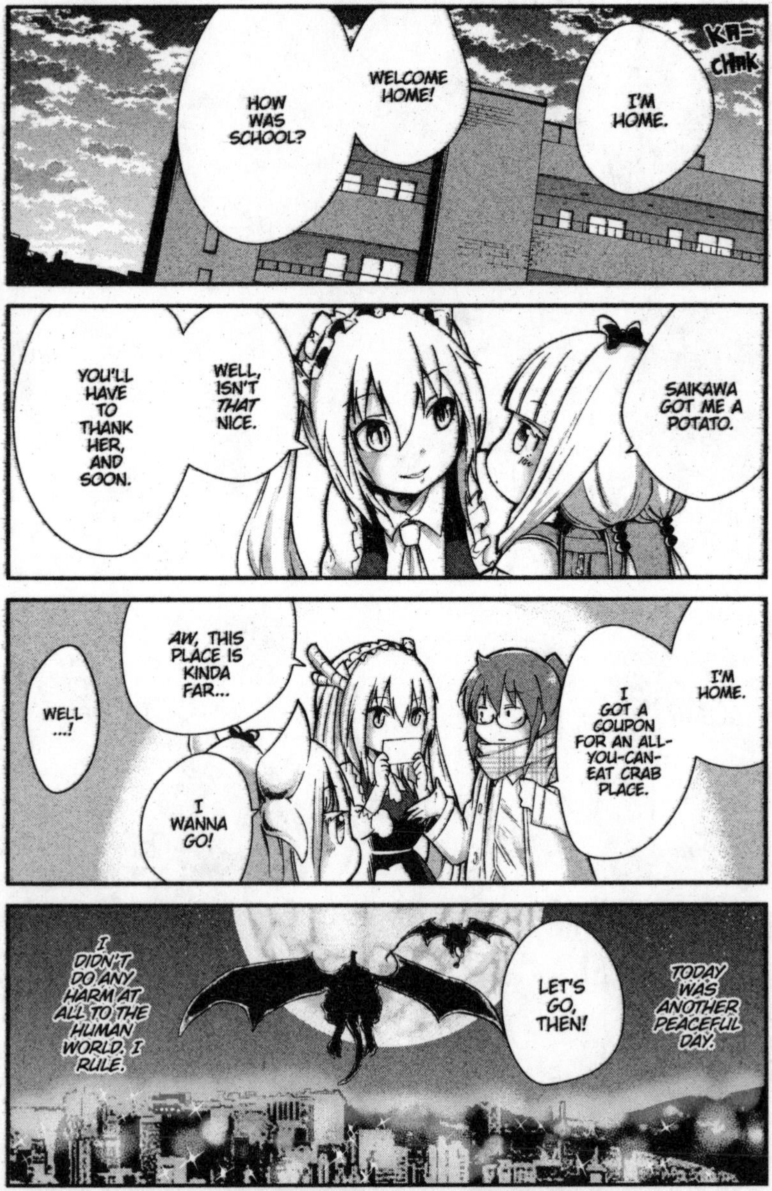
KA-CHNK
I'M HOME.
WELCOME HOME!
HOW WAS SCHOOL?
SAIKAWA GOT ME A POTATO.
WELL, ISN'T *THAT* NICE.
YOU'LL HAVE TO THANK HER, AND SOON.
I'M HOME.
I GOT A COUPON FOR AN ALL-YOU-CAN-EAT CRAB PLACE.
AW, THIS PLACE IS KINDA FAR...
I WANNA GO!
WELL ...!
TODAY WAS ANOTHER PEACEFUL DAY.
LET'S GO, THEN!
I DIDN'T DO ANY HARM AT ALL TO THE HUMAN WORLD. I RULE.

TIME FOR KANNA/END

Yum.

Miss Kobayashi's
Dragon Maid
Miss Kobayashi's
Dragon Maid
Miss Kobayashi's
Dragon Maid
Miss Kobayashi's
Dragon Maid

Miss Kobayashi's Dragon Maid
Kanna's Daily Life

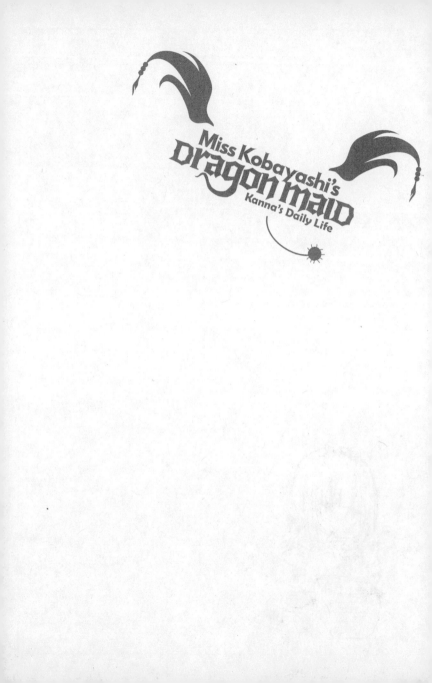

KANNA AND THAT KID

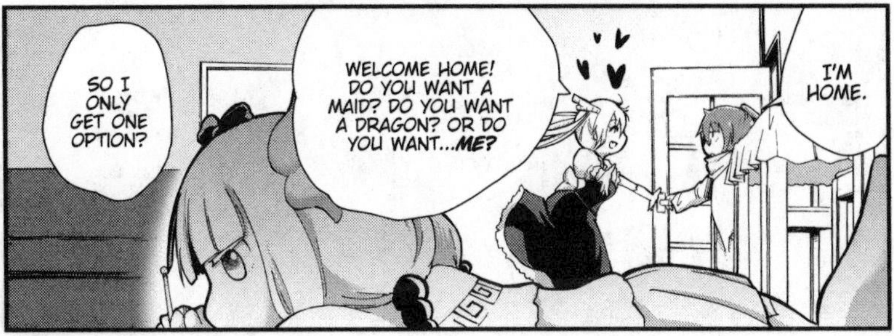
I'M HOME.
WELCOME HOME! DO YOU WANT A MAID? DO YOU WANT A DRAGON? OR DO YOU WANT...**ME?**
SO I ONLY GET ONE OPTION?

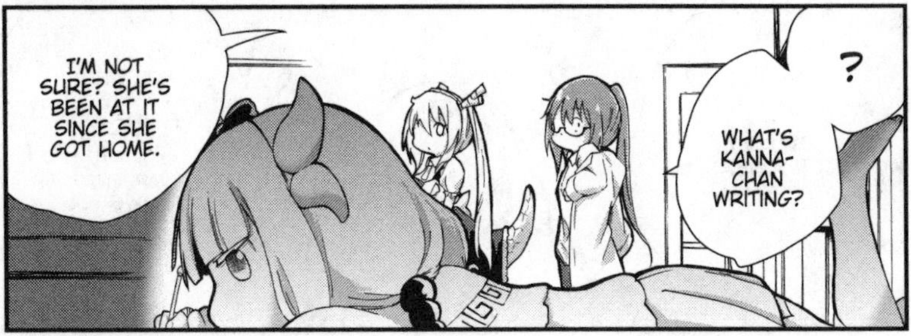
?
WHAT'S KANNA-CHAN WRITING?
I'M NOT SURE? SHE'S BEEN AT IT SINCE SHE GOT HOME.

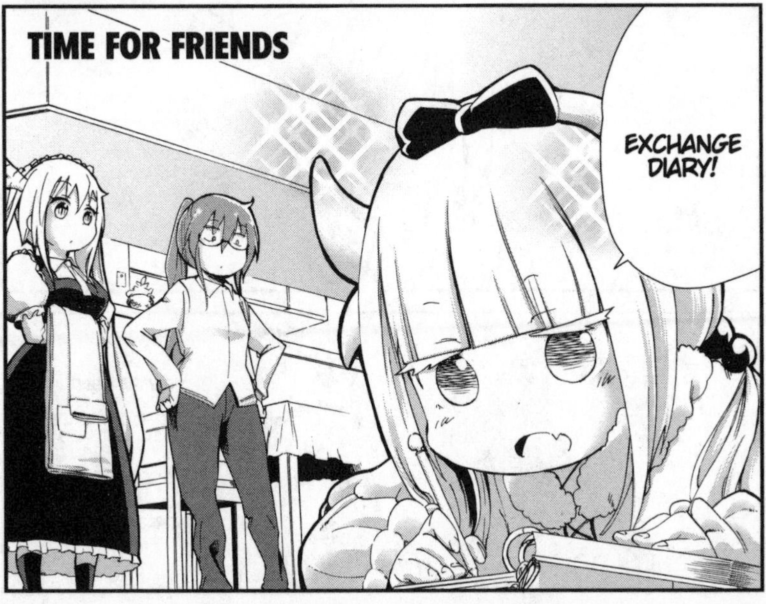
TIME FOR FRIENDS
EXCHANGE DIARY!

DARK HISTORY

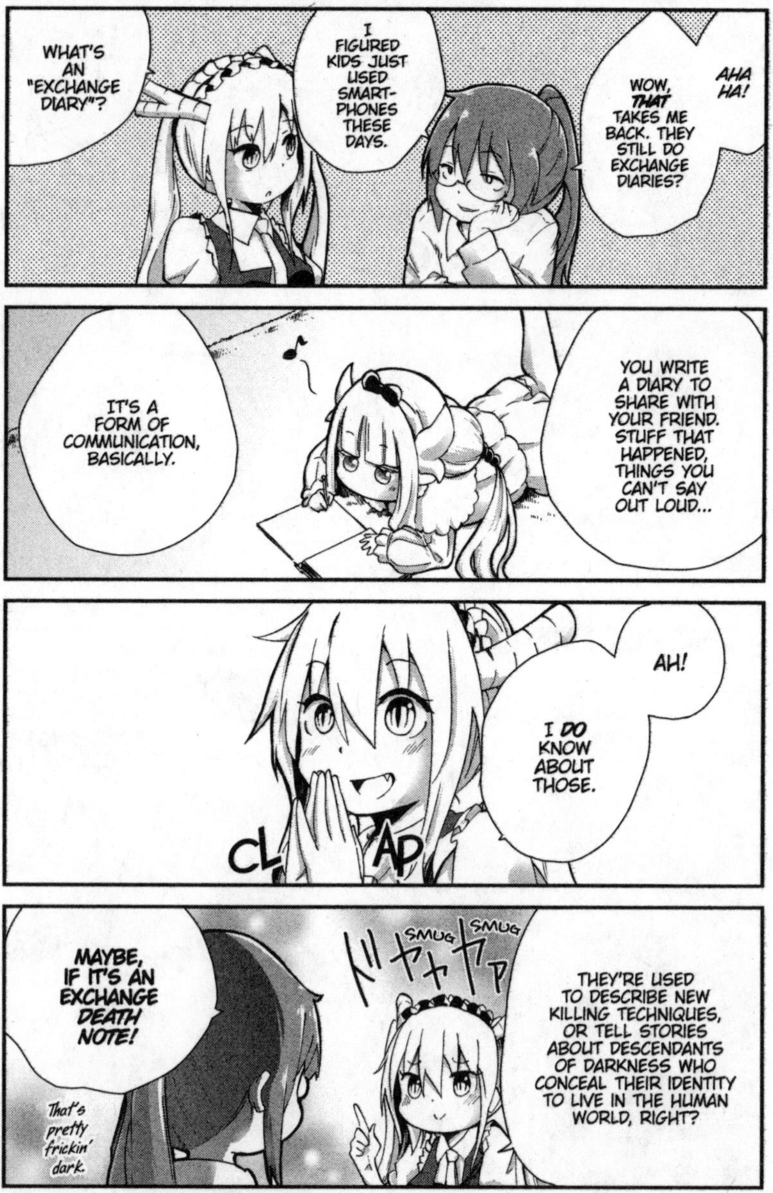
AHA HA!
WOW, THAT TAKES ME BACK. THEY STILL DO EXCHANGE DIARIES?
I FIGURED KIDS JUST USED SMART-PHONES THESE DAYS.
WHAT'S AN "EXCHANGE DIARY"?
YOU WRITE A DIARY TO SHARE WITH YOUR FRIEND. STUFF THAT HAPPENED, THINGS YOU CAN'T SAY OUT LOUD...
IT'S A FORM OF COMMUNICATION, BASICALLY.
AH!
I DO KNOW ABOUT THOSE.
CLAP
SMUG SMUG
THEY'RE USED TO DESCRIBE NEW KILLING TECHNIQUES, OR TELL STORIES ABOUT DESCENDANTS OF DARKNESS WHO CONCEAL THEIR IDENTITY TO LIVE IN THE HUMAN WORLD, RIGHT?
MAYBE, IF IT'S AN EXCHANGE DEATH NOTE!
That's pretty frickin' dark.

OVER MY DEAD BODY

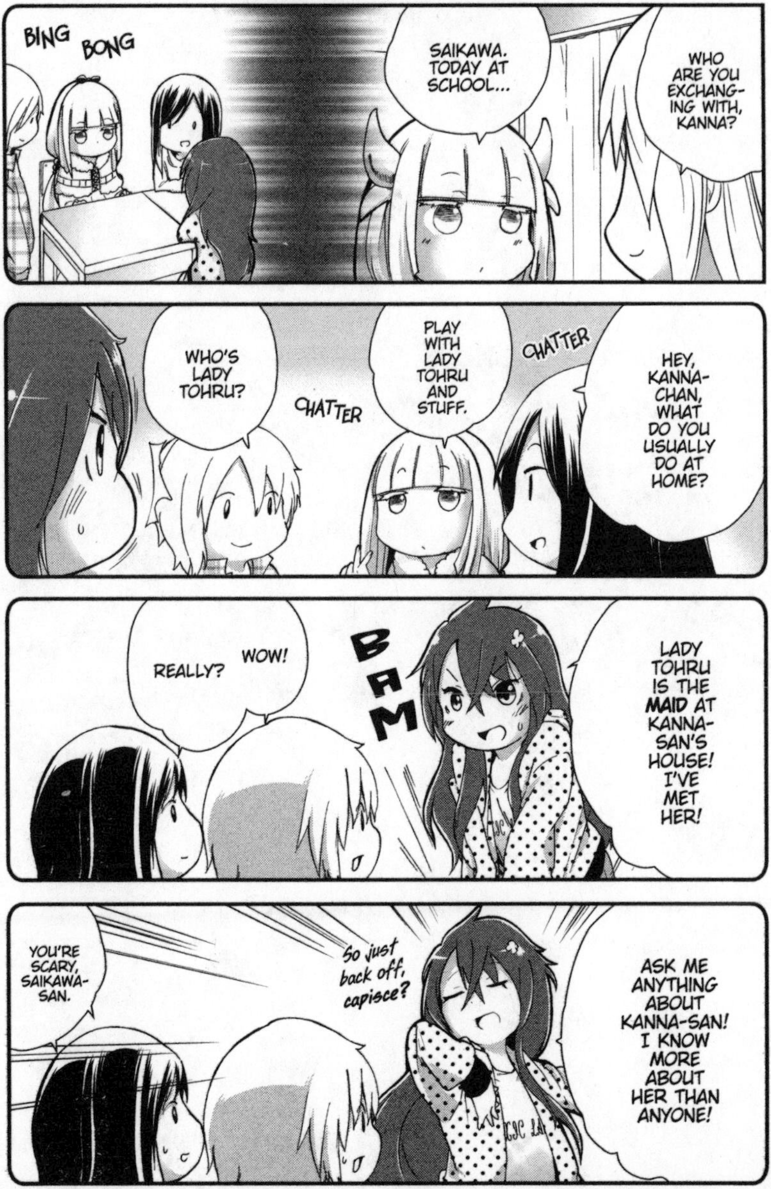
WHO ARE YOU EXCHANGING WITH, KANNA?
SAIKAWA. TODAY AT SCHOOL...
BING BONG
HEY, KANNA-CHAN, WHAT DO YOU USUALLY DO AT HOME?
CHATTER
PLAY WITH LADY TOHRU AND STUFF.
CHATTER
WHO'S LADY TOHRU?
LADY TOHRU IS THE MAID AT KANNA-SAN'S HOUSE! I'VE MET HER!
BAM
WOW!
REALLY?
ASK ME ANYTHING ABOUT KANNA-SAN! I KNOW MORE ABOUT HER THAN ANYONE!
So just back off, capisce?
YOU'RE SCARY, SAIKAWA-SAN.

LOVE MAKES YOU WANT TO KNOW MORE

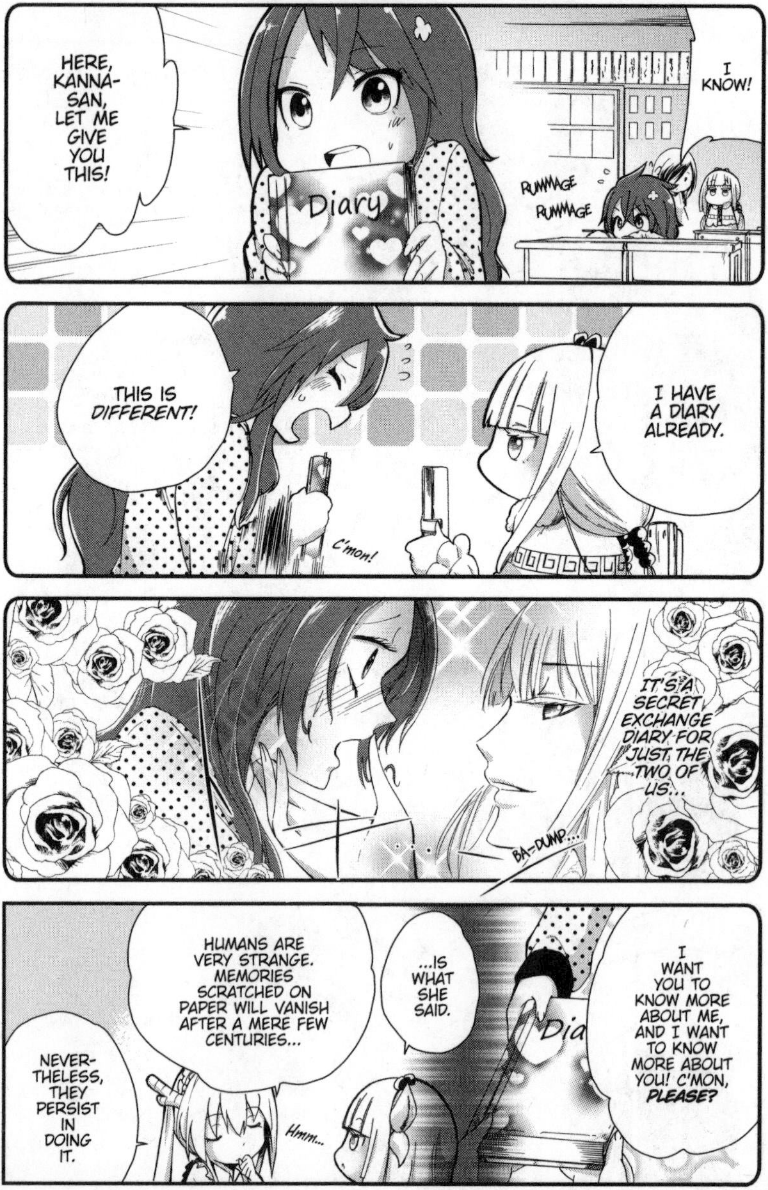
I KNOW!
RUMMAGE RUMMAGE
HERE, KANNA-SAN, LET ME GIVE YOU THIS!
Diary
I HAVE A DIARY ALREADY.
THIS IS DIFFERENT!
C'mon!
IT'S A SECRET EXCHANGE DIARY FOR JUST THE TWO OF US...
BA-DUMP...
I WANT YOU TO KNOW MORE ABOUT ME, AND I WANT TO KNOW MORE ABOUT YOU! C'MON, **PLEASE?**
Dia
...IS WHAT SHE SAID.
HUMANS ARE VERY STRANGE. MEMORIES SCRATCHED ON PAPER WILL VANISH AFTER A MERE FEW CENTURIES...
NEVERTHELESS, THEY PERSIST IN DOING IT.
Hmm...

RIGHT! WE'LL JUST HAVE TO LOOK!

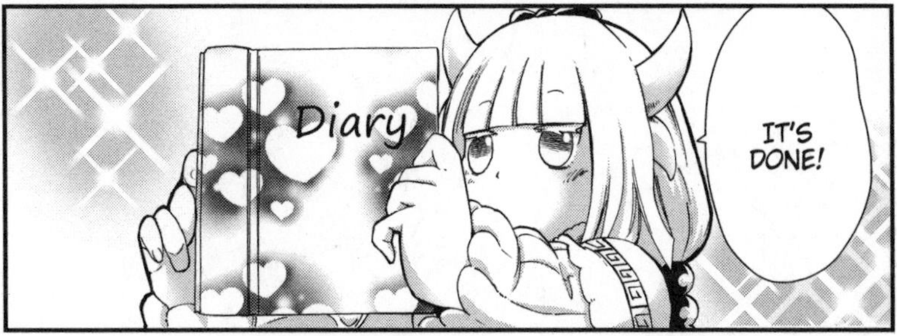
IT'S DONE!
Diary

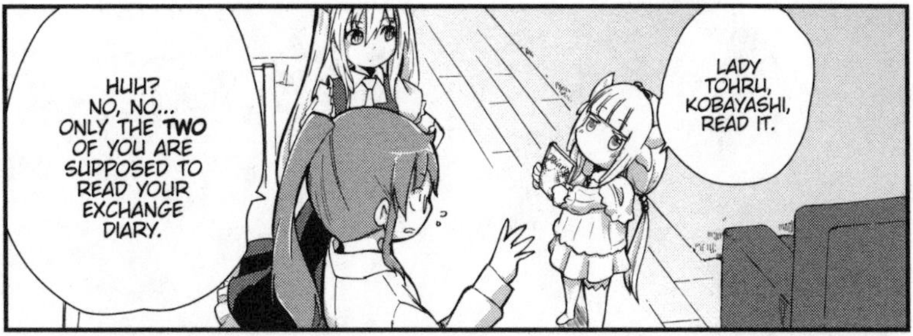
LADY TOHRU, KOBAYASHI, READ IT.
HUH? NO, NO... ONLY THE TWO OF YOU ARE SUPPOSED TO READ YOUR EXCHANGE DIARY.

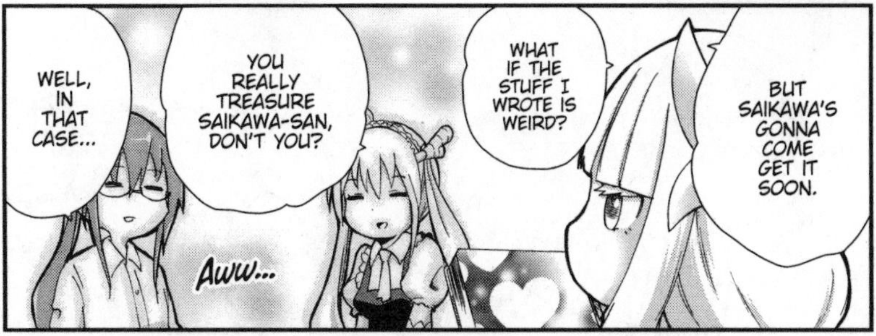
BUT SAIKAWA'S GONNA COME GET IT SOON.
WHAT IF THE STUFF I WROTE IS WEIRD?
YOU REALLY TREASURE SAIKAWA-SAN, DON'T YOU?
WELL, IN THAT CASE...
Aww...

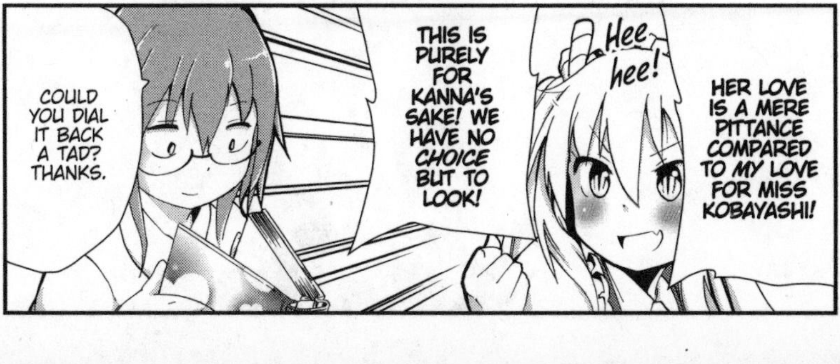
HER LOVE IS A MERE PITTANCE COMPARED TO MY LOVE FOR MISS KOBAYASHI!
Hee hee!
THIS IS PURELY FOR KANNA'S SAKE! WE HAVE NO CHOICE BUT TO LOOK!
COULD YOU DIAL IT BACK A TAD? THANKS.

GREETINGS...

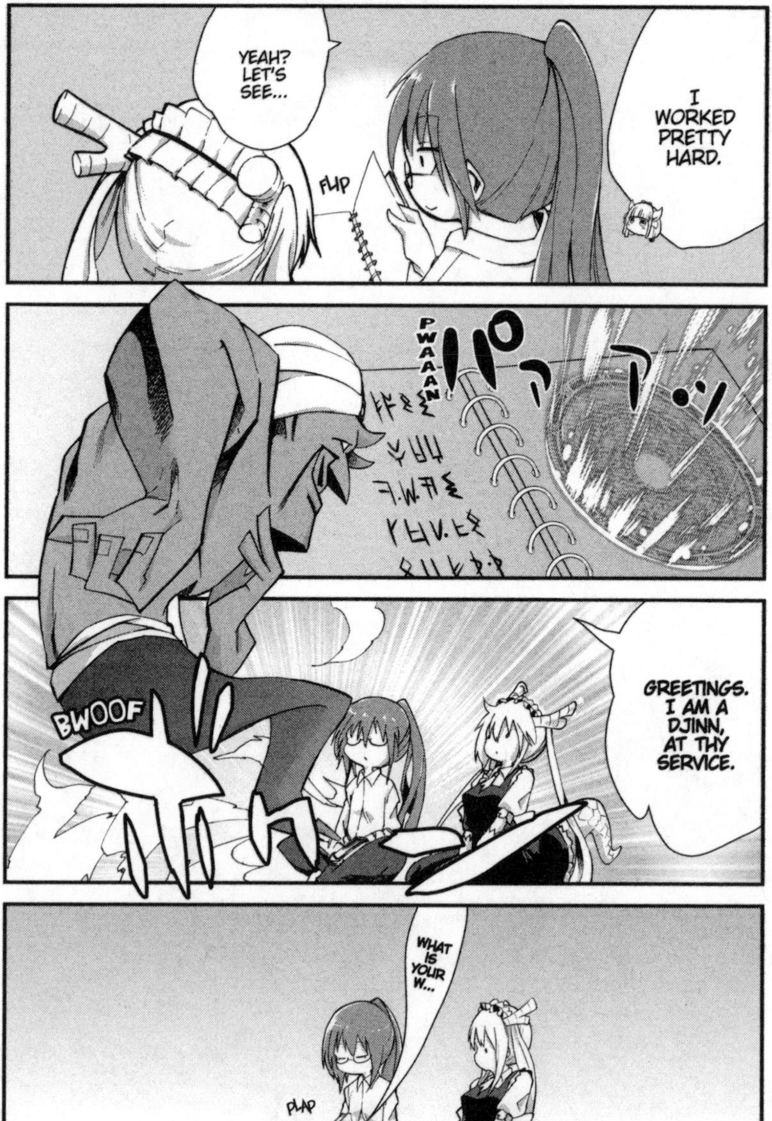
I WORKED PRETTY HARD.
YEAH? LET'S SEE...
FLIP
PWAAAAN
GREETINGS. I AM A DJINN, AT THY SERVICE.
BWOOF
WHAT IS YOUR W...
PLAP

WHAT IS YOUR W...

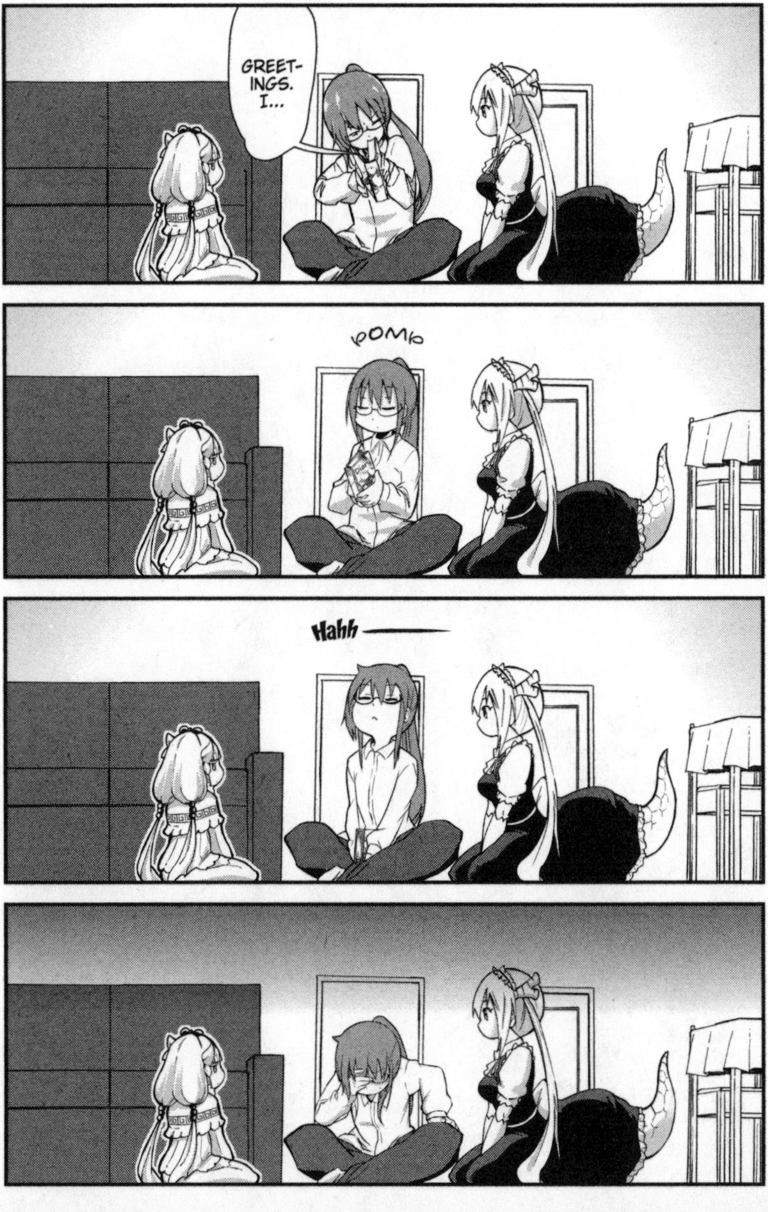
GREET-INGS. I...
POMP
Hahh ——

A LITTLE TOO GOOD!

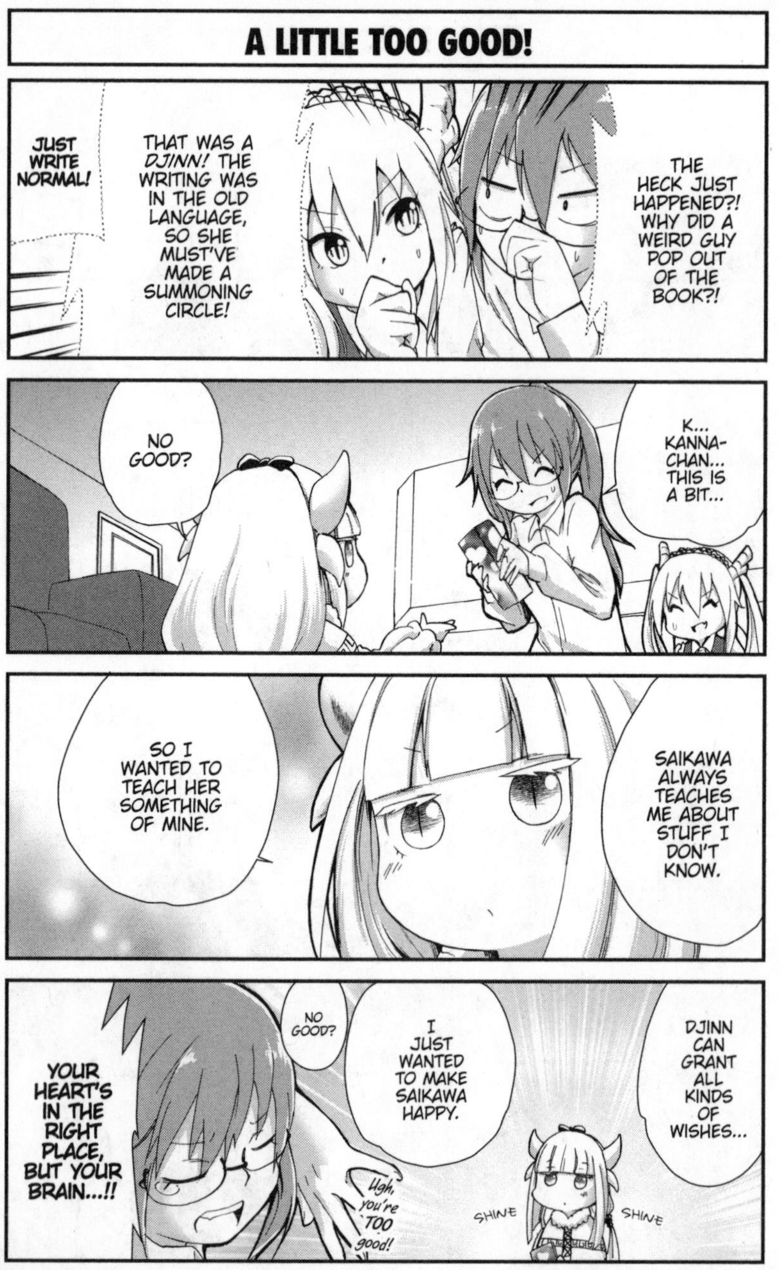
THE HECK JUST HAPPENED?! WHY DID A WEIRD GUY POP OUT OF THE BOOK?!
THAT WAS A DJINN! THE WRITING WAS IN THE OLD LANGUAGE, SO SHE MUST'VE MADE A SUMMONING CIRCLE!
JUST WRITE NORMAL!
K... KANNA-CHAN... THIS IS A BIT...
NO GOOD?
SAIKAWA ALWAYS TEACHES ME ABOUT STUFF I DON'T KNOW.
SO I WANTED TO TEACH HER SOMETHING OF MINE.
DJINN CAN GRANT ALL KINDS OF WISHES...
I JUST WANTED TO MAKE SAIKAWA HAPPY.
NO GOOD?
SHINE
SHINE
Ugh, you're TOO good!
YOUR HEART'S IN THE RIGHT PLACE, BUT YOUR BRAIN...!!

I'LL DO MY BEST!

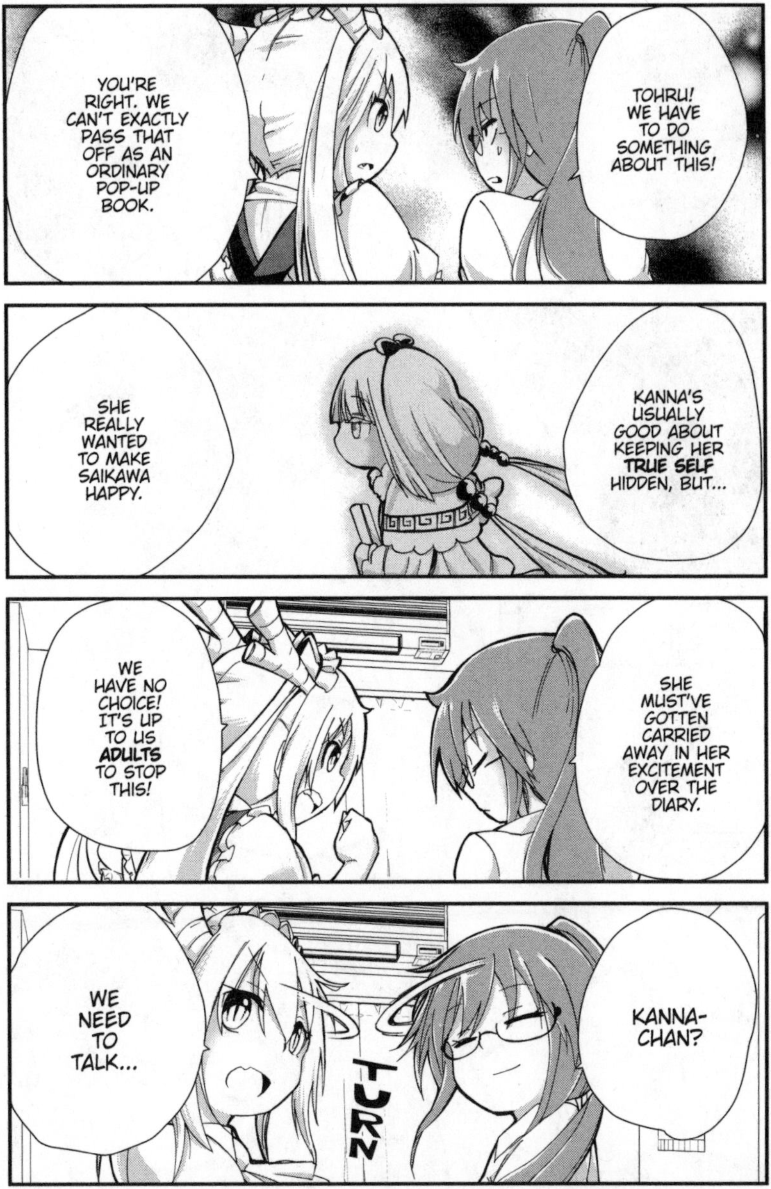
TOHRU! WE HAVE TO DO SOMETHING ABOUT THIS!
YOU'RE RIGHT. WE CAN'T EXACTLY PASS THAT OFF AS AN ORDINARY POP-UP BOOK.
KANNA'S USUALLY GOOD ABOUT KEEPING HER **TRUE SELF** HIDDEN, BUT...
SHE REALLY WANTED TO MAKE SAIKAWA HAPPY.
SHE MUST'VE GOTTEN CARRIED AWAY IN HER EXCITEMENT OVER THE DIARY.
WE HAVE NO CHOICE! IT'S UP TO US **ADULTS** TO STOP THIS!
KANNA-CHAN?
TURN
WE NEED TO TALK...

TOO LATE

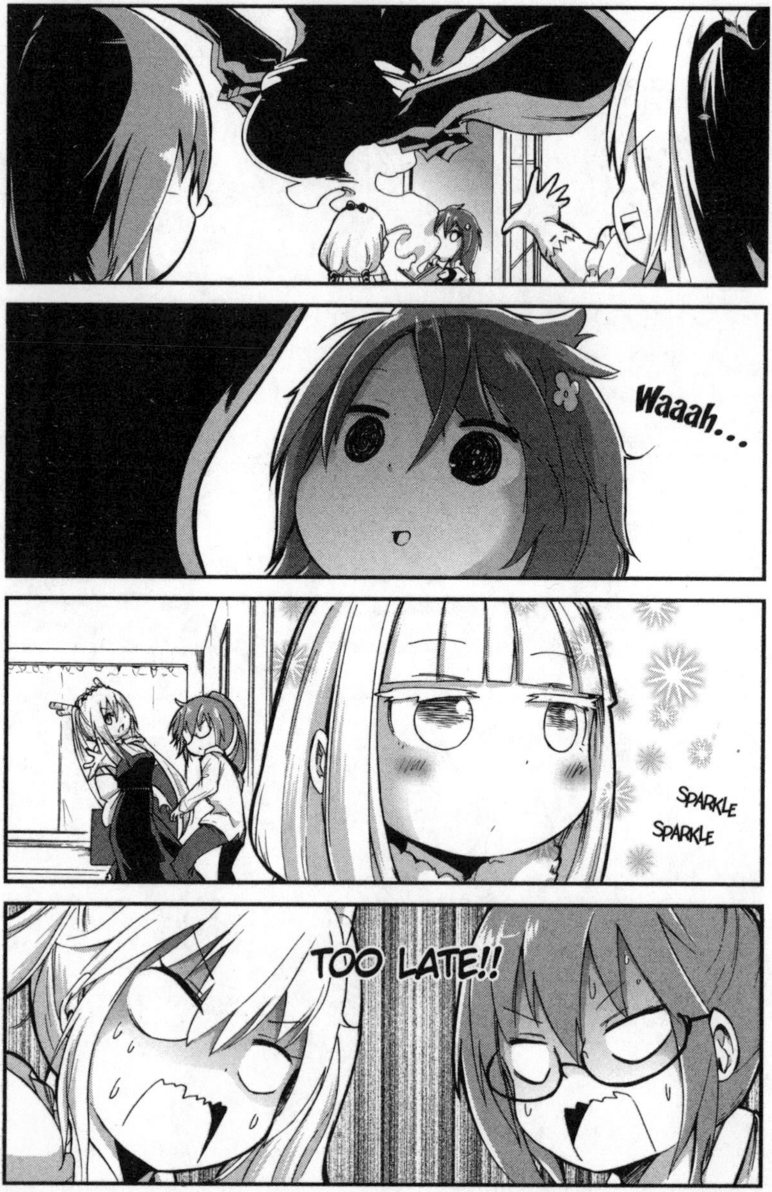

GET BACK!

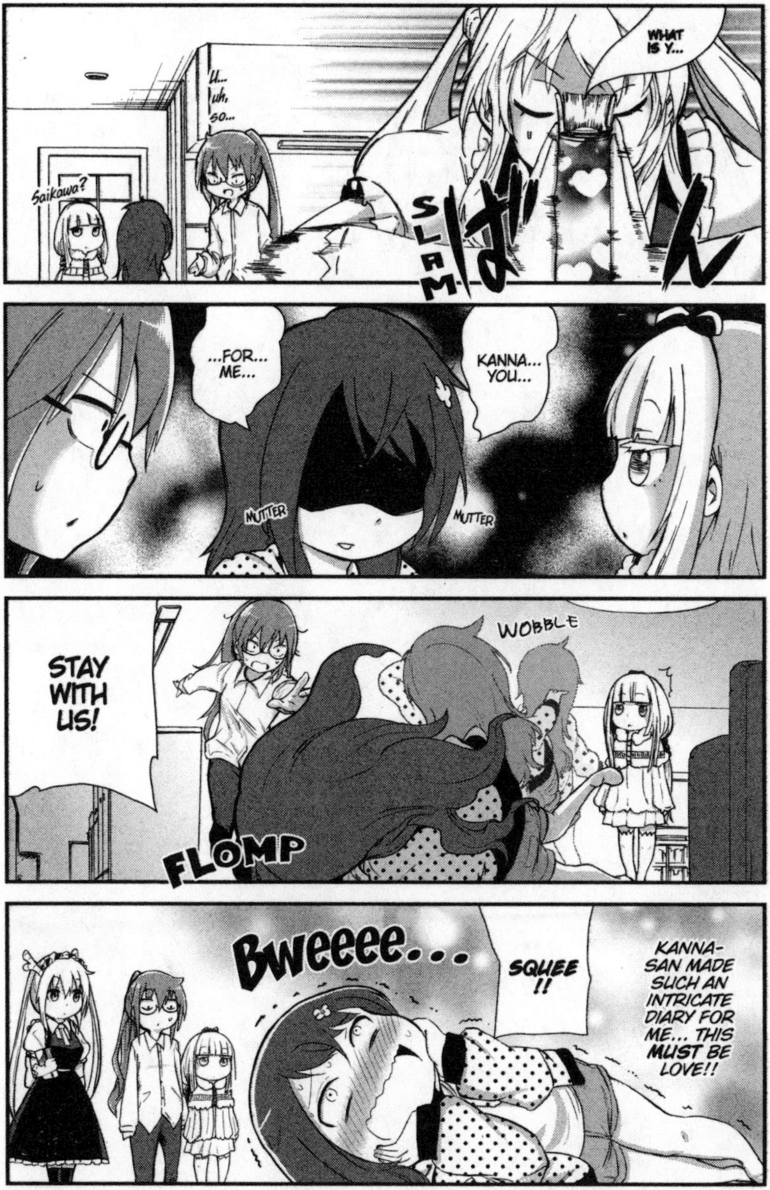

WHAT IS Y...
SLAM
ばん
U... uh, so...
Saikawa?
KANNA... YOU...
...FOR... ME...
MUTTER
MUTTER
WOBBLE
STAY WITH US!
FLOMP
KANNA-SAN MADE SUCH AN INTRICATE DIARY FOR ME... THIS **MUST** BE LOVE!!
SQUEE !!
Bweeee...

WHAT IS LOVE? ACCEPTANCE!

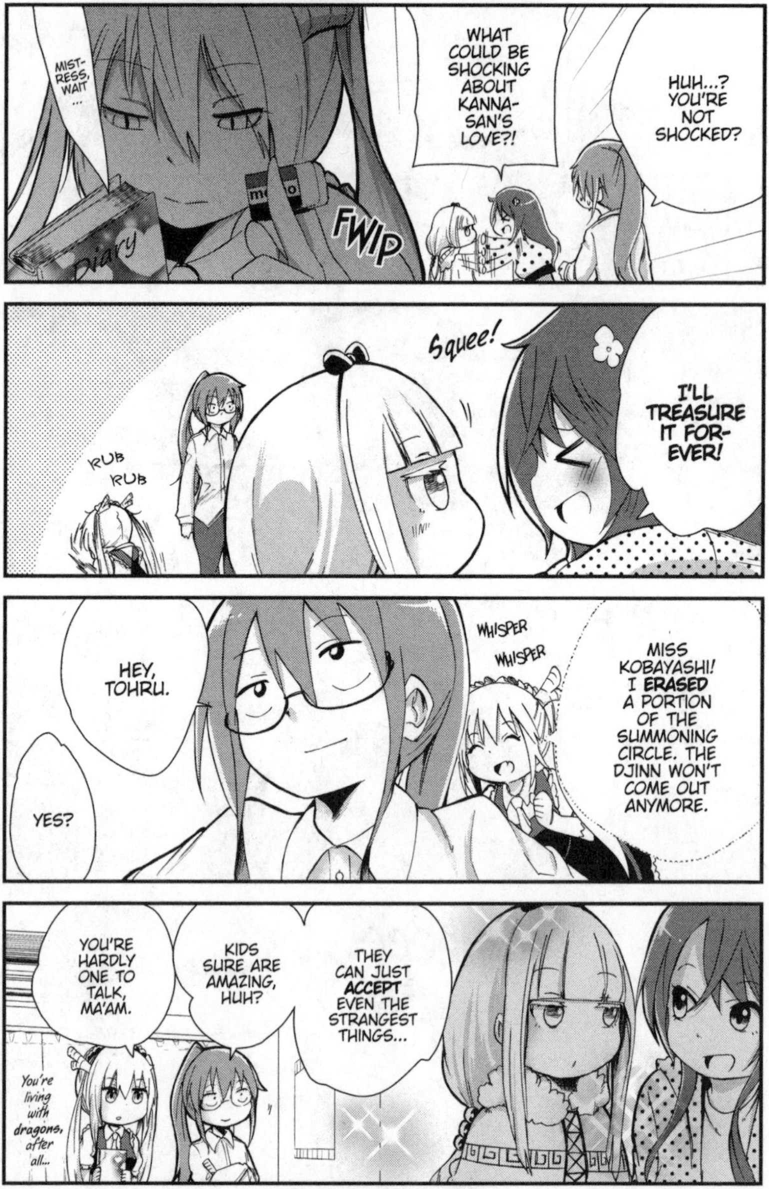
HUH...? YOU'RE NOT SHOCKED?
WHAT COULD BE SHOCKING ABOUT KANNA-SAN'S LOVE?!
MISTRESS, WAIT...
memo
FWIP
Diary
I'LL TREASURE IT FOREVER!
Squee!
RUB RUB
MISS KOBAYASHI! I **ERASED** A PORTION OF THE SUMMONING CIRCLE. THE DJINN WON'T COME OUT ANYMORE.
WHISPER WHISPER
HEY, TOHRU.
YES?
THEY CAN JUST **ACCEPT** EVEN THE STRANGEST THINGS...
KIDS SURE ARE AMAZING, HUH?
YOU'RE HARDLY ONE TO TALK, MA'AM.
You're living with dragons, after all...

TIME FOR FRIENDS/END

Miss Kobayashi's Dragon Maid
Kanna's Daily Life

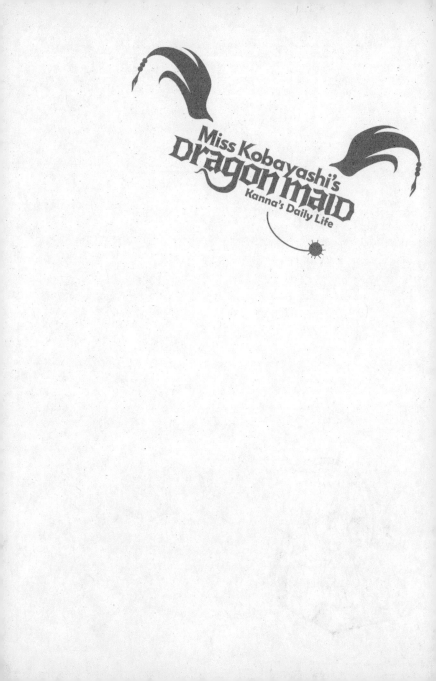

GREETINGS

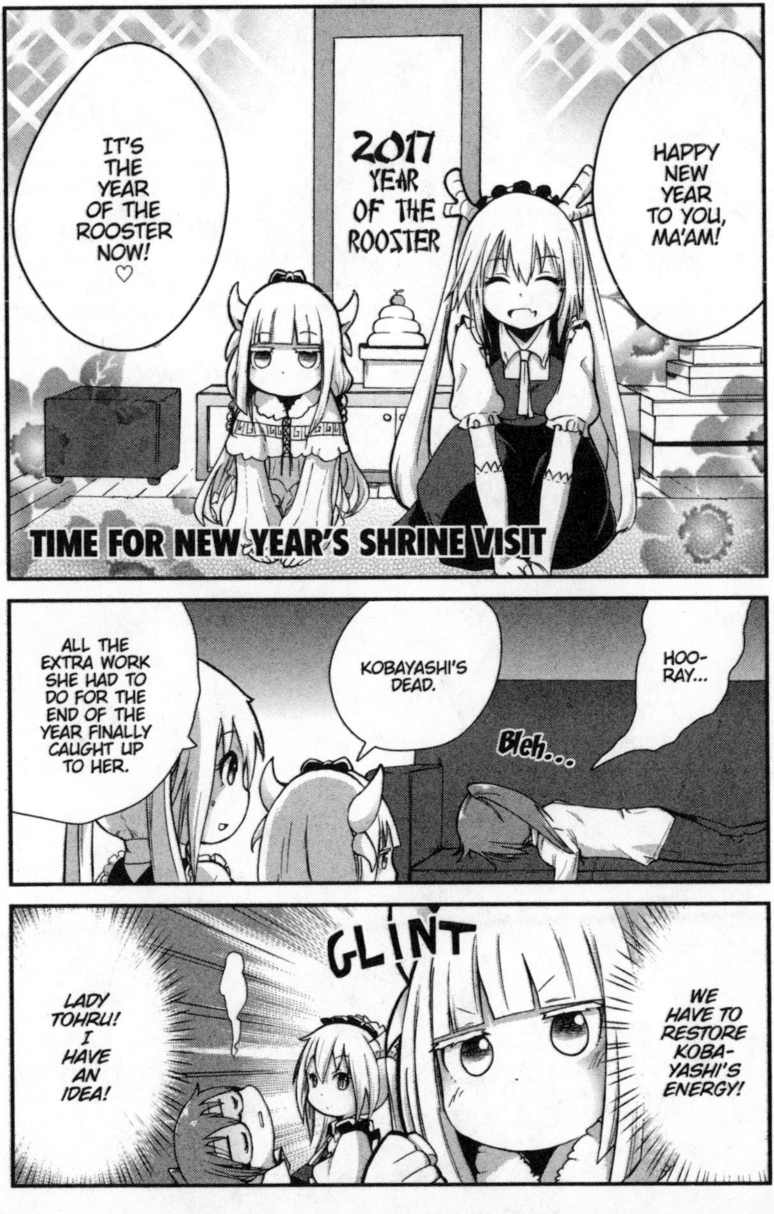
HAPPY NEW YEAR TO YOU, MA'AM!
2017 YEAR OF THE ROOSTER
IT'S THE YEAR OF THE ROOSTER NOW! ♡
TIME FOR NEW YEAR'S SHRINE VISIT
HOO-RAY...
Bleh...
KOBAYASHI'S DEAD.
ALL THE EXTRA WORK SHE HAD TO DO FOR THE END OF THE YEAR FINALLY CAUGHT UP TO HER.
GLINT
WE HAVE TO RESTORE KOBA-YASHI'S ENERGY!
LADY TOHRU! I HAVE AN IDEA!

PHOENIX

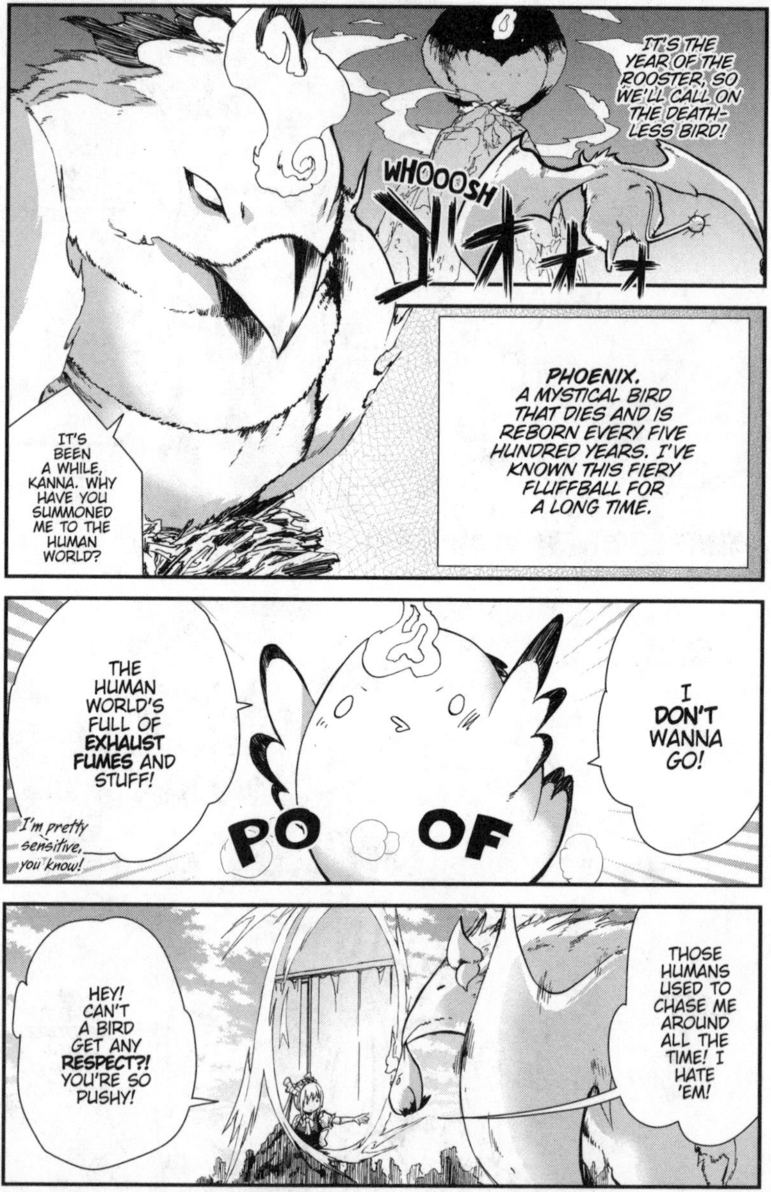
IT'S THE YEAR OF THE ROOSTER, SO WE'LL CALL ON THE DEATH-LESS BIRD!
WHOOOSH
ゴオオオ
PHOENIX. A MYSTICAL BIRD THAT DIES AND IS REBORN EVERY FIVE HUNDRED YEARS. I'VE KNOWN THIS FIERY FLUFFBALL FOR A LONG TIME.
IT'S BEEN A WHILE, KANNA. WHY HAVE YOU SUMMONED ME TO THE HUMAN WORLD?
I **DON'T** WANNA GO!
THE HUMAN WORLD'S FULL OF **EXHAUST FUMES** AND STUFF!
I'm pretty sensitive, you know!
POOF
THOSE HUMANS USED TO CHASE ME AROUND ALL THE TIME! I HATE 'EM!
HEY! CAN'T A BIRD GET ANY **RESPECT?!** YOU'RE SO PUSHY!

GOOD VIBRATIONS

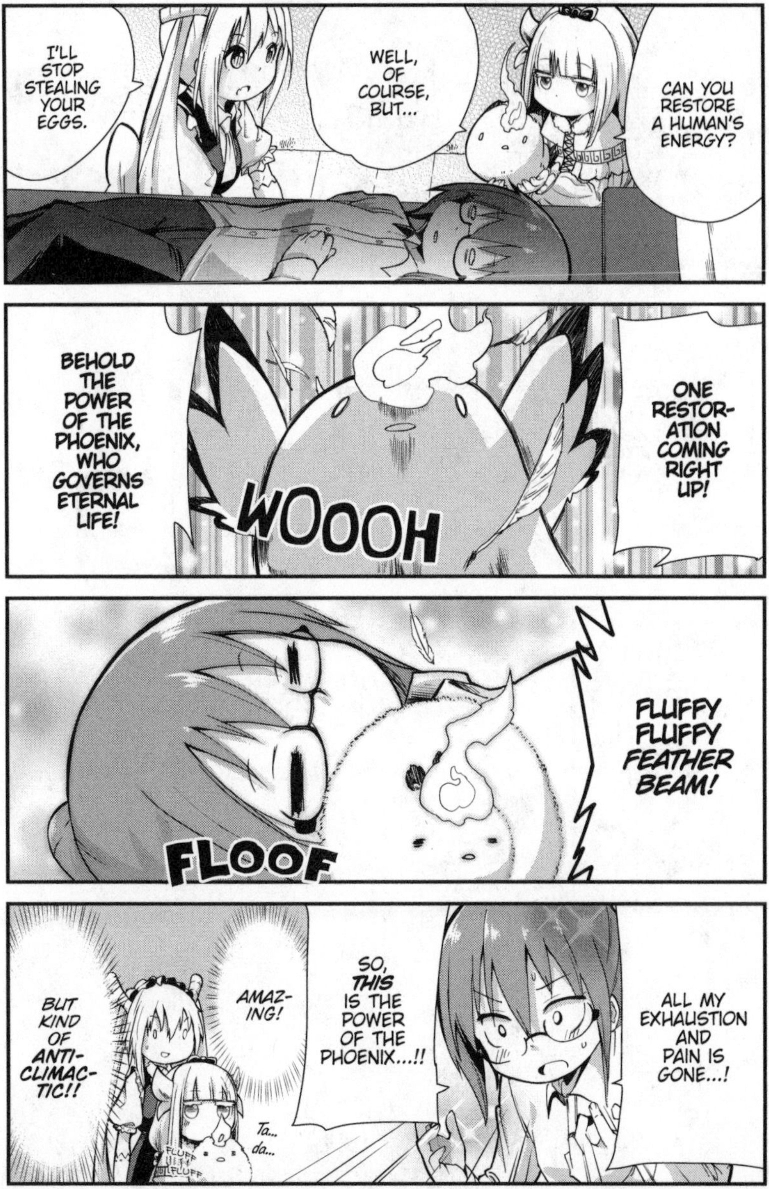
CAN YOU RESTORE A HUMAN'S ENERGY?
WELL, OF COURSE, BUT...
I'LL STOP STEALING YOUR EGGS.
ONE RESTORATION COMING RIGHT UP!
BEHOLD THE POWER OF THE PHOENIX, WHO GOVERNS ETERNAL LIFE!
WOOOH
FLUFFY FLUFFY FEATHER BEAM!
FLOOF
ALL MY EXHAUSTION AND PAIN IS GONE...!
SO, THIS IS THE POWER OF THE PHOENIX...!!
AMAZING!
BUT KIND OF ANTI-CLIMACTIC!!
Ta... da...

GODS VS. MONSTERS 2017

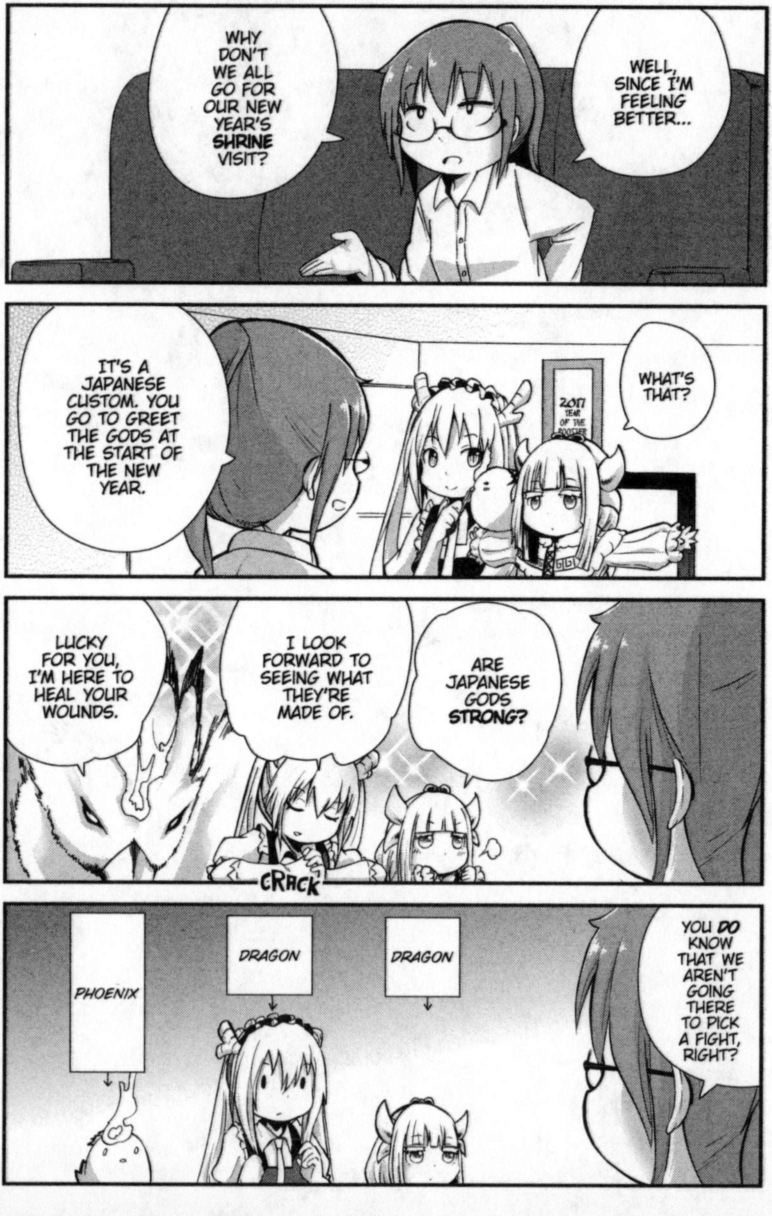
WELL, SINCE I'M FEELING BETTER...
WHY DON'T WE ALL GO FOR OUR NEW YEAR'S **SHRINE** VISIT?
WHAT'S THAT?
2017 YEAR OF THE
IT'S A JAPANESE CUSTOM. YOU GO TO GREET THE GODS AT THE START OF THE NEW YEAR.
ARE JAPANESE GODS **STRONG?**
I LOOK FORWARD TO SEEING WHAT THEY'RE MADE OF.
LUCKY FOR YOU, I'M HERE TO HEAL YOUR WOUNDS.
CRACK
YOU ***DO*** KNOW THAT WE AREN'T GOING THERE TO PICK A FIGHT, RIGHT?
DRAGON
DRAGON
PHOENIX

SAIKAWA-SAN'S SUNDAY BEST

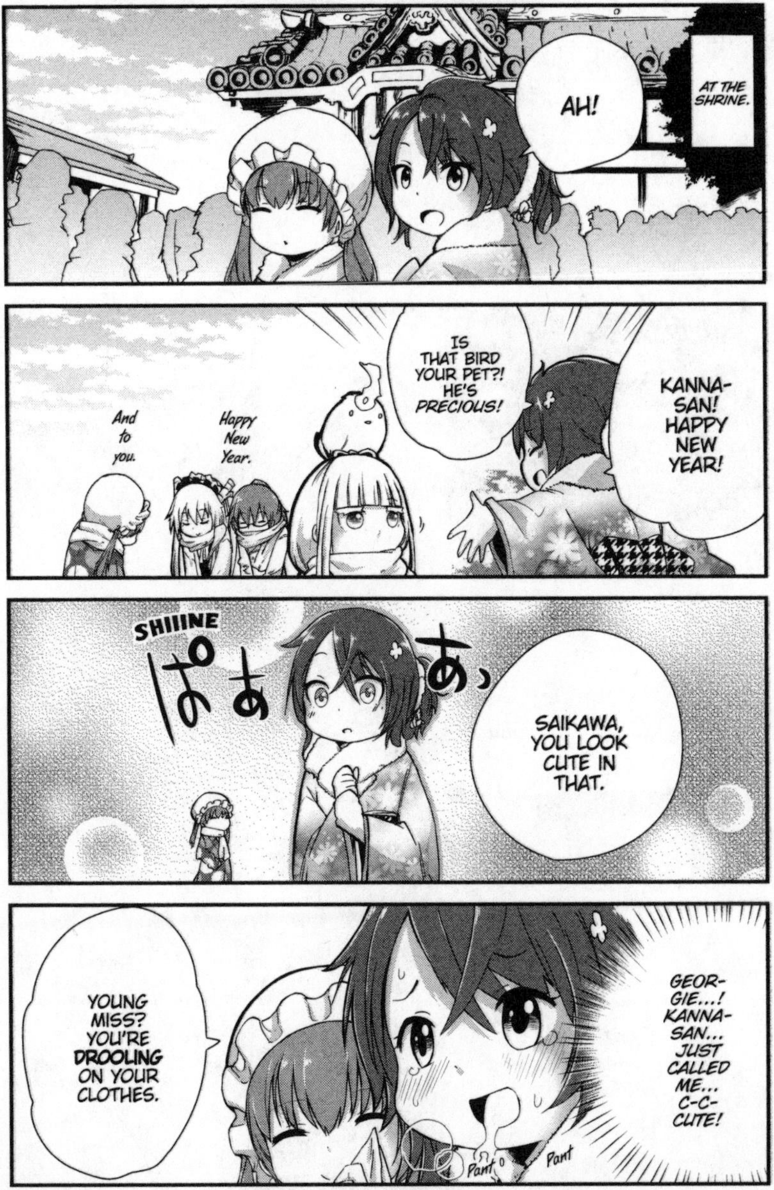

AT THE SHRINE.
AH!
KANNA-SAN! HAPPY NEW YEAR!
IS THAT BIRD YOUR PET?! HE'S PRECIOUS!
Happy New Year.
And to you.
SAIKAWA, YOU LOOK CUTE IN THAT.
SHIIINE
ぱぁあ
GEORGIE...! KANNA-SAN... JUST CALLED ME... C-C-CUTE!
YOUNG MISS? YOU'RE DROOLING ON YOUR CLOTHES.
Pant
Pant

KANNA'S IN HOT WATER!

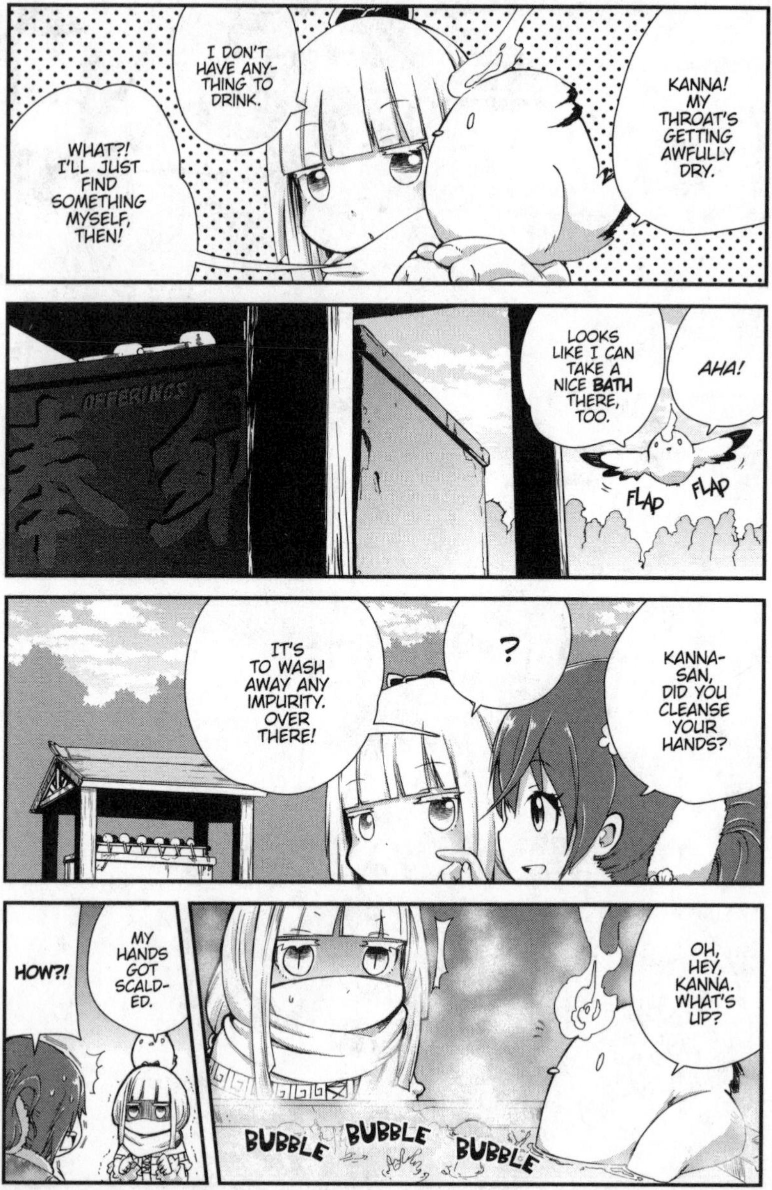
KANNA! MY THROAT'S GETTING AWFULLY DRY.
I DON'T HAVE ANY-THING TO DRINK.
WHAT?! I'LL JUST FIND SOMETHING MYSELF, THEN!
AHA!
LOOKS LIKE I CAN TAKE A NICE BATH THERE, TOO.
FLAP FLAP
OFFERINGS
KANNA-SAN, DID YOU CLEANSE YOUR HANDS?
?
IT'S TO WASH AWAY ANY IMPURITY. OVER THERE!
OH, HEY, KANNA. WHAT'S UP?
BUBBLE BUBBLE BUBBLE
MY HANDS GOT SCALD-ED.
HOW?!

KANNA IS HERE!

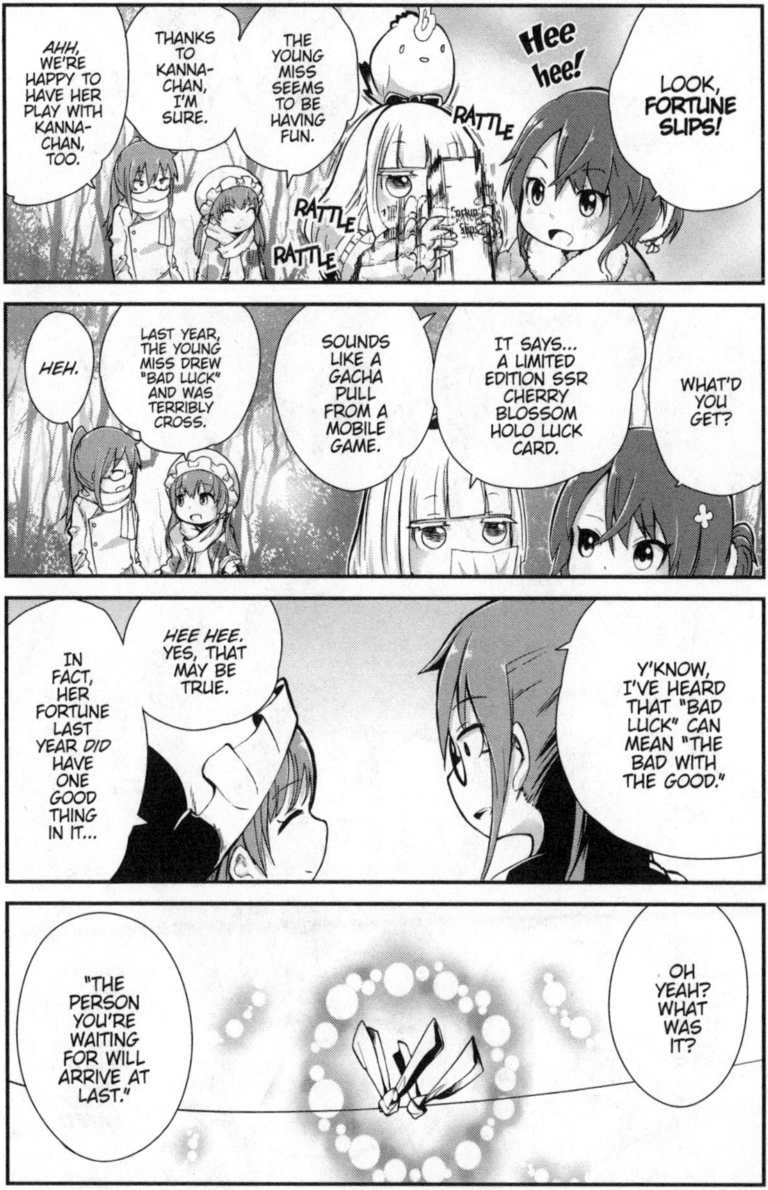
LOOK, FORTUNE SLIPS!
Hee hee!
RATTLE
RATTLE
RATTLE
THE YOUNG MISS SEEMS TO BE HAVING FUN.
THANKS TO KANNA-CHAN, I'M SURE.
AHH, WE'RE HAPPY TO HAVE HER PLAY WITH KANNA-CHAN, TOO.
WHAT'D YOU GET?
IT SAYS... A LIMITED EDITION SSR CHERRY BLOSSOM HOLO LUCK CARD.
SOUNDS LIKE A GACHA PULL FROM A MOBILE GAME.
LAST YEAR, THE YOUNG MISS DREW "BAD LUCK" AND WAS TERRIBLY CROSS.
HEH.
Y'KNOW, I'VE HEARD THAT "BAD LUCK" CAN MEAN "THE BAD WITH THE GOOD."
HEE HEE. YES, THAT MAY BE TRUE.
IN FACT, HER FORTUNE LAST YEAR *DID* HAVE ONE GOOD THING IN IT...
OH YEAH? WHAT WAS IT?
"THE PERSON YOU'RE WAITING FOR WILL ARRIVE AT LAST."

SAIKAWA-SAN ON A RAMPAGE

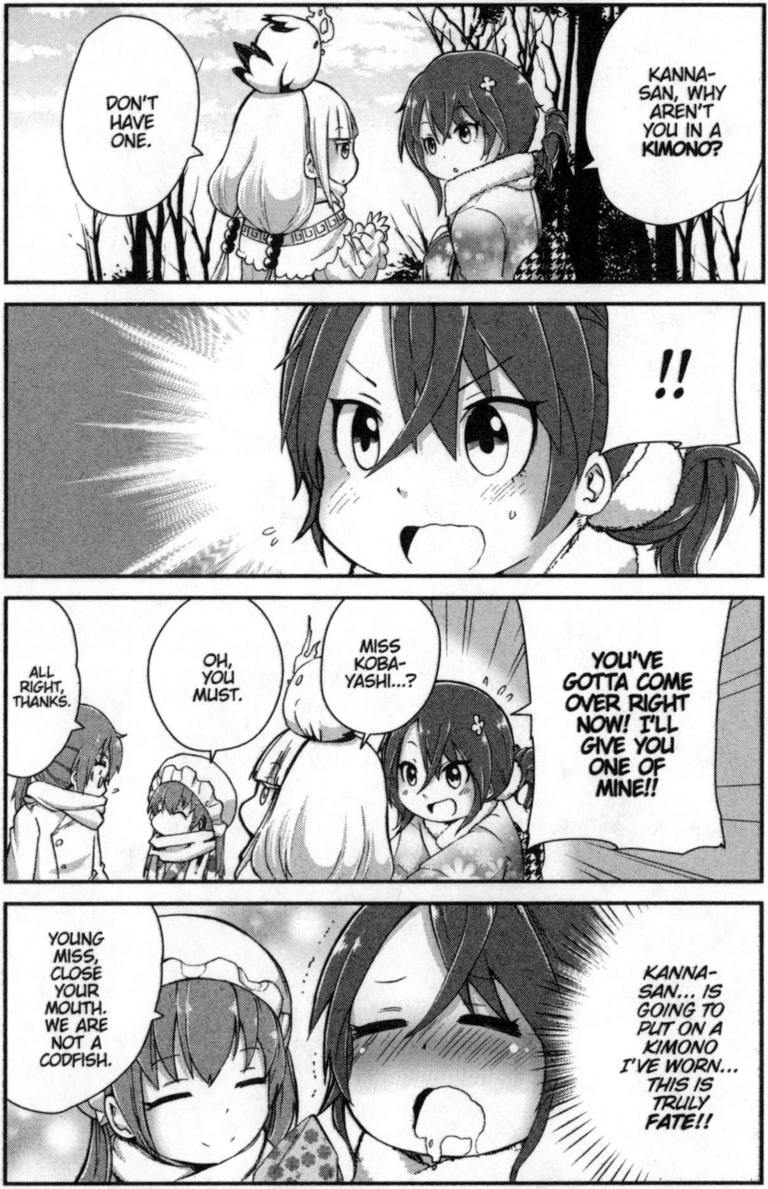
KANNA-SAN, WHY AREN'T YOU IN A KIMONO?
DON'T HAVE ONE.
!!
YOU'VE GOTTA COME OVER RIGHT NOW! I'LL GIVE YOU ONE OF MINE!!
MISS KOBA-YASHI...?
OH, YOU MUST.
ALL RIGHT, THANKS.
KANNA-SAN... IS GOING TO PUT ON A KIMONO I'VE WORN... THIS IS TRULY FATE!!
YOUNG MISS, CLOSE YOUR MOUTH. WE ARE NOT A CODFISH.

KANNA'S TRIBULATIONS

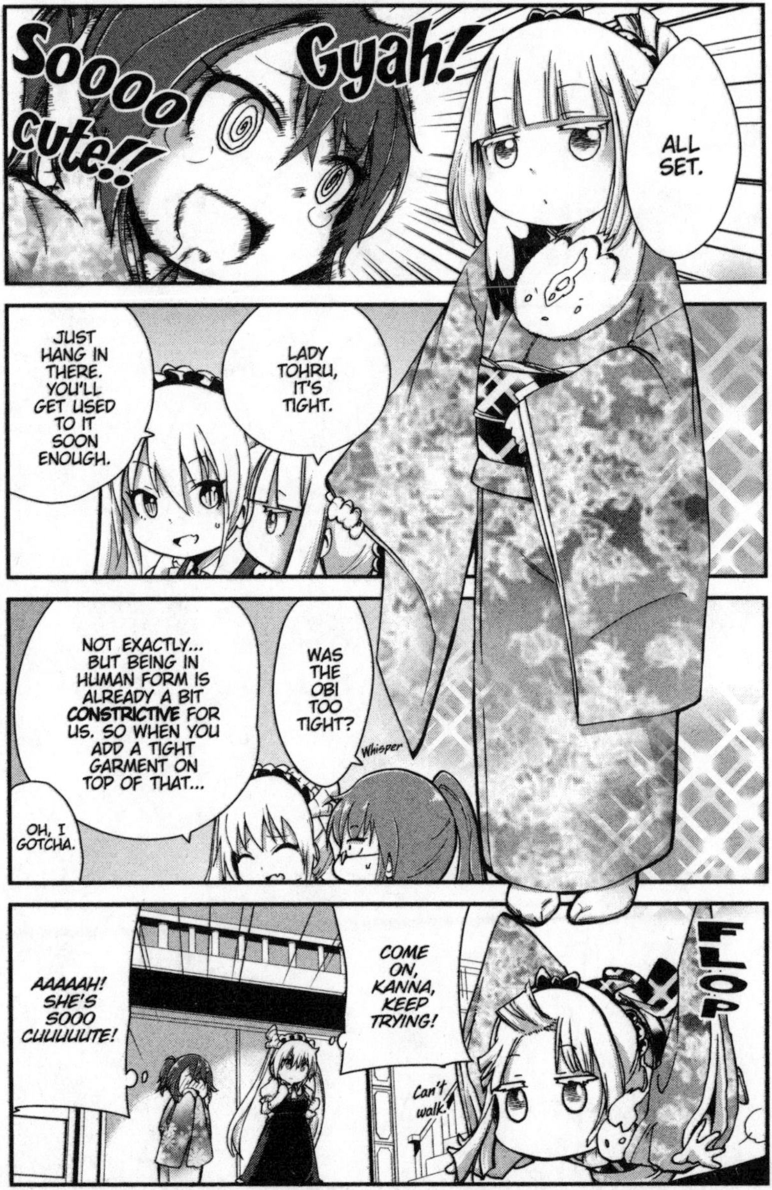
ALL SET.
Gyah!
Soooo cute!!
LADY TOHRU, IT'S TIGHT.
JUST HANG IN THERE. YOU'LL GET USED TO IT SOON ENOUGH.
Whisper
WAS THE OBI TOO TIGHT?
NOT EXACTLY... BUT BEING IN HUMAN FORM IS ALREADY A BIT **CONSTRICTIVE** FOR US. SO WHEN YOU ADD A TIGHT GARMENT ON TOP OF THAT...
OH, I GOTCHA.
FLOP
Can't walk.
COME ON, KANNA, KEEP TRYING!
AAAAAH! SHE'S SOOO CUUUUUTE!

HANETSUKI

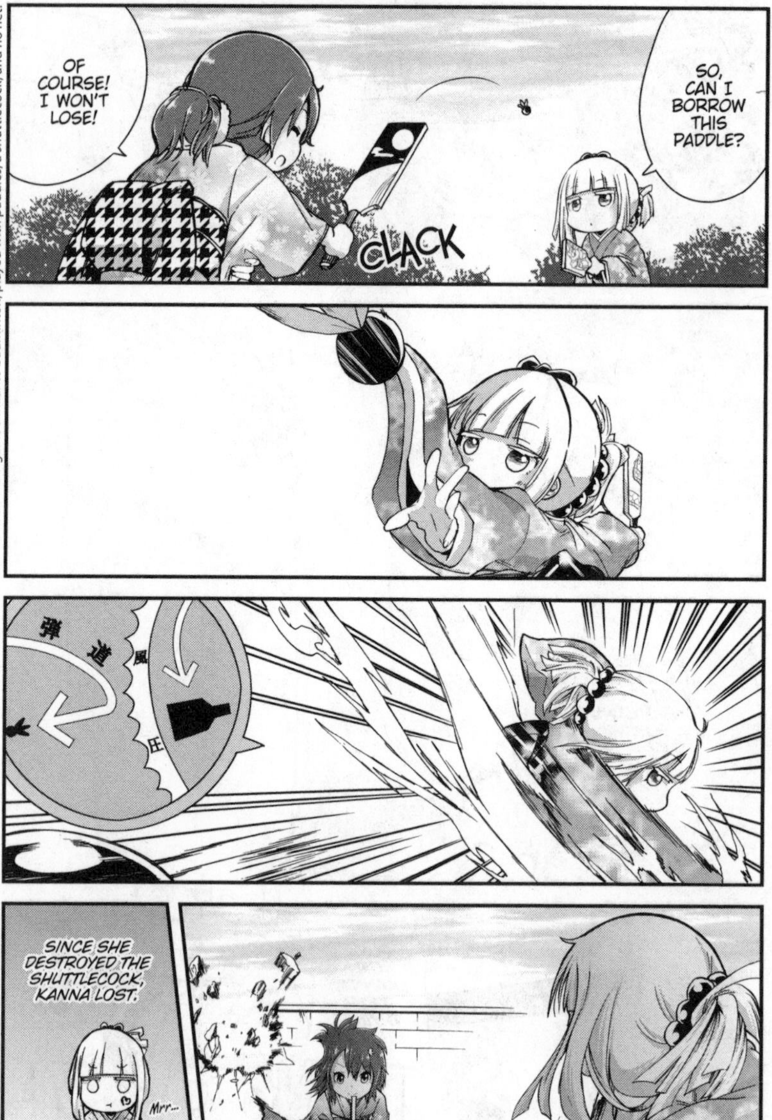
SO, CAN I BORROW THIS PADDLE?
OF COURSE! I WON'T LOSE!
CLACK
弾道
風
圧
SINCE SHE DESTROYED THE SHUTTLECOCK, KANNA LOST.
Mrr...

※ Hanetsuki is a game similar to badminton, played with paddles, a shuttlecock, and no net.

ME

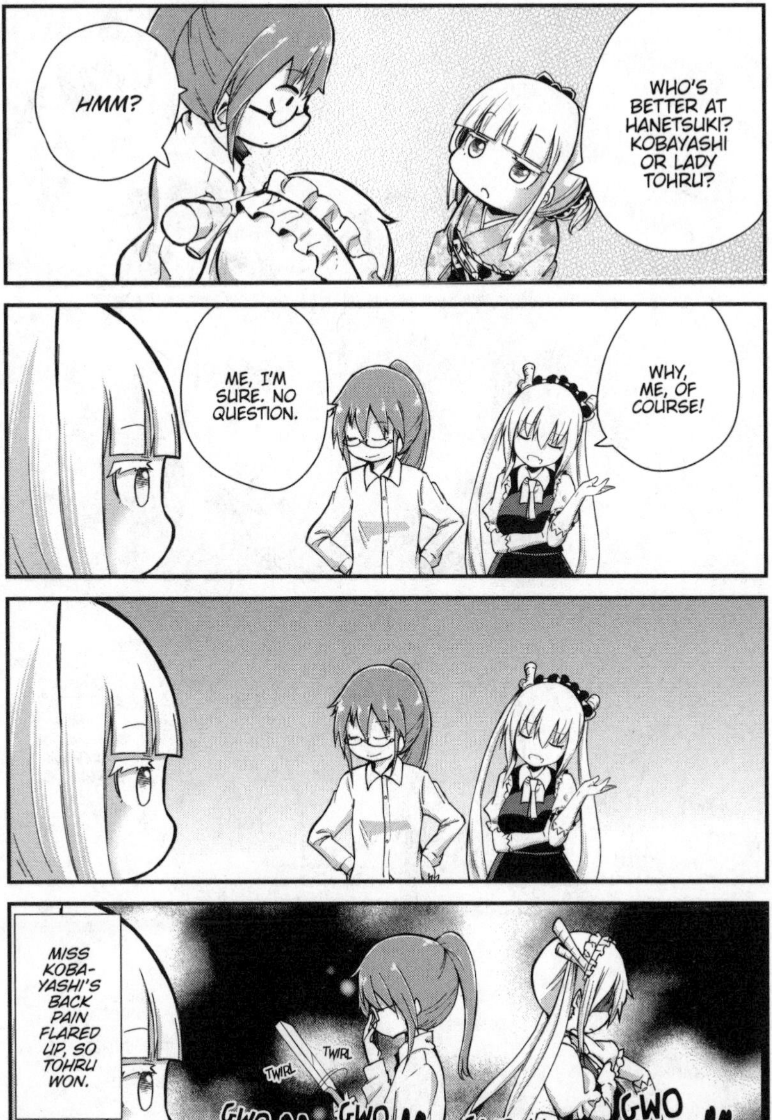
WHO'S BETTER AT HANETSUKI? KOBAYASHI OR LADY TOHRU?
HMM?
WHY, ME, OF COURSE!
ME, I'M SURE. NO QUESTION.
MISS KOBA-YASHI'S BACK PAIN FLARED UP, SO TOHRU WON.
TWIRL
TWIRL
GWO
GWO
GWO
GWO

ANOTHER GOOD YEAR

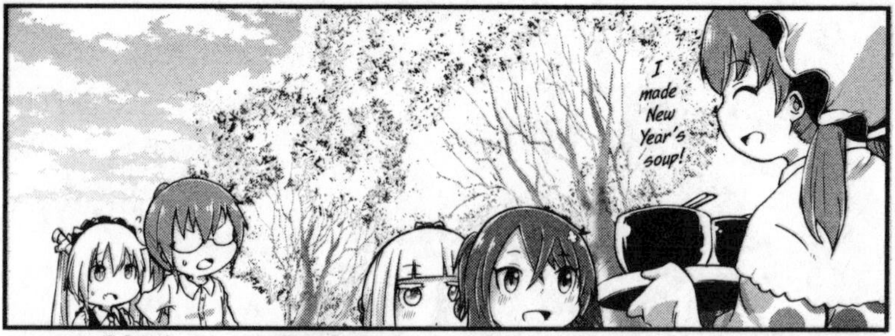
I made New Year's soup!

※ Ozōni is a soup made with mochi rice cake and vegetables. It is traditionally served on New Year's.

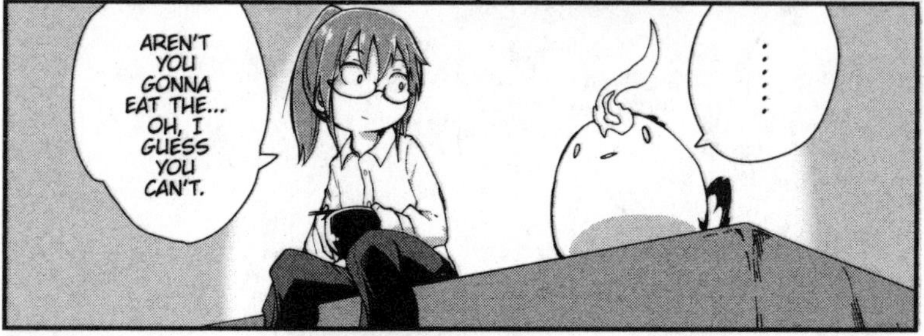
......
AREN'T YOU GONNA EAT THE... OH, I GUESS YOU CAN'T.

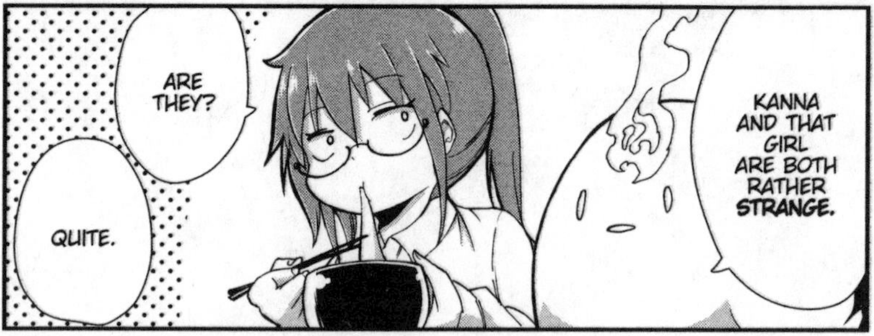
KANNA AND THAT GIRL ARE BOTH RATHER **STRANGE.**
ARE THEY?
QUITE.

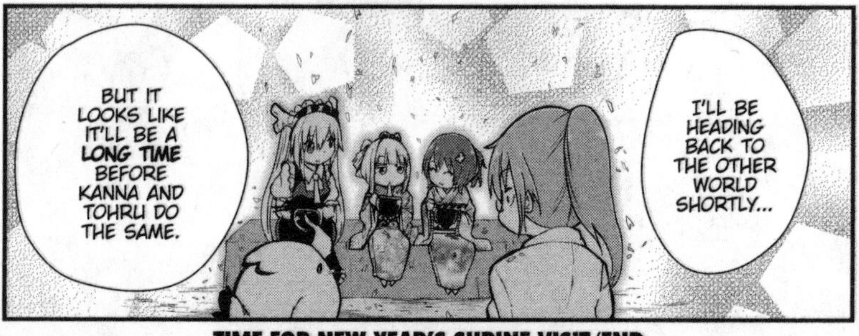
I'LL BE HEADING BACK TO THE OTHER WORLD SHORTLY...
BUT IT LOOKS LIKE IT'LL BE A **LONG TIME** BEFORE KANNA AND TOHRU DO THE SAME.

TIME FOR NEW YEAR'S SHRINE VISIT/END

We match! ♥

Miss Kobayashi's Dragon Maid
Kanna's Daily Life

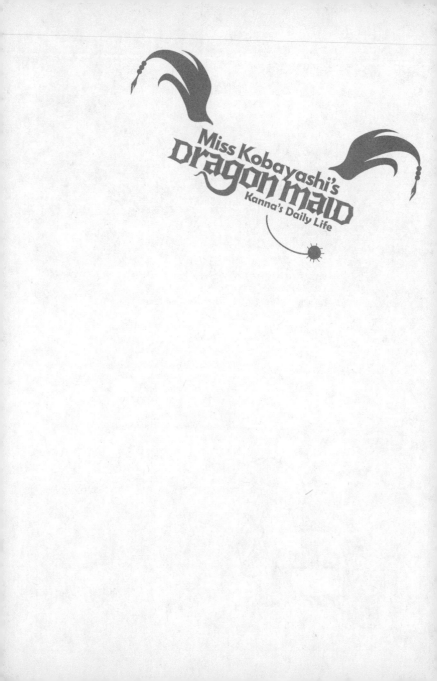

JACK FROST

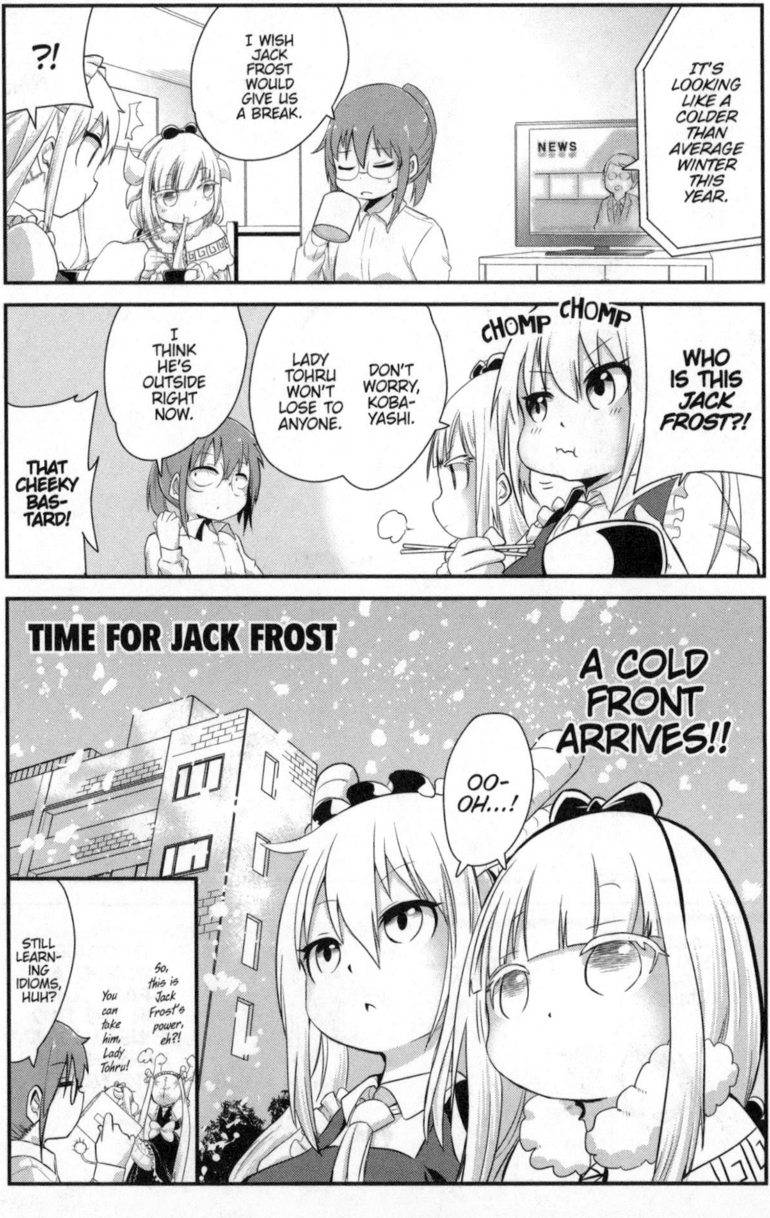
IT'S LOOKING LIKE A COLDER THAN AVERAGE WINTER THIS YEAR.
I WISH JACK FROST WOULD GIVE US A BREAK.
?!
WHO IS THIS JACK FROST?!
CHOMP CHOMP
DON'T WORRY, KOBA-YASHI.
LADY TOHRU WON'T LOSE TO ANYONE.
I THINK HE'S OUTSIDE RIGHT NOW.
THAT CHEEKY BAS-TARD!
TIME FOR JACK FROST
A COLD FRONT ARRIVES!!
OO-OH...!
So, this is Jack Frost's power, eh?!
You can take him, Lady Tohru!
STILL LEARNING IDIOMS, HUH?

SAIKAWA'S IGLOO RULES

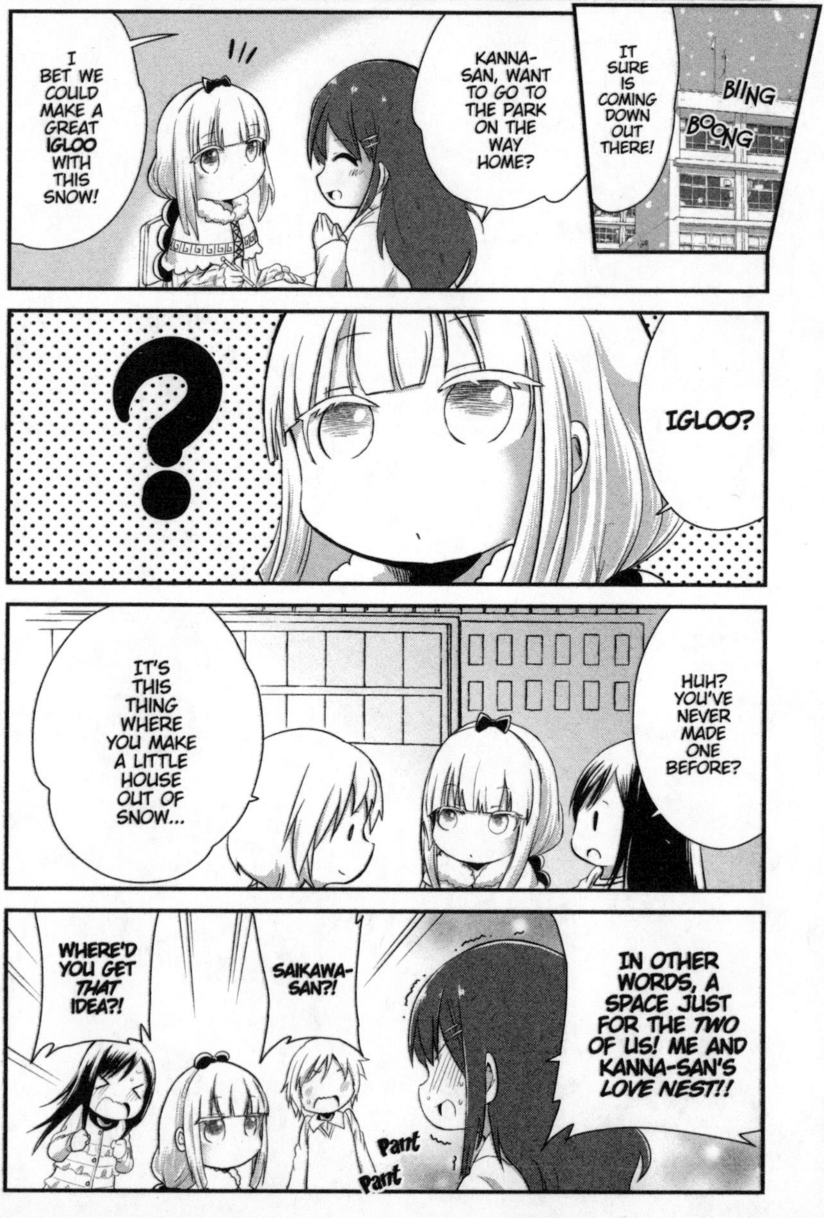
BIING
BOONG
IT SURE IS COMING DOWN OUT THERE!
KANNA-SAN, WANT TO GO TO THE PARK ON THE WAY HOME?
I BET WE COULD MAKE A GREAT IGLOO WITH THIS SNOW!
IGLOO?
HUH? YOU'VE NEVER MADE ONE BEFORE?
IT'S THIS THING WHERE YOU MAKE A LITTLE HOUSE OUT OF SNOW...
IN OTHER WORDS, A SPACE JUST FOR THE TWO OF US! ME AND KANNA-SAN'S LOVE NEST!!
Pant
Pant
SAIKAWA-SAN?!
WHERE'D YOU GET THAT IDEA?!

KANNA'S ANTI-FREEZING PLAN

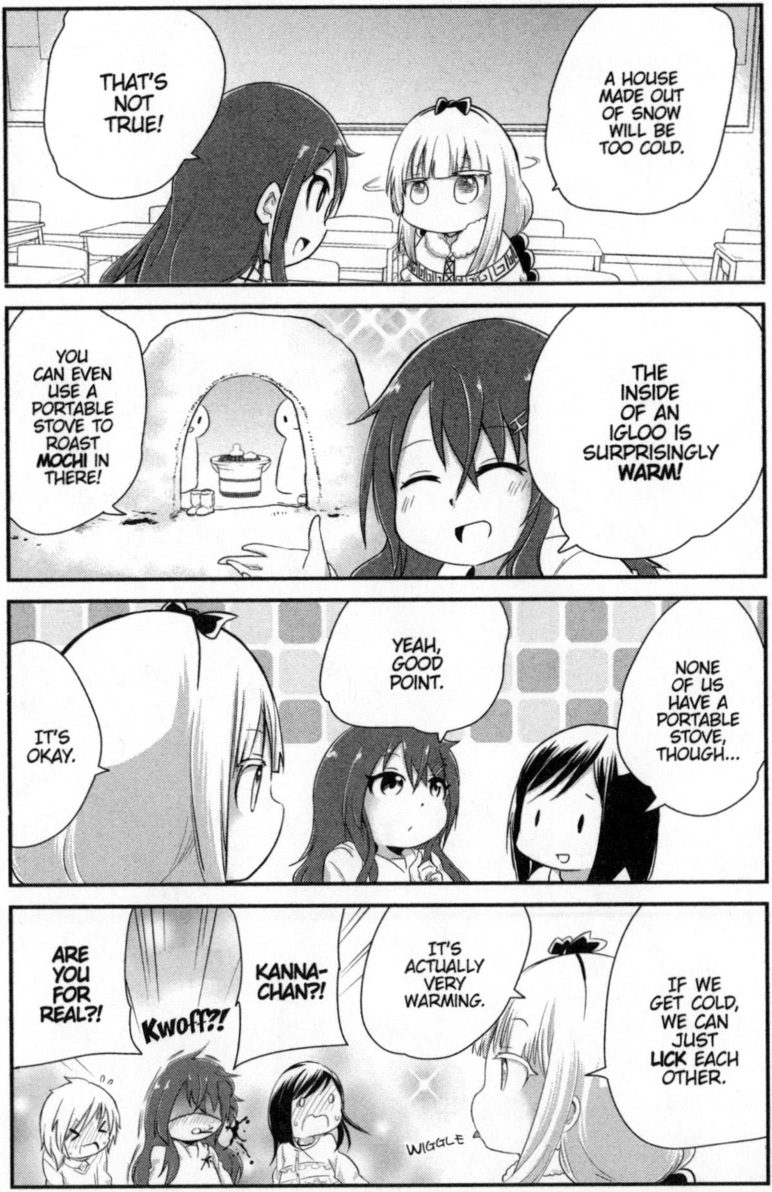
A HOUSE MADE OUT OF SNOW WILL BE TOO COLD.
THAT'S NOT TRUE!
THE INSIDE OF AN IGLOO IS SURPRISINGLY **WARM!**
YOU CAN EVEN USE A PORTABLE STOVE TO ROAST **MOCHI** IN THERE!
NONE OF US HAVE A PORTABLE STOVE, THOUGH...
YEAH, GOOD POINT.
IT'S OKAY.
IF WE GET COLD, WE CAN JUST **LICK** EACH OTHER.
IT'S ACTUALLY VERY WARMING.
KANNA-CHAN?!
ARE YOU FOR REAL?!
Kwoff?!
WIGGLE

SEE YOU TOMORROW

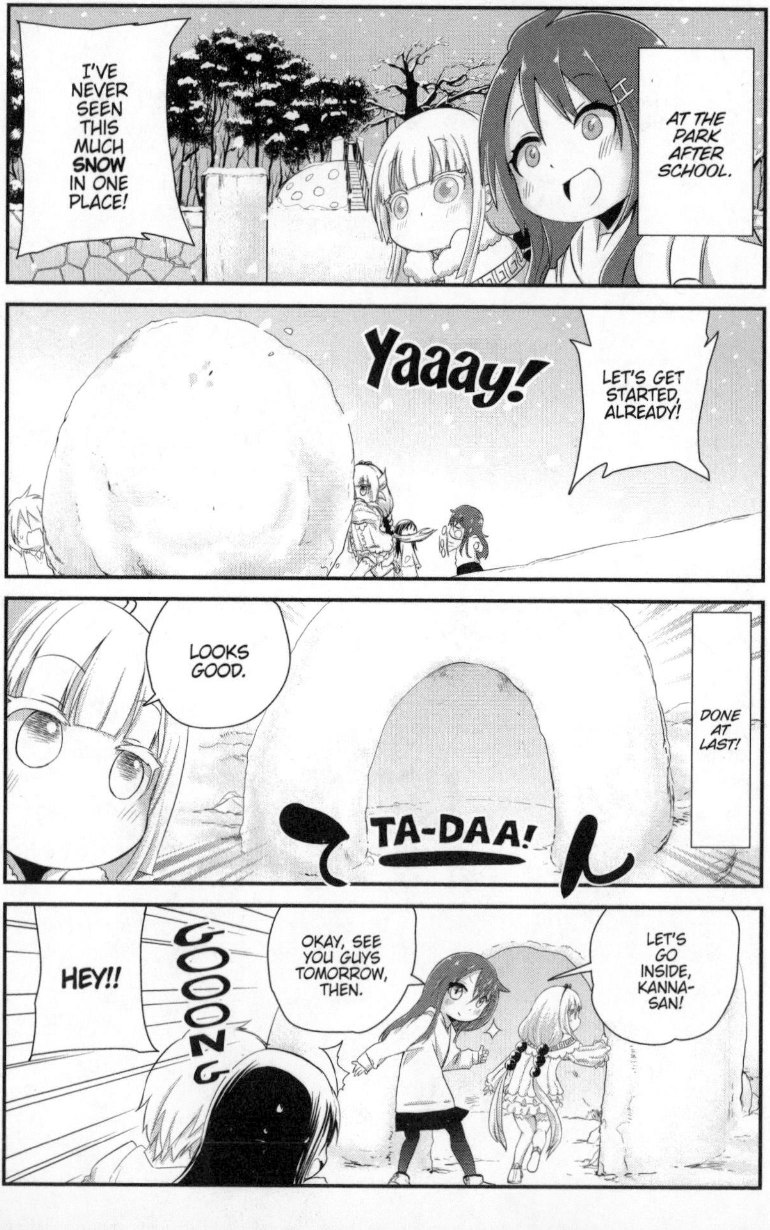
AT THE PARK AFTER SCHOOL.
I'VE NEVER SEEN THIS MUCH SNOW IN ONE PLACE!
LET'S GET STARTED, ALREADY!
Yaaay!
DONE AT LAST!
TA-DAA!
LOOKS GOOD.
LET'S GO INSIDE, KANNA-SAN!
OKAY, SEE YOU GUYS TOMORROW, THEN.
GOOON
HEY!!

LIKE *THE WOMAN IN THE DUNES*

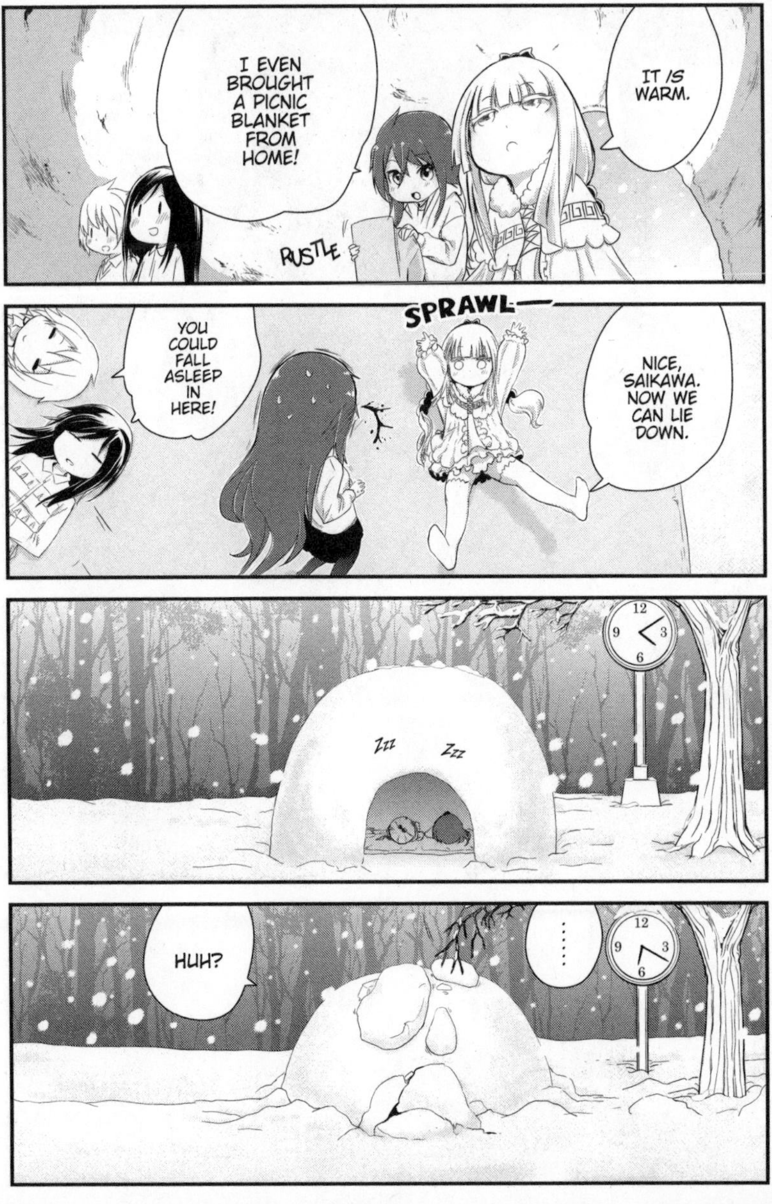

IT IS WARM.
I EVEN BROUGHT A PICNIC BLANKET FROM HOME!
RUSTLE
SPRAWL—
NICE, SAIKAWA. NOW WE CAN LIE DOWN.
YOU COULD FALL ASLEEP IN HERE!
12 3 6 9
Zzz
Zzz
12 3 6 9
......
HUH?

※The Woman in the Dunes is a Japanese novel and film about a widow who traps a young schoolteacher in a house buried in sand.

KANNA CAN BE KIND

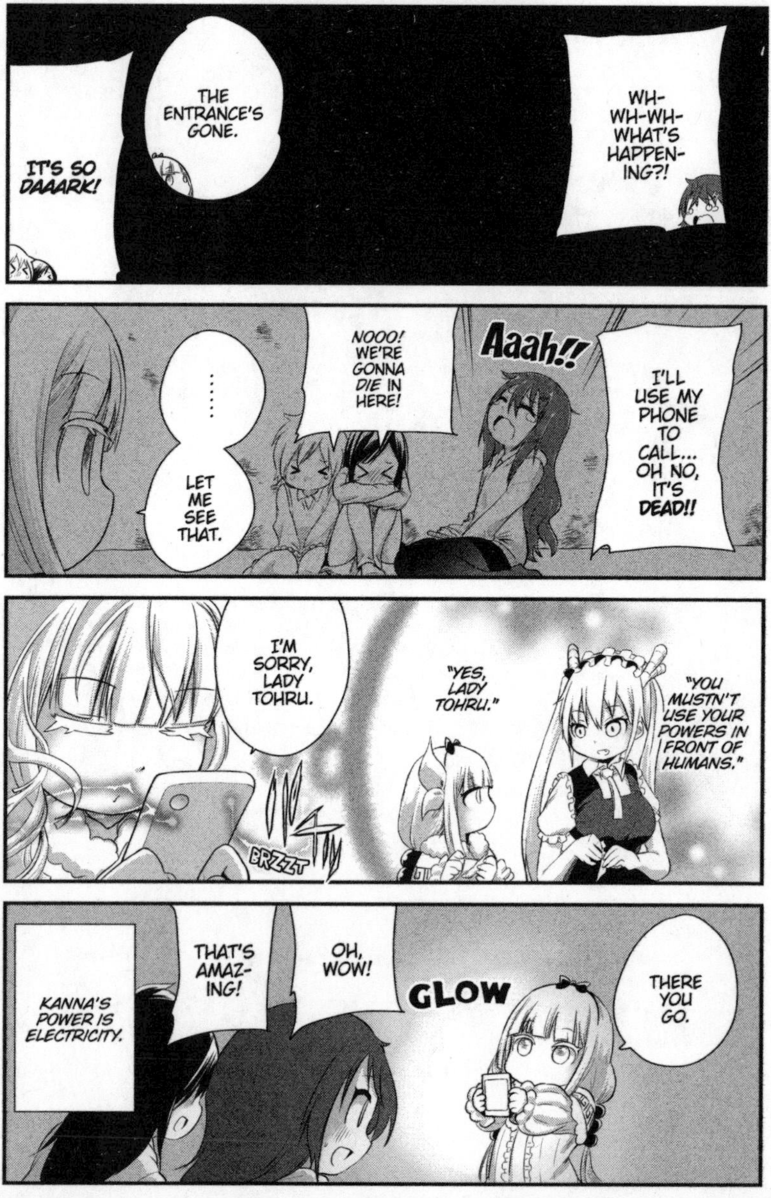
WH-WH-WH-WHAT'S HAPPENING?!
THE ENTRANCE'S GONE.
IT'S SO DAAARK!
I'LL USE MY PHONE TO CALL... OH NO, IT'S DEAD!!
Aaah!!
NOOO! WE'RE GONNA DIE IN HERE!
......
LET ME SEE THAT.
"YOU MUSTN'T USE YOUR POWERS IN FRONT OF HUMANS."
"YES, LADY TOHRU."
I'M SORRY, LADY TOHRU.
BRZZZT
THERE YOU GO.
GLOW
OH, WOW!
THAT'S AMAZING!
KANNA'S POWER IS ELECTRICITY.

RIGHT

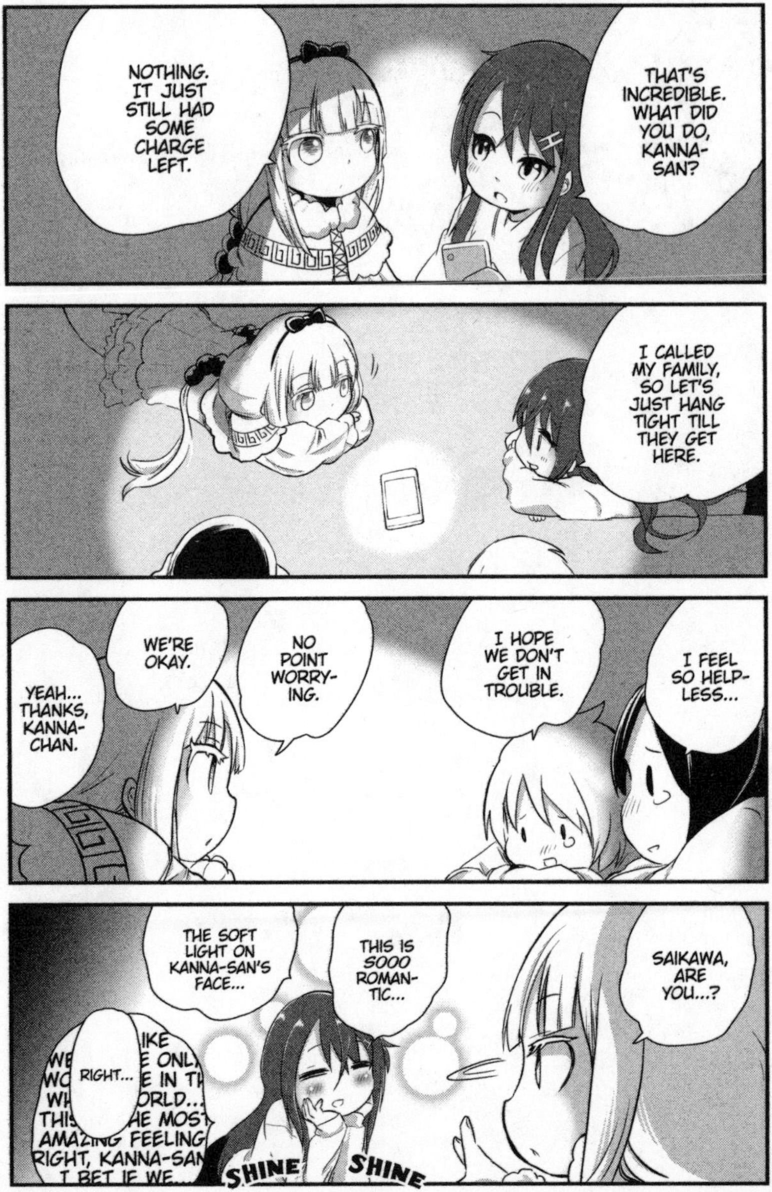
THAT'S INCREDIBLE. WHAT DID YOU DO, KANNA-SAN?
NOTHING. IT JUST STILL HAD SOME CHARGE LEFT.
I CALLED MY FAMILY, SO LET'S JUST HANG TIGHT TILL THEY GET HERE.
I FEEL SO HELP-LESS...
I HOPE WE DON'T GET IN TROUBLE.
NO POINT WORRY-ING.
WE'RE OKAY.
YEAH... THANKS, KANNA-CHAN.
SAIKAWA, ARE YOU...?
THIS IS SOOO ROMAN-TIC...
THE SOFT LIGHT ON KANNA-SAN'S FACE...
AMAZING FEELING
RIGHT, KANNA-SAN
RIGHT...
SHINE
SHINE

THE GOD OF SALVATION APPEARS!

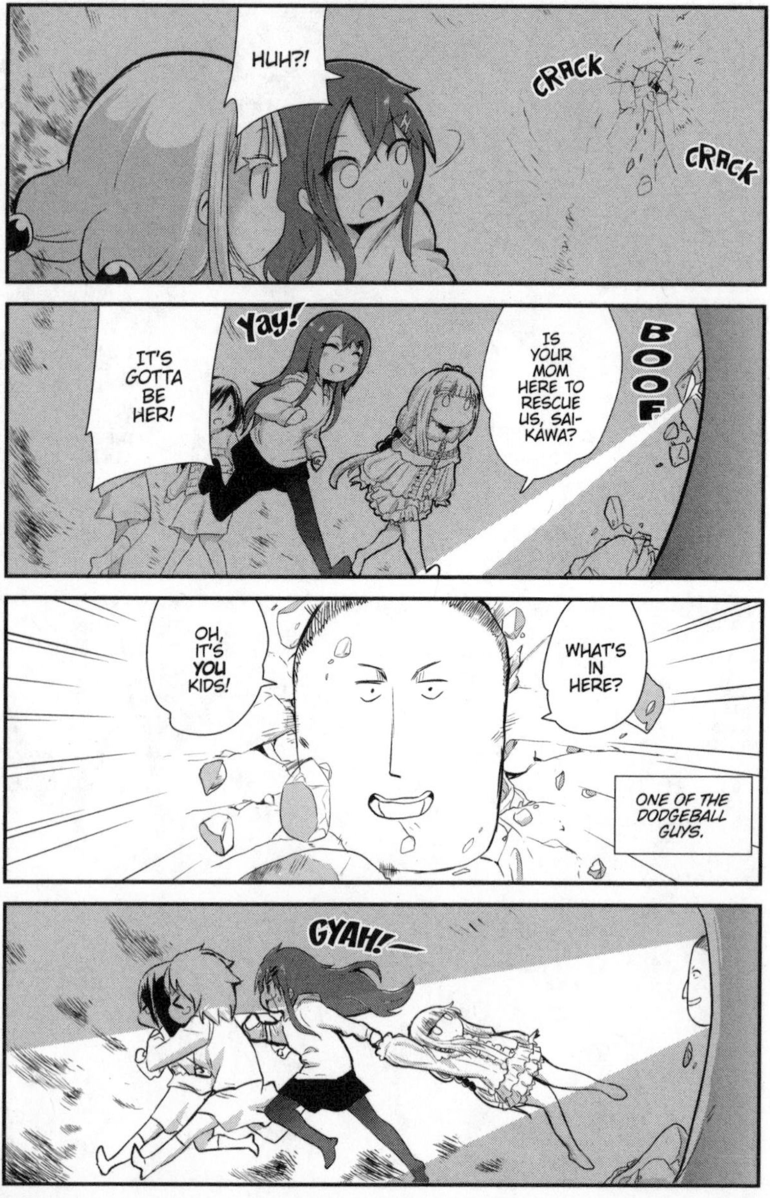
CRACK
CRACK
HUH?!
BOOF
IS YOUR MOM HERE TO RESCUE US, SAI-KAWA?
Yay!
IT'S GOTTA BE HER!
WHAT'S IN HERE?
ONE OF THE DODGEBALL GUYS.
OH, IT'S YOU KIDS!
GYAH!—

I DON'T LIKE HIM!

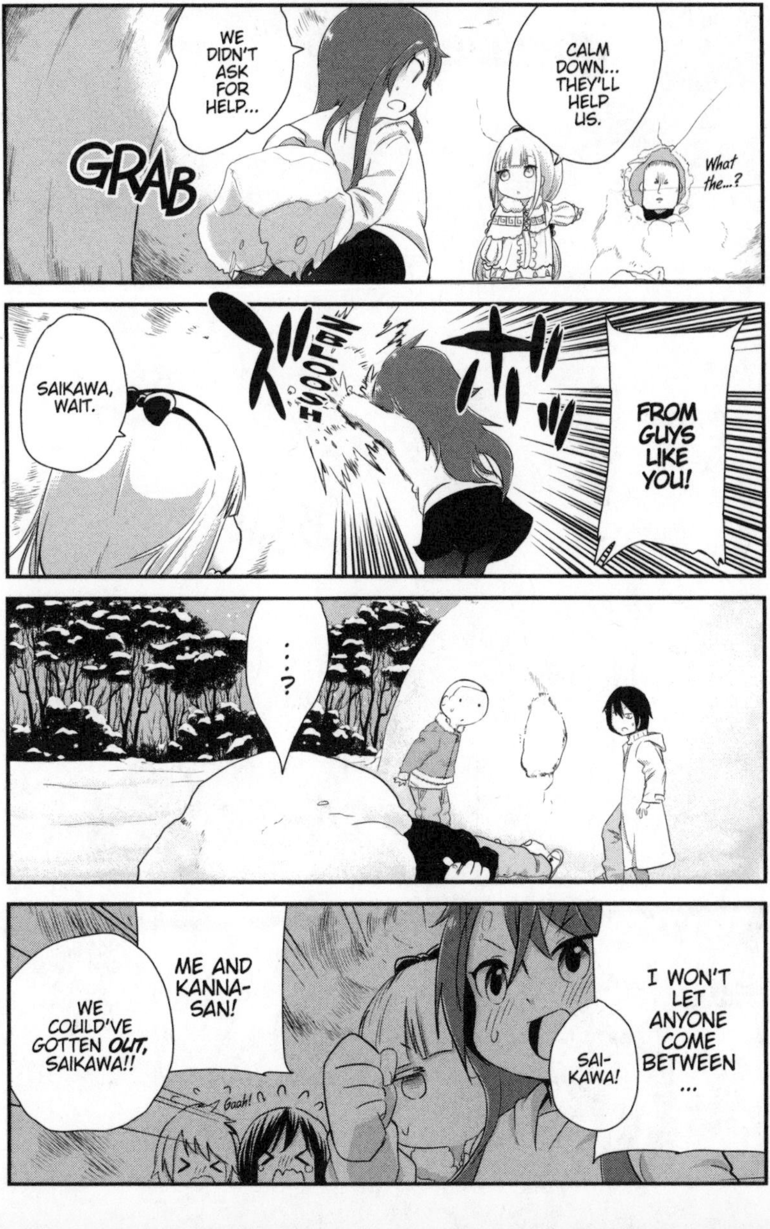

What the...?
CALM DOWN... THEY'LL HELP US.
WE DIDN'T ASK FOR HELP...
GRAB
FROM GUYS LIKE YOU!
SPLOOSH
SAIKAWA, WAIT.
...?
I WON'T LET ANYONE COME BETWEEN ...
SAI-KAWA!
ME AND KANNA-SAN!
WE COULD'VE GOTTEN *OUT*, SAIKAWA!!
Gaah!

KANNA TAKES A STAND!

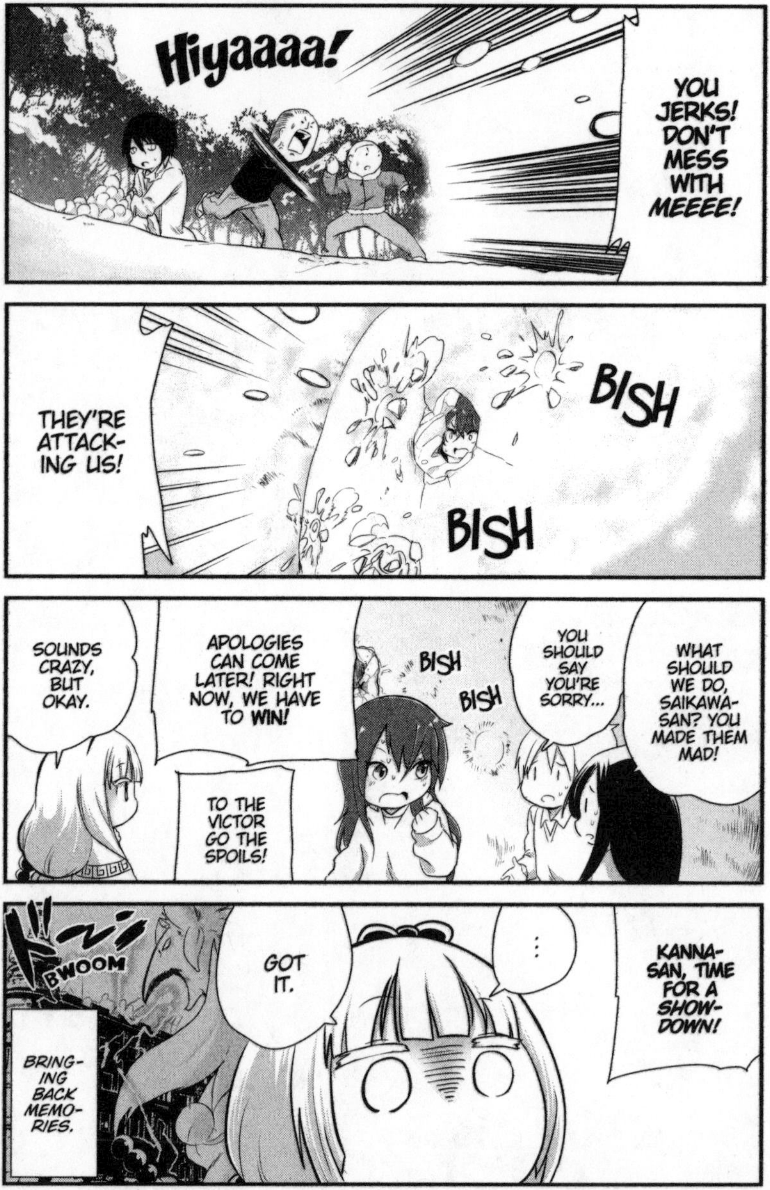
YOU JERKS! DON'T MESS WITH MEEEE!
Hiyaaaa!
BISH
BISH
THEY'RE ATTACK-ING US!
WHAT SHOULD WE DO, SAIKAWA-SAN? YOU MADE THEM MAD!
YOU SHOULD SAY YOU'RE SORRY...
BISH
BISH
APOLOGIES CAN COME LATER! RIGHT NOW, WE HAVE TO WIN!
TO THE VICTOR GO THE SPOILS!
SOUNDS CRAZY, BUT OKAY.
KANNA-SAN, TIME FOR A SHOW-DOWN!
...
GOT IT.
BWOOM
BRING-ING BACK MEMO-RIES.

PRETENDING TO UNDERSTAND

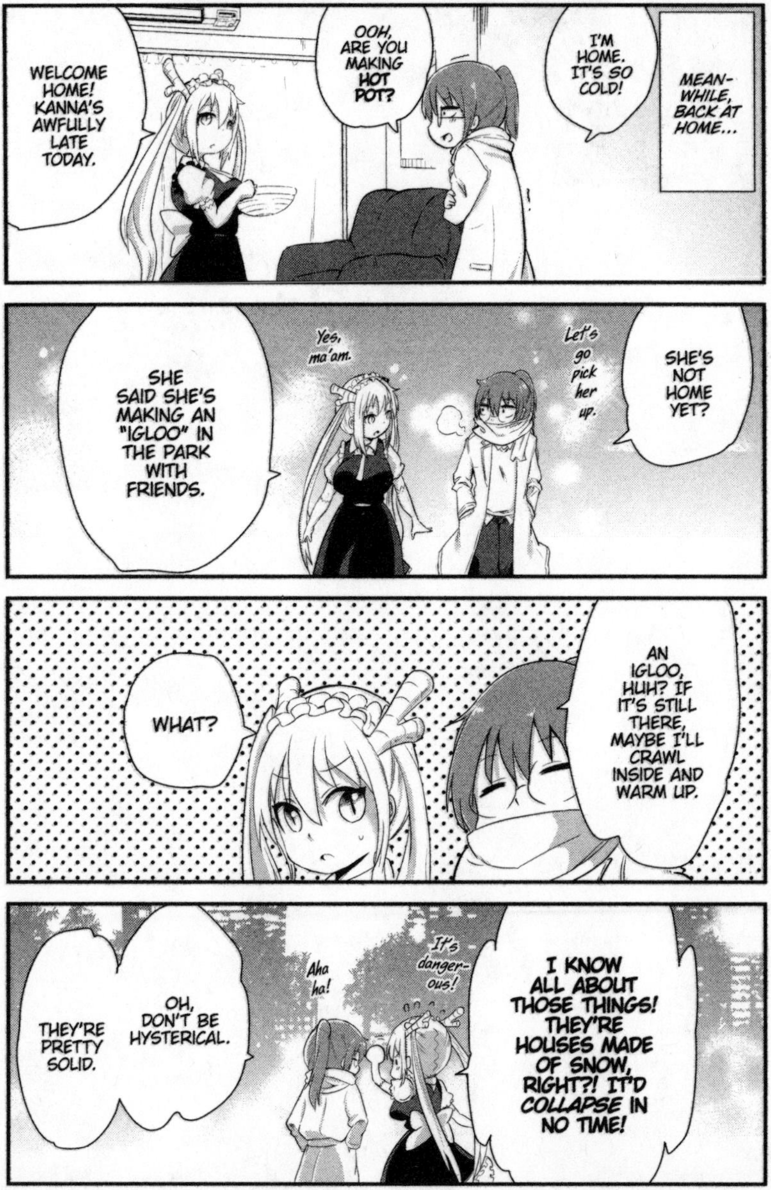
MEAN-WHILE, BACK AT HOME...
I'M HOME. IT'S SO COLD!
OOH, ARE YOU MAKING HOT POT?
WELCOME HOME! KANNA'S AWFULLY LATE TODAY.
SHE'S NOT HOME YET?
Let's go pick her up.
Yes, ma'am.
SHE SAID SHE'S MAKING AN "IGLOO" IN THE PARK WITH FRIENDS.
AN IGLOO, HUH? IF IT'S STILL THERE, MAYBE I'LL CRAWL INSIDE AND WARM UP.
WHAT?
I KNOW ALL ABOUT THOSE THINGS! THEY'RE HOUSES MADE OF SNOW, RIGHT?! IT'D COLLAPSE IN NO TIME!
It's danger-ous!
Aha ha!
OH, DON'T BE HYSTERICAL.
THEY'RE PRETTY SOLID.

NOT WHAT THEY EXPECTED

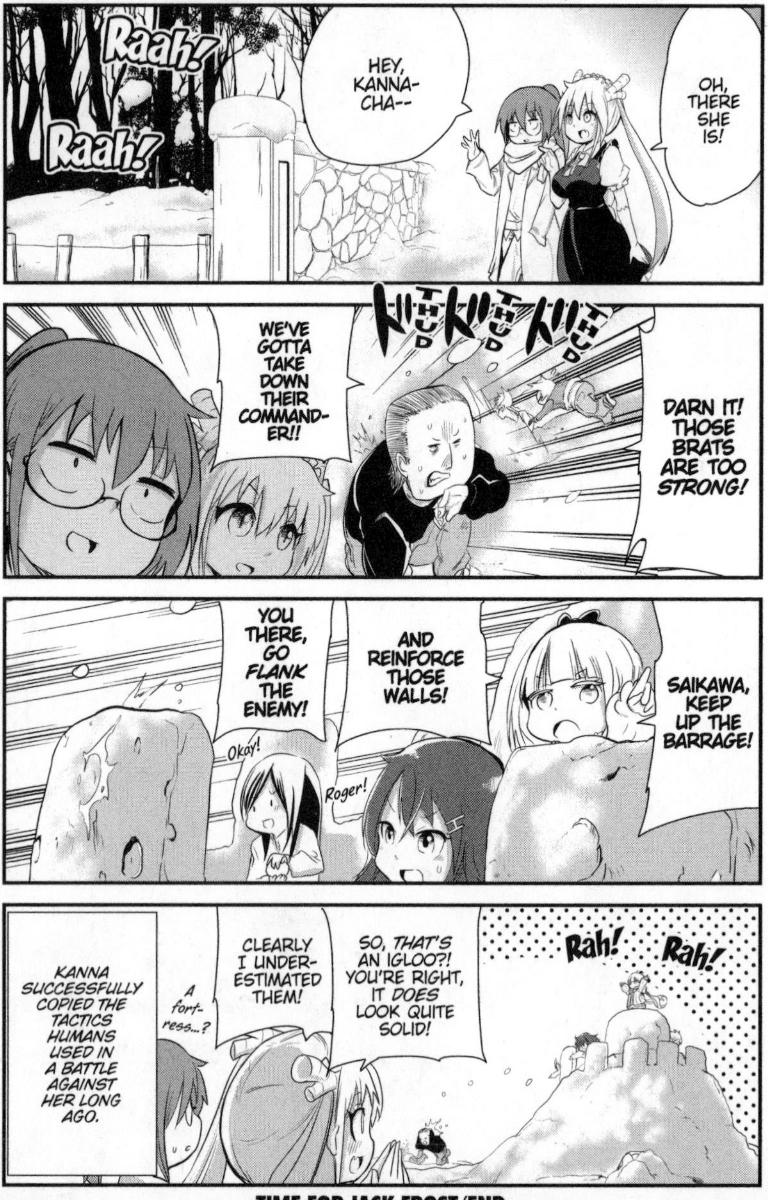
OH, THERE SHE IS!
HEY, KANNA-CHA--
Raah!
Raah!
DARN IT! THOSE BRATS ARE TOO STRONG!
THUD THUD THUD
WE'VE GOTTA TAKE DOWN THEIR COMMANDER!!
SAIKAWA, KEEP UP THE BARRAGE!
AND REINFORCE THOSE WALLS!
YOU THERE, GO FLANK THE ENEMY!
Roger!
Okay!
Rah! Rah!
SO, THAT'S AN IGLOO?! YOU'RE RIGHT, IT DOES LOOK QUITE SOLID!
CLEARLY I UNDER-ESTIMATED THEM!
A fort-ress...?
KANNA SUCCESSFULLY COPIED THE TACTICS HUMANS USED IN A BATTLE AGAINST HER LONG AGO.

TIME FOR JACK FROST/END

TOO HIGH OF A MOUNTAIN

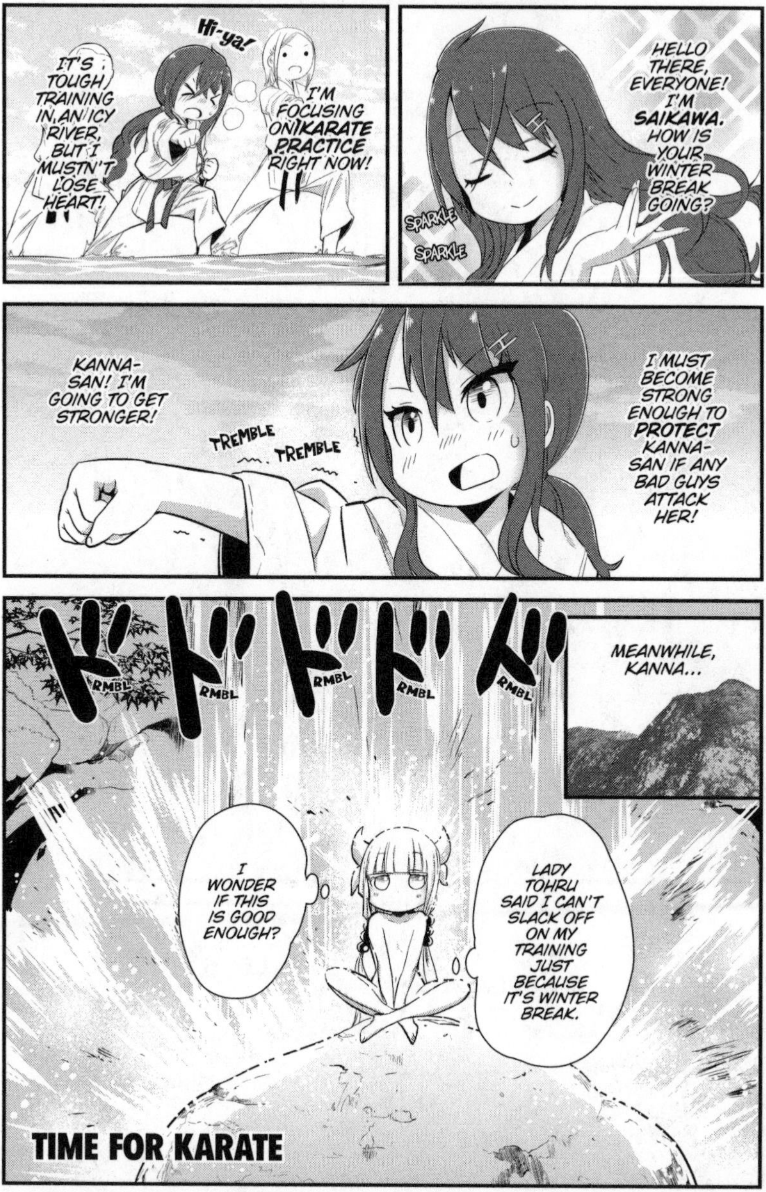
HELLO THERE, EVERYONE! I'M SAIKAWA. HOW IS YOUR WINTER BREAK GOING?
SPARKLE
SPARKLE
Hi-ya!
I'M FOCUSING ON KARATE PRACTICE RIGHT NOW!
IT'S TOUGH TRAINING IN AN ICY RIVER, BUT I MUSTN'T LOSE HEART!
I MUST BECOME STRONG ENOUGH TO PROTECT KANNA-SAN IF ANY BAD GUYS ATTACK HER!
KANNA-SAN! I'M GOING TO GET STRONGER!
TREMBLE
TREMBLE
MEANWHILE, KANNA...
RMBL
RMBL
RMBL
RMBL
RMBL
LADY TOHRU SAID I CAN'T SLACK OFF ON MY TRAINING JUST BECAUSE IT'S WINTER BREAK.
I WONDER IF THIS IS GOOD ENOUGH?

TIME FOR KARATE

AFFINITY

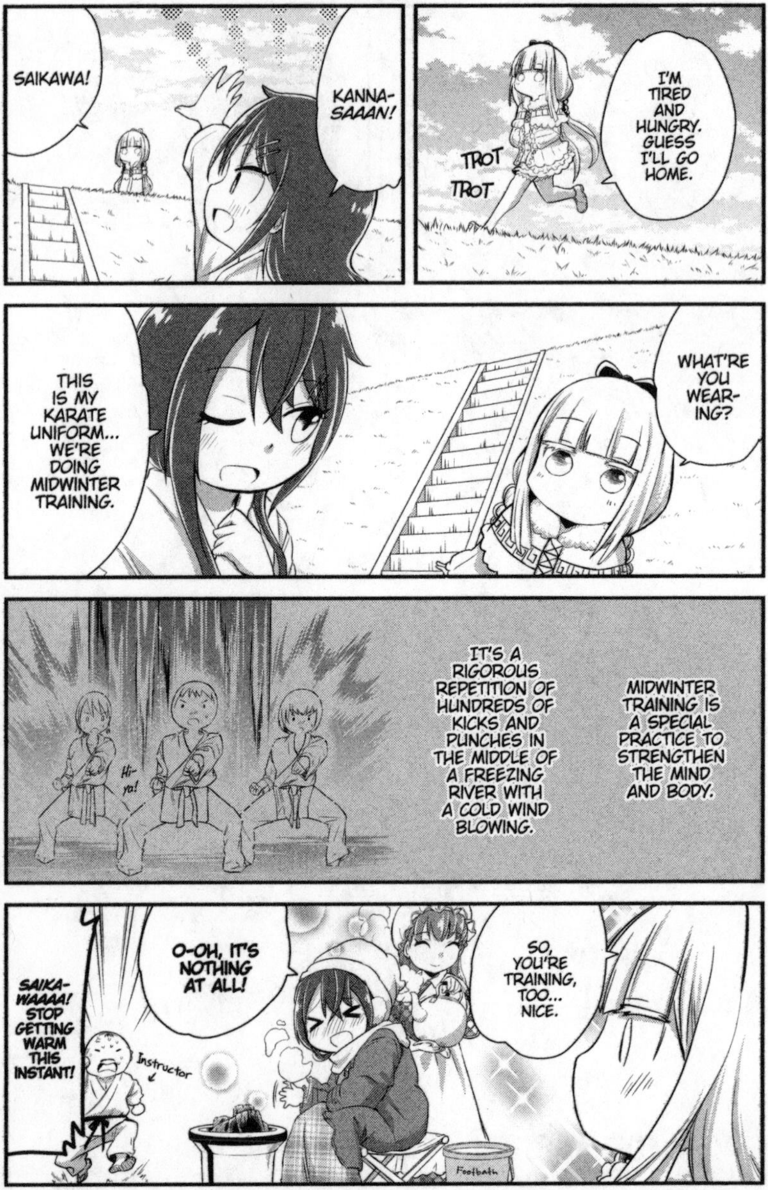
I'M TIRED AND HUNGRY. GUESS I'LL GO HOME.
TROT TROT
KANNA-SAAAN!
SAIKAWA!
WHAT'RE YOU WEAR-ING?
THIS IS MY KARATE UNIFORM... WE'RE DOING MIDWINTER TRAINING.
MIDWINTER TRAINING IS A SPECIAL PRACTICE TO STRENGTHEN THE MIND AND BODY.
IT'S A RIGOROUS REPETITION OF HUNDREDS OF KICKS AND PUNCHES IN THE MIDDLE OF A FREEZING RIVER WITH A COLD WIND BLOWING.
Hi-ya!
SO, YOU'RE TRAINING, TOO... NICE.
O-OH, IT'S NOTHING AT ALL!
SAIKA-WAAAA! STOP GETTING WARM THIS INSTANT!
Instructor
Footbath

KANNA'S SUDDEN AIRHEAD ATTACK!

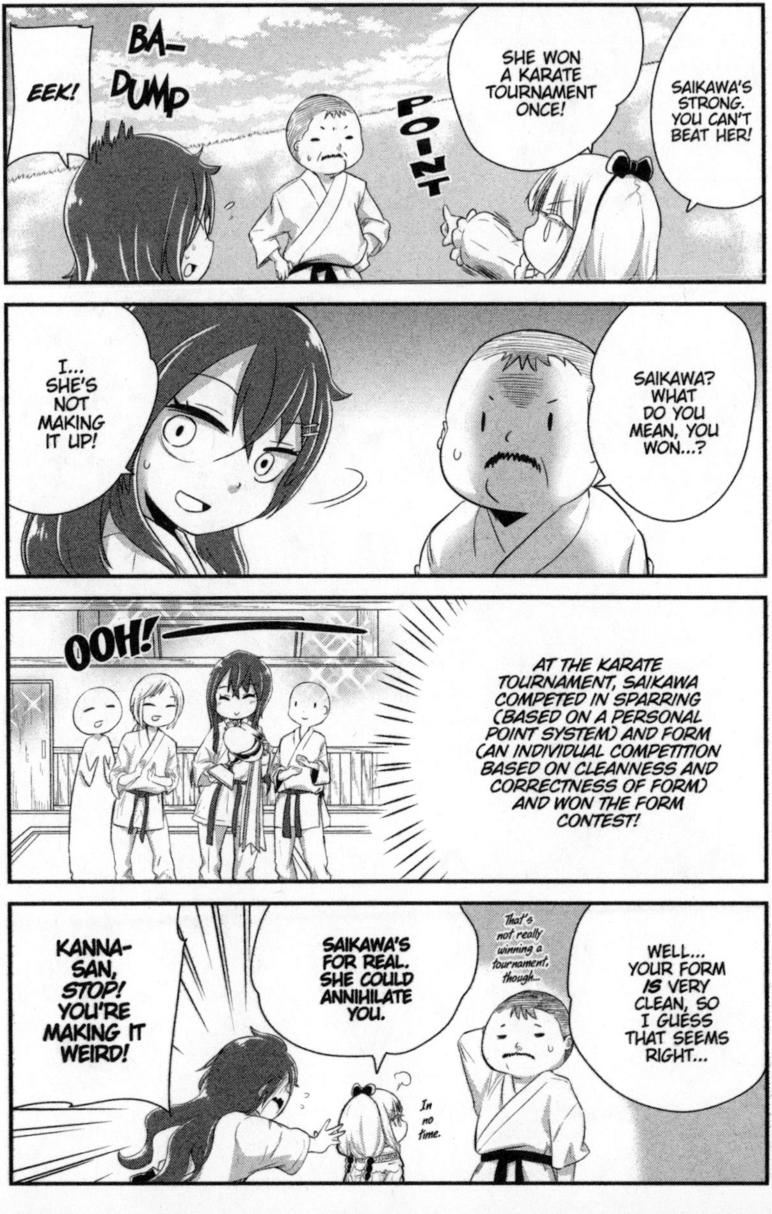

SAIKAWA'S STRONG. YOU CAN'T BEAT HER!
SHE WON A KARATE TOURNAMENT ONCE!
POINT
BA-DUMP
EEK!
SAIKAWA? WHAT DO YOU MEAN, YOU WON...?
I... SHE'S NOT MAKING IT UP!
AT THE KARATE TOURNAMENT, SAIKAWA COMPETED IN SPARRING (BASED ON A PERSONAL POINT SYSTEM) AND FORM (AN INDIVIDUAL COMPETITION BASED ON CLEANNESS AND CORRECTNESS OF FORM) AND WON THE FORM CONTEST!
OOH!
WELL... YOUR FORM IS VERY CLEAN, SO I GUESS THAT SEEMS RIGHT...
That's not really winning a tournament, though...
SAIKAWA'S FOR REAL. SHE COULD ANNIHILATE YOU.
In no time.
KANNA-SAN, STOP! YOU'RE MAKING IT WEIRD!

READ THE ROOM, WILL YOU? (1)

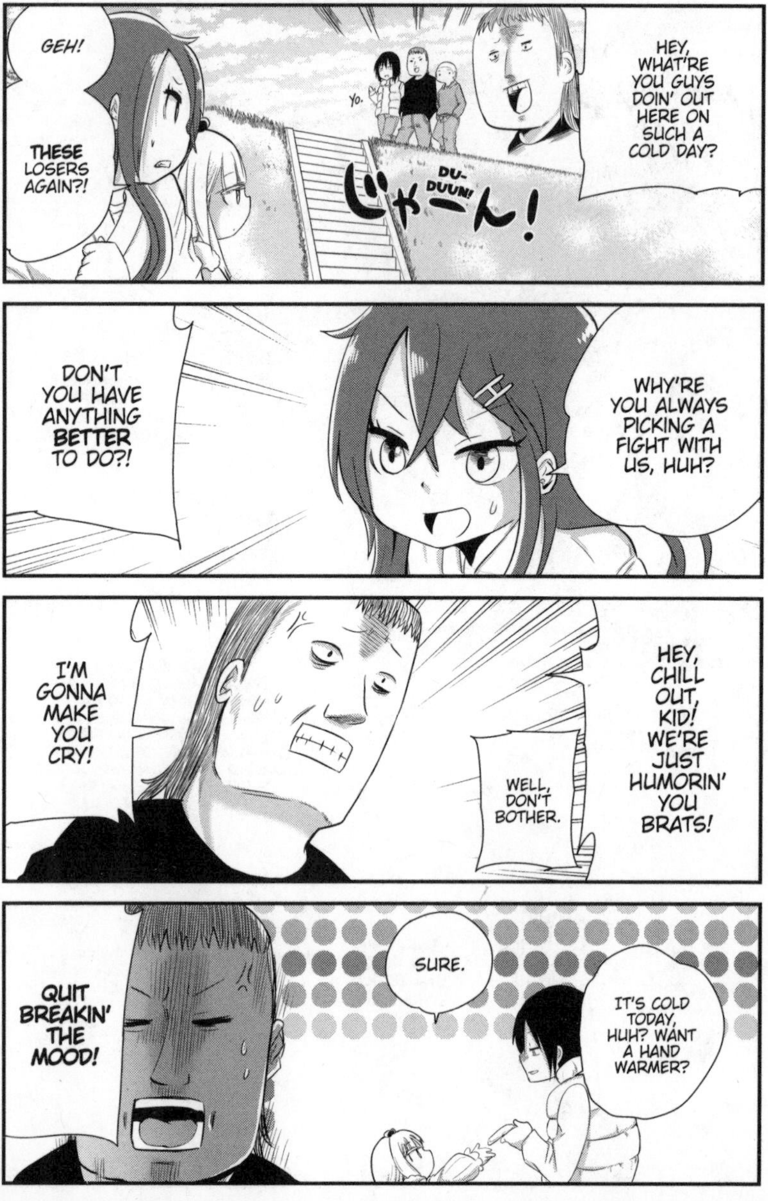
HEY, WHAT'RE YOU GUYS DOIN' OUT HERE ON SUCH A COLD DAY?
YO.
GEH!
THESE LOSERS AGAIN?!
DU-DUUN!
じゃーん!
WHY'RE YOU ALWAYS PICKING A FIGHT WITH US, HUH?
DON'T YOU HAVE ANYTHING BETTER TO DO?!
HEY, CHILL OUT, KID! WE'RE JUST HUMORIN' YOU BRATS!
WELL, DON'T BOTHER.
I'M GONNA MAKE YOU CRY!
IT'S COLD TODAY, HUH? WANT A HAND WARMER?
SURE.
QUIT BREAKIN' THE MOOD!

READ THE ROOM, WILL YOU? (2)

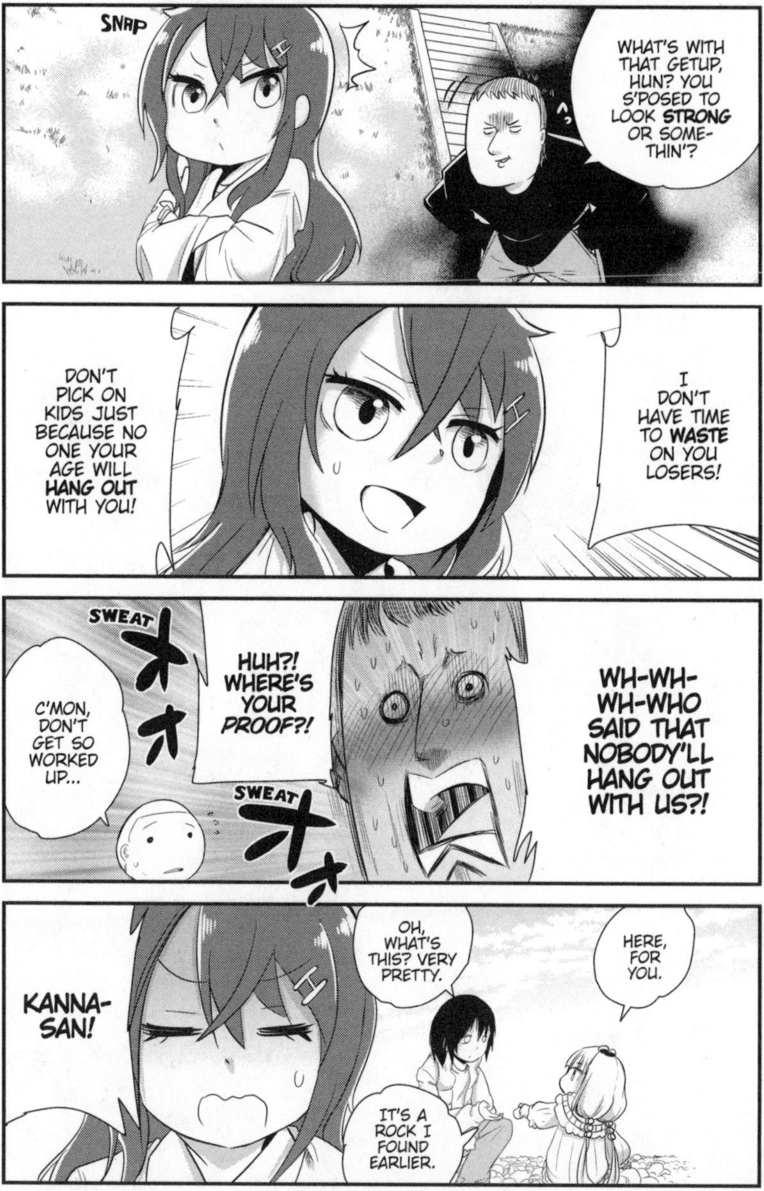
WHAT'S WITH THAT GETUP, HUH? YOU S'POSED TO LOOK **STRONG** OR SOME-THIN'?
SNAP
I DON'T HAVE TIME TO **WASTE** ON YOU LOSERS!
DON'T PICK ON KIDS JUST BECAUSE NO ONE YOUR AGE WILL **HANG OUT** WITH YOU!
WH-WH-WH-WHO SAID THAT NOBODY'LL HANG OUT WITH US?!
SWEAT
HUH?! WHERE'S YOUR *PROOF*?!
SWEAT
C'MON, DON'T GET SO WORKED UP...
HERE, FOR YOU.
OH, WHAT'S THIS? VERY PRETTY.
IT'S A ROCK I FOUND EARLIER.
KANNA-SAN!

BIRTH OF A BEAR-KILLER

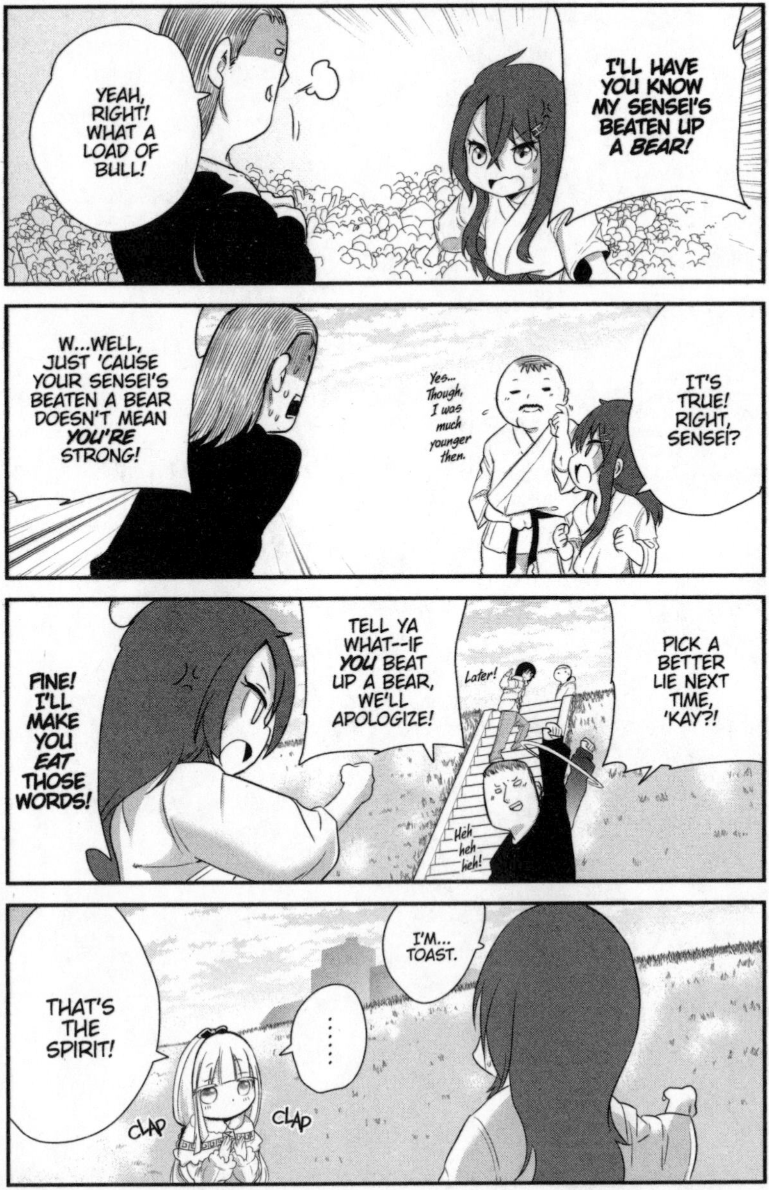
I'LL HAVE YOU KNOW MY SENSEI'S BEATEN UP A *BEAR!*
YEAH, RIGHT! WHAT A LOAD OF BULL!
IT'S TRUE! RIGHT, SENSEI?
Yes... Though, I was much younger then.
W...WELL, JUST 'CAUSE YOUR SENSEI'S BEATEN A BEAR DOESN'T MEAN *YOU'RE* STRONG!
PICK A BETTER LIE NEXT TIME, 'KAY?!
Later!
TELL YA WHAT--IF *YOU* BEAT UP A BEAR, WE'LL APOLOGIZE!
Heh heh heh!
FINE! I'LL MAKE YOU *EAT* THOSE WORDS!
I'M... TOAST.
......
THAT'S THE SPIRIT!
CLAP
CLAP

YOU CAN DO IT

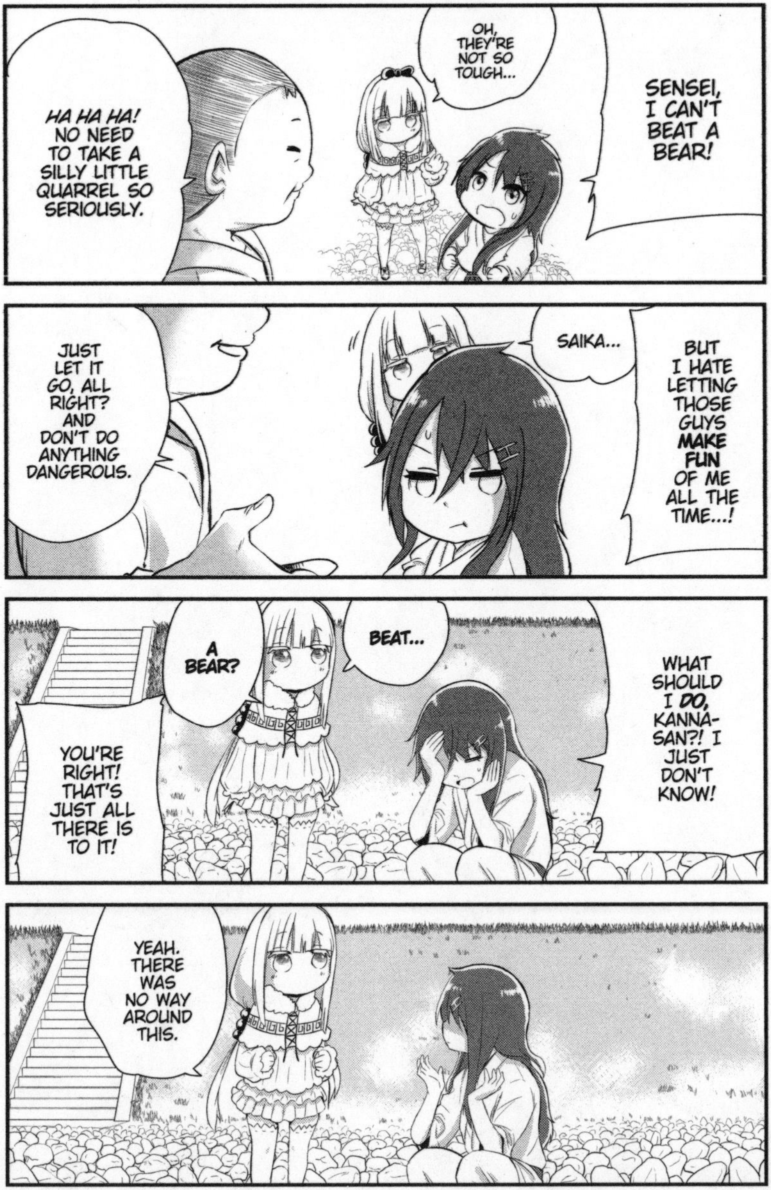
SENSEI, I CAN'T BEAT A BEAR!
OH, THEY'RE NOT SO TOUGH...
HA HA HA! NO NEED TO TAKE A SILLY LITTLE QUARREL SO SERIOUSLY.
BUT I HATE LETTING THOSE GUYS MAKE FUN OF ME ALL THE TIME...!
SAIKA...
JUST LET IT GO, ALL RIGHT? AND DON'T DO ANYTHING DANGEROUS.
WHAT SHOULD I DO, KANNA-SAN?! I JUST DON'T KNOW!
BEAT...
A BEAR?
YOU'RE RIGHT! THAT'S JUST ALL THERE IS TO IT!
YEAH. THERE WAS NO WAY AROUND THIS.

KARATE OBSESSION

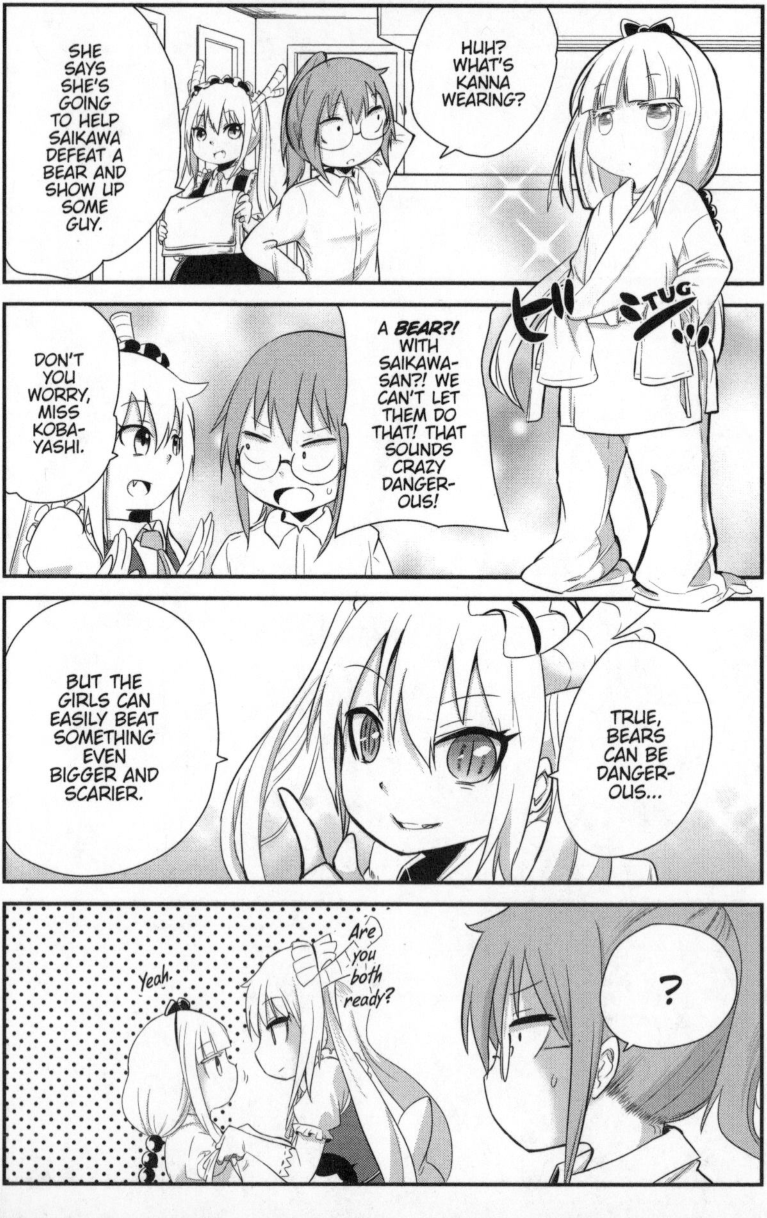
HUH? WHAT'S KANNA WEARING?
SHE SAYS SHE'S GOING TO HELP SAIKAWA DEFEAT A BEAR AND SHOW UP SOME GUY.
TUG
A ***BEAR?!*** WITH SAIKAWA-SAN?! WE CAN'T LET THEM DO THAT! THAT SOUNDS CRAZY DANGER-OUS!
DON'T YOU WORRY, MISS KOBA-YASHI.
TRUE, BEARS CAN BE DANGER-OUS...
BUT THE GIRLS CAN EASILY BEAT SOMETHING EVEN BIGGER AND SCARIER.
?
Are you both ready?
Yeah.

LUCOA MADE THE FUR

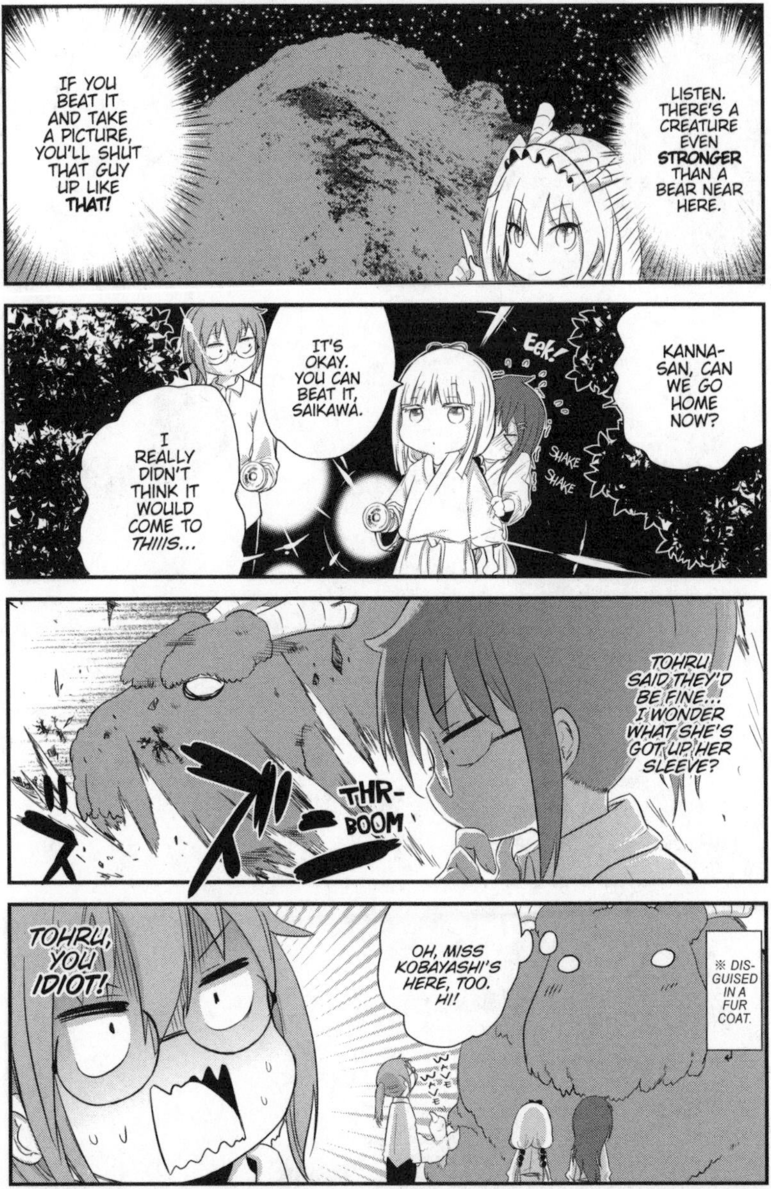
LISTEN. THERE'S A CREATURE EVEN STRONGER THAN A BEAR NEAR HERE.
IF YOU BEAT IT AND TAKE A PICTURE, YOU'LL SHUT THAT GUY UP LIKE THAT!
KANNA-SAN, CAN WE GO HOME NOW?
Eek!
SHAKE SHAKE
IT'S OKAY. YOU CAN BEAT IT, SAIKAWA.
I REALLY DIDN'T THINK IT WOULD COME TO THIIIS...
TOHRU SAID THEY'D BE FINE...! I WONDER WHAT SHE'S GOT UP HER SLEEVE?
THR-BOOM
※ DIS-GUISED IN A FUR COAT.
OH, MISS KOBAYASHI'S HERE, TOO. HI!
WAVE WAVE
TOHRU, YOU IDIOT!

SPINNING KICK

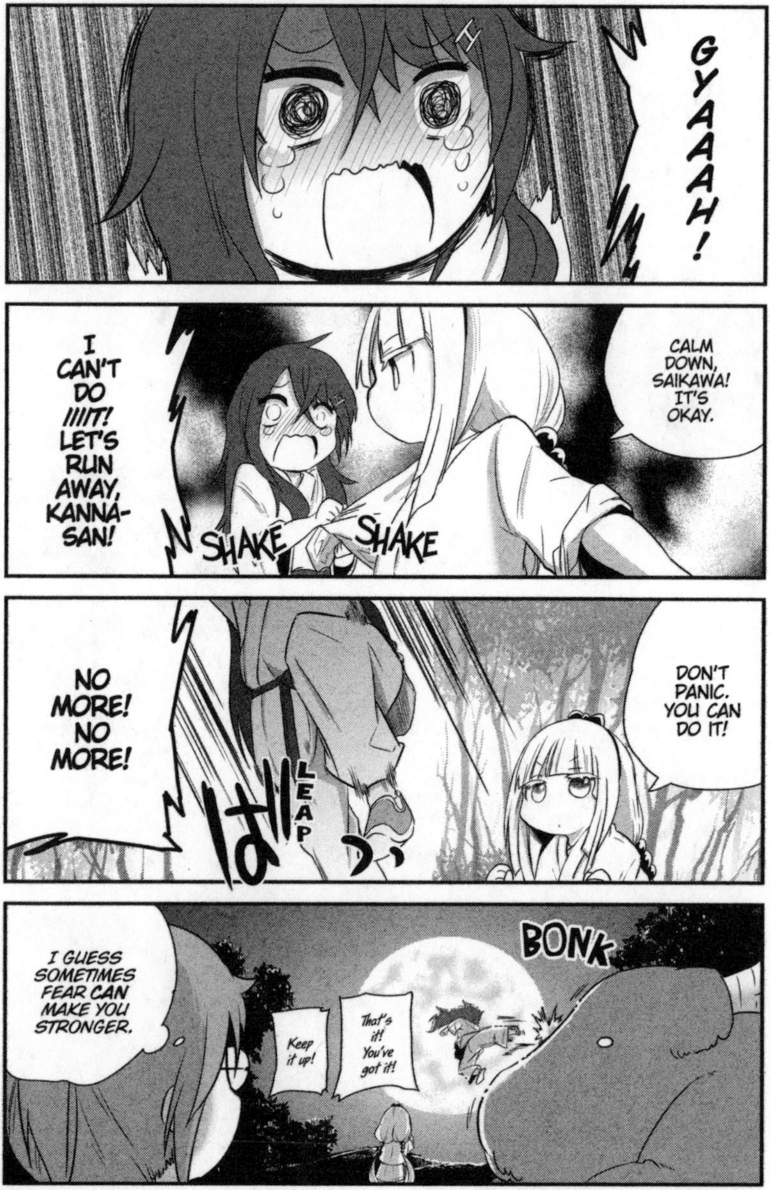
GYAAAH!
CALM DOWN, SAIKAWA! IT'S OKAY.
SHAKE SHAKE
I CAN'T DO IIIIT! LET'S RUN AWAY, KANNA-SAN!
DON'T PANIC. YOU CAN DO IT!
LEAP
NO MORE! NO MORE!
BONK
That's it! You've got it!
Keep it up!
I GUESS SOMETIMES FEAR CAN MAKE YOU STRONGER.

BEAR KILLER--NO, DRAGON KILLER SAIKAWA

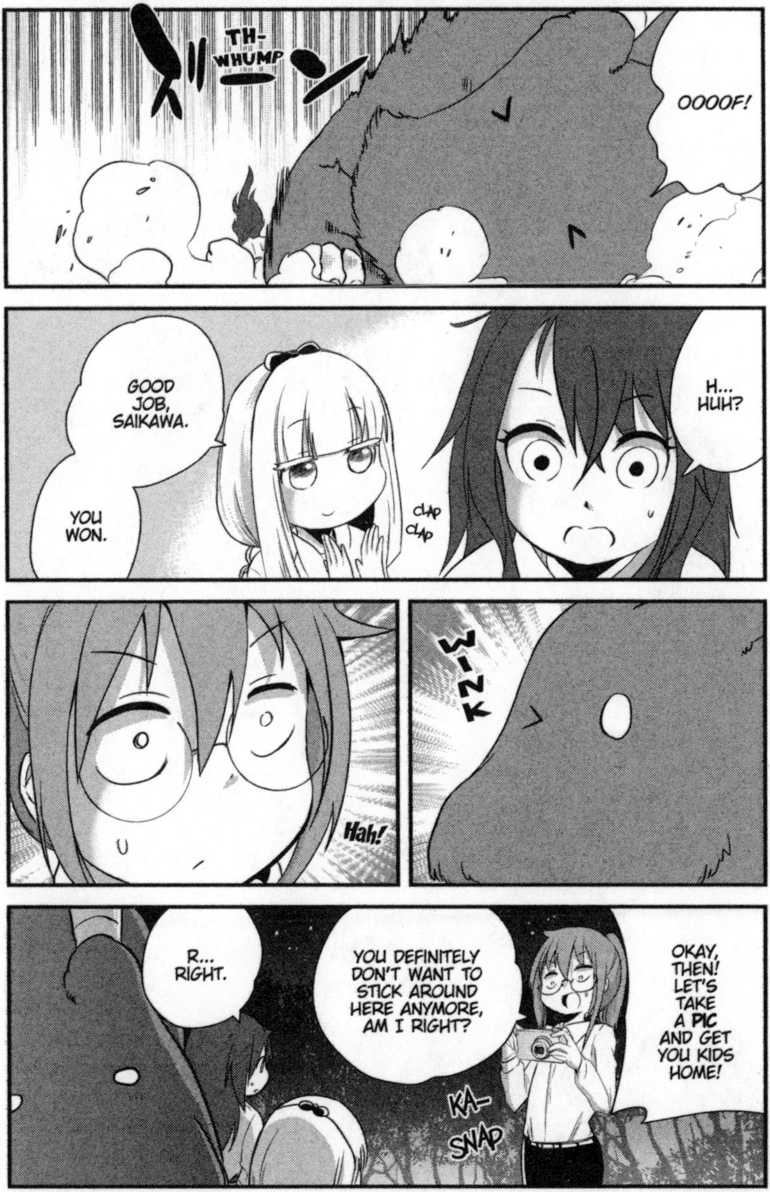
OOOOF!
TH-WHUMP
H... HUH?
CLAP CLAP
GOOD JOB, SAIKAWA.
YOU WON.
WINK
Hah!
OKAY, THEN! LET'S TAKE A PIC AND GET YOU KIDS HOME!
KA-SNAP
YOU DEFINITELY DON'T WANT TO STICK AROUND HERE ANYMORE, AM I RIGHT?
R... RIGHT.

SAIKAWA IS ALREADY KANNA'S KNIGHT

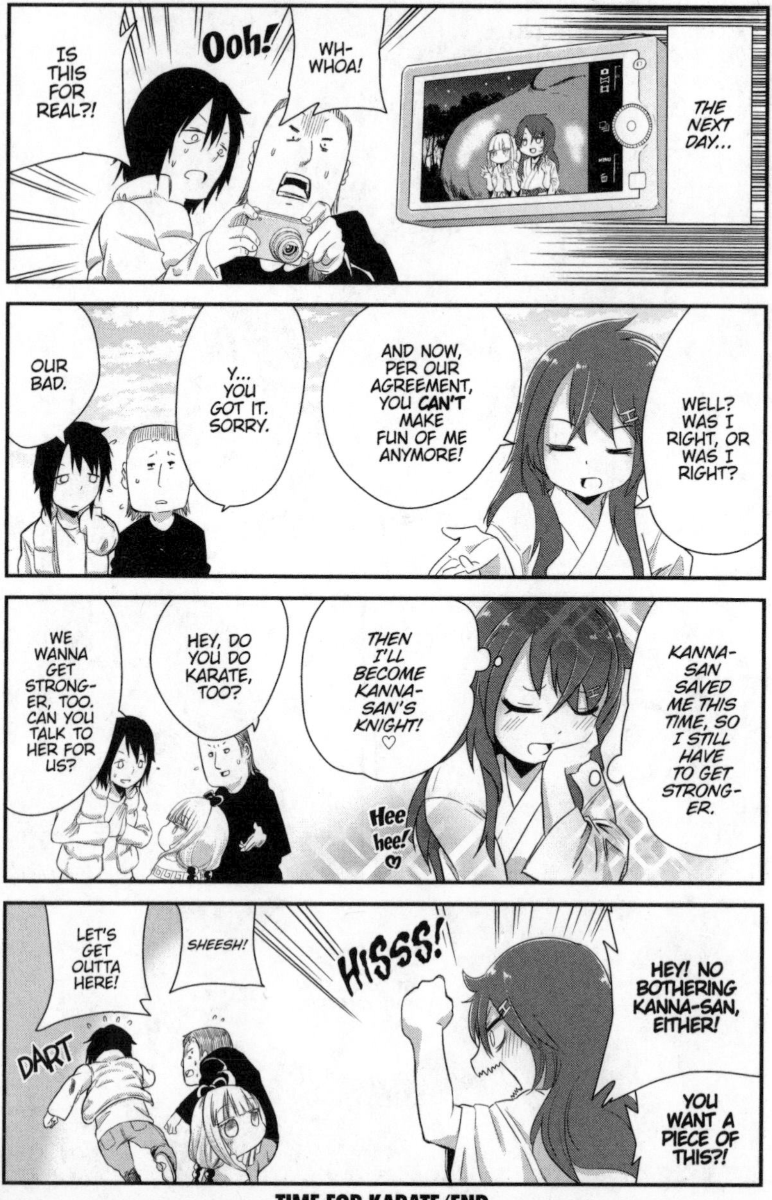
THE NEXT DAY...
WH-WHOA!
Ooh!
IS THIS FOR REAL?!
WELL? WAS I RIGHT, OR WAS I RIGHT?
AND NOW, PER OUR AGREEMENT, YOU **CAN'T** MAKE FUN OF ME ANYMORE!
Y... YOU GOT IT. SORRY.
OUR BAD.
KANNA-SAN SAVED ME THIS TIME, SO I STILL HAVE TO GET STRONGER.
THEN I'LL BECOME KANNA-SAN'S KNIGHT! ♡
Hee hee! ♡
HEY, DO YOU DO KARATE, TOO?
WE WANNA GET STRONGER, TOO. CAN YOU TALK TO HER FOR US?
HEY! NO BOTHERING KANNA-SAN, EITHER!
HISSS!
SHEESH!
LET'S GET OUTTA HERE!
YOU WANT A PIECE OF THIS?!
DART

TIME FOR KARATE/END

Working
on the
disguise.

Make it
convincing,
please!

Miss Kobayashi's Dragon Maid
Kanna's Daily Life

VALENTINE START

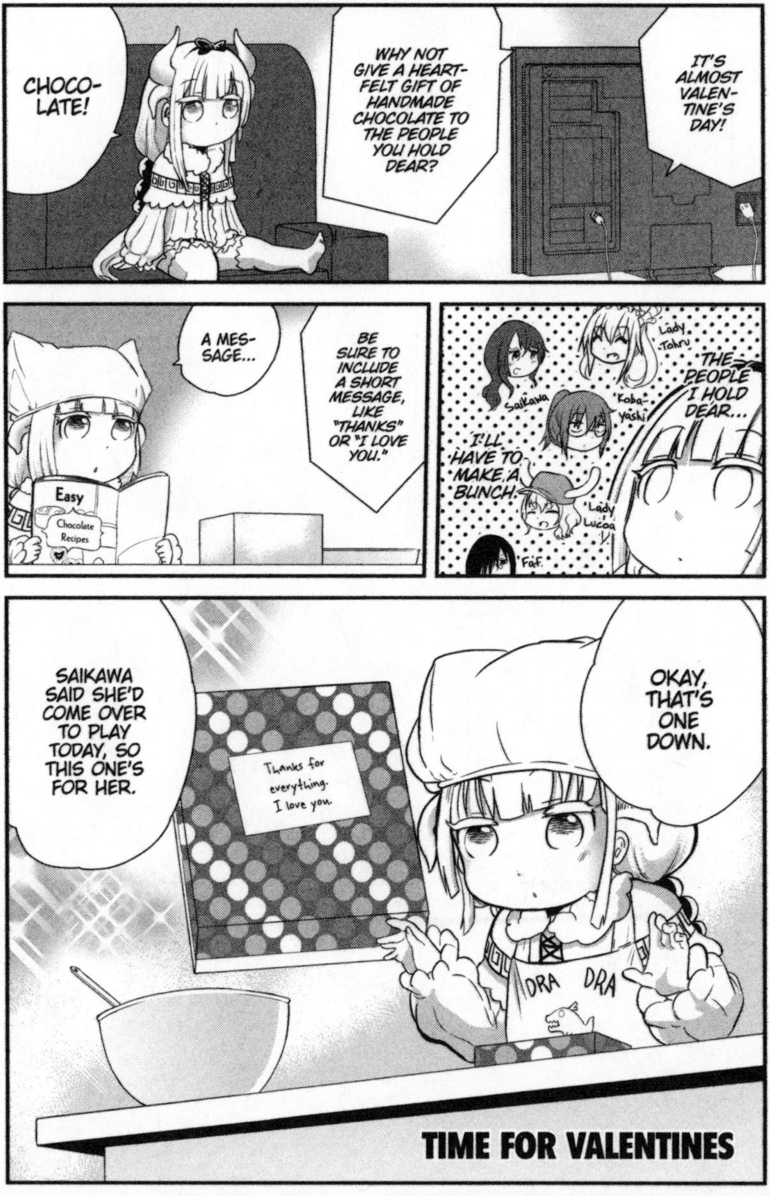
IT'S ALMOST VALENTINE'S DAY!
WHY NOT GIVE A HEARTFELT GIFT OF HANDMADE CHOCOLATE TO THE PEOPLE YOU HOLD DEAR?
CHOCOLATE!
THE PEOPLE I HOLD DEAR...
Lady Tohru
Saikawa
Kobayashi
I'LL HAVE TO MAKE A BUNCH.
Lady Lucoa
Faf.
BE SURE TO INCLUDE A SHORT MESSAGE, LIKE "THANKS" OR "I LOVE YOU."
A MESSAGE...
Easy
Chocolate Recipes
OKAY, THAT'S ONE DOWN.
SAIKAWA SAID SHE'D COME OVER TO PLAY TODAY, SO THIS ONE'S FOR HER.
Thanks for everything. I love you.
DRA DRA
TIME FOR VALENTINES

ILULU AWAKENS

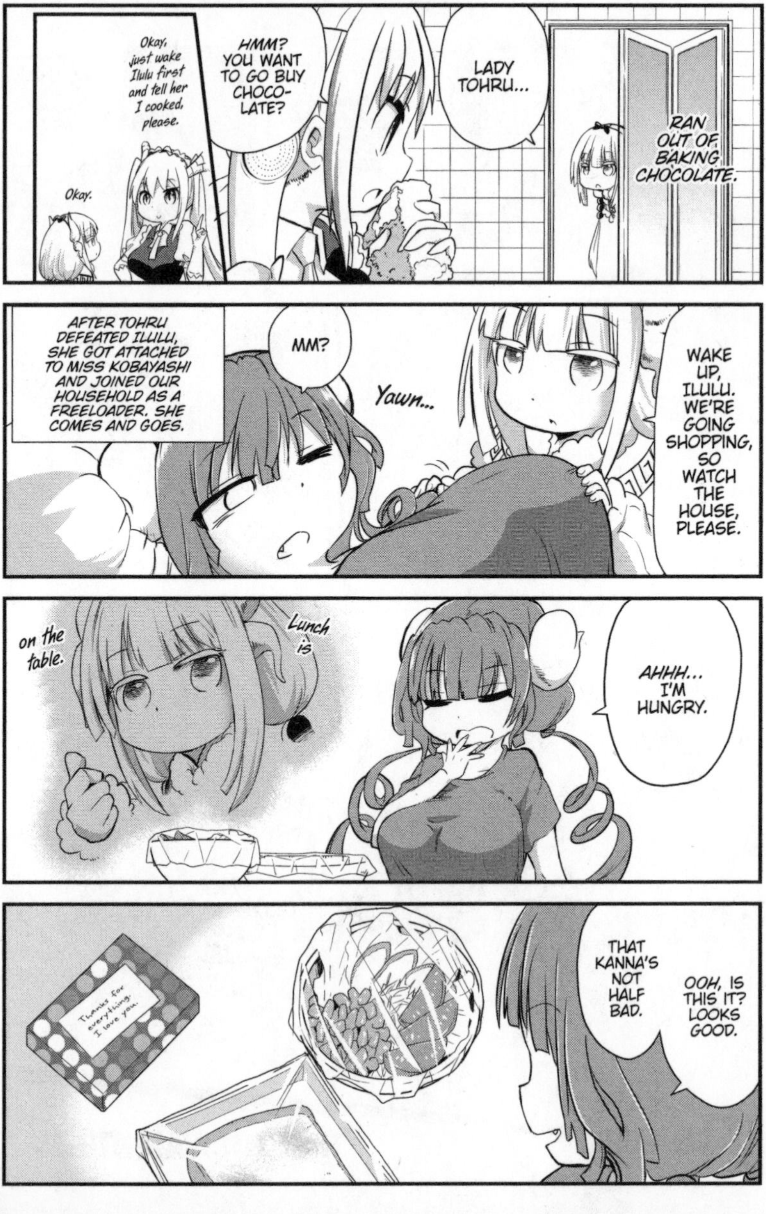
RAN OUT OF BAKING CHOCOLATE.
LADY TOHRU...
HMM? YOU WANT TO GO BUY CHOCOLATE?
Okay, just wake Ilulu first and tell her I cooked, please.
Okay.
WAKE UP, ILULU. WE'RE GOING SHOPPING, SO WATCH THE HOUSE, PLEASE.
Yawn...
MM?
AFTER TOHRU DEFEATED ILULU, SHE GOT ATTACHED TO MISS KOBAYASHI AND JOINED OUR HOUSEHOLD AS A FREELOADER. SHE COMES AND GOES.
AHHH... I'M HUNGRY.
Lunch is
on the table.
OOH, IS THIS IT? LOOKS GOOD.
THAT KANNA'S NOT HALF BAD.
Thanks for everything. I love you.

MY BLOODY VALENTINE

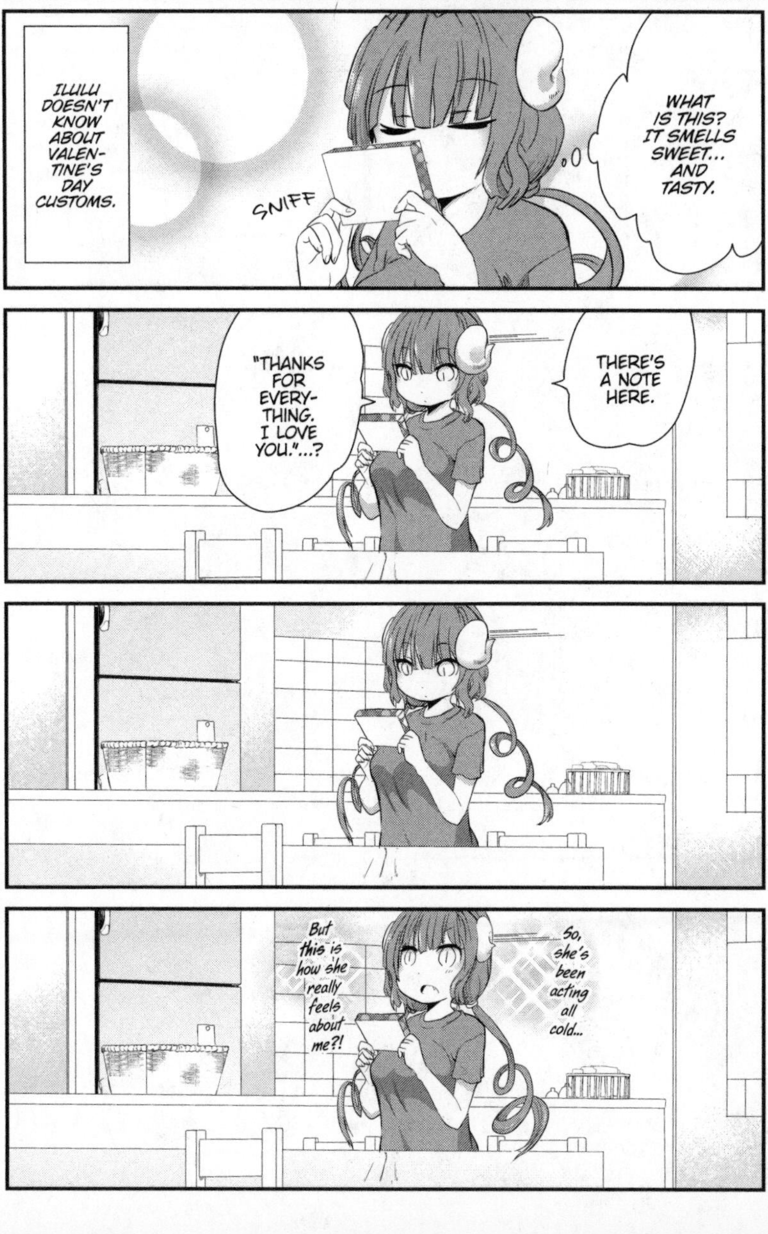
WHAT IS THIS? IT SMELLS SWEET... AND TASTY.
ILULU DOESN'T KNOW ABOUT VALENTINE'S DAY CUSTOMS.
SNIFF
THERE'S A NOTE HERE.
"THANKS FOR EVERYTHING. I LOVE YOU."...?
So, she's been acting all cold...
But this is how she really feels about me?!

ILULU AND SAIKAWA (1)

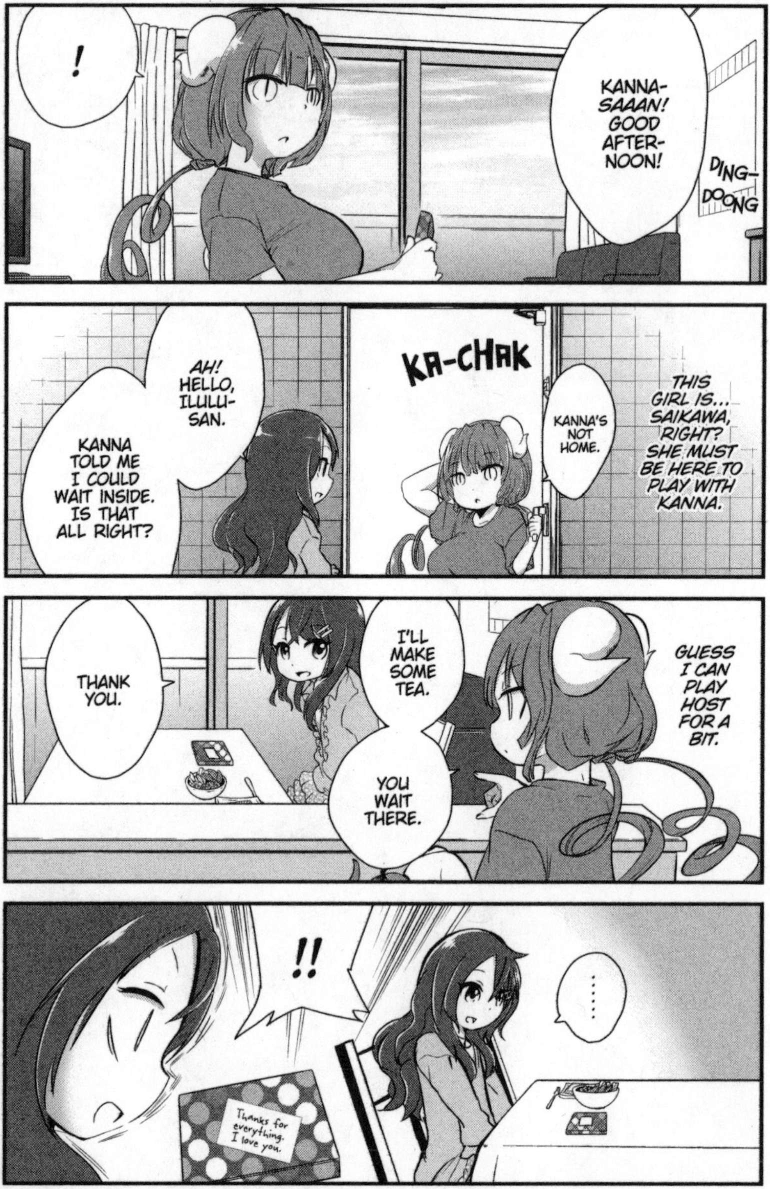
DING-DOONG
KANNA-SAAAN! GOOD AFTER-NOON!
!
THIS GIRL IS... SAIKAWA, RIGHT? SHE MUST BE HERE TO PLAY WITH KANNA.
KANNA'S NOT HOME.
KA-CHAK
AH! HELLO, ILULU-SAN.
KANNA TOLD ME I COULD WAIT INSIDE. IS THAT ALL RIGHT?
GUESS I CAN PLAY HOST FOR A BIT.
I'LL MAKE SOME TEA.
YOU WAIT THERE.
THANK YOU.
......
!!
Thanks for everything. I love you.

ILULU AND SAIKAWA (2)

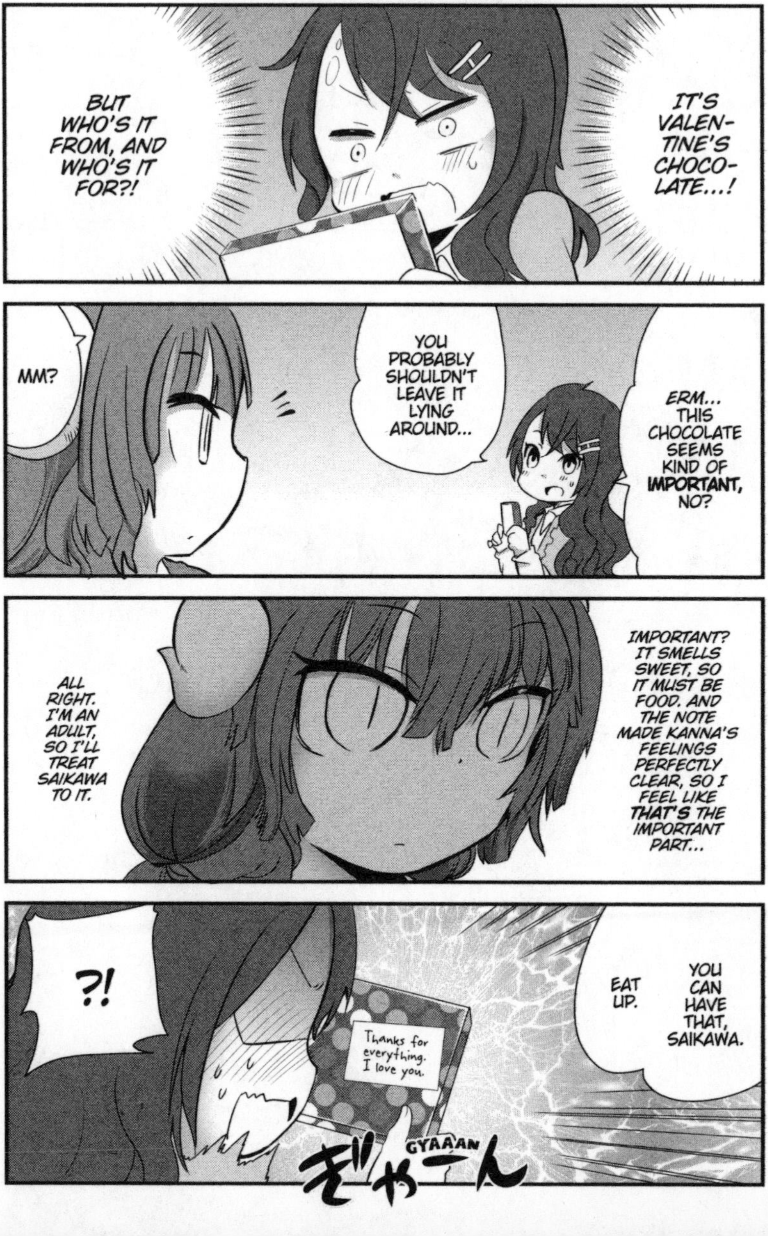
IT'S VALENTINE'S CHOCOLATE...!
BUT WHO'S IT FROM, AND WHO'S IT FOR?!
ERM... THIS CHOCOLATE SEEMS KIND OF **IMPORTANT**, NO?
YOU PROBABLY SHOULDN'T LEAVE IT LYING AROUND...
MM?
IMPORTANT? IT SMELLS SWEET, SO IT MUST BE FOOD. AND THE NOTE MADE KANNA'S FEELINGS PERFECTLY CLEAR, SO I FEEL LIKE **THAT'S** THE IMPORTANT PART...
ALL RIGHT. I'M AN ADULT, SO I'LL TREAT SAIKAWA TO IT.
YOU CAN HAVE THAT, SAIKAWA.
EAT UP.
Thanks for everything. I love you.
?!
GYAAAN
ぎゃーん

ILULU AND SAIKAWA (3)

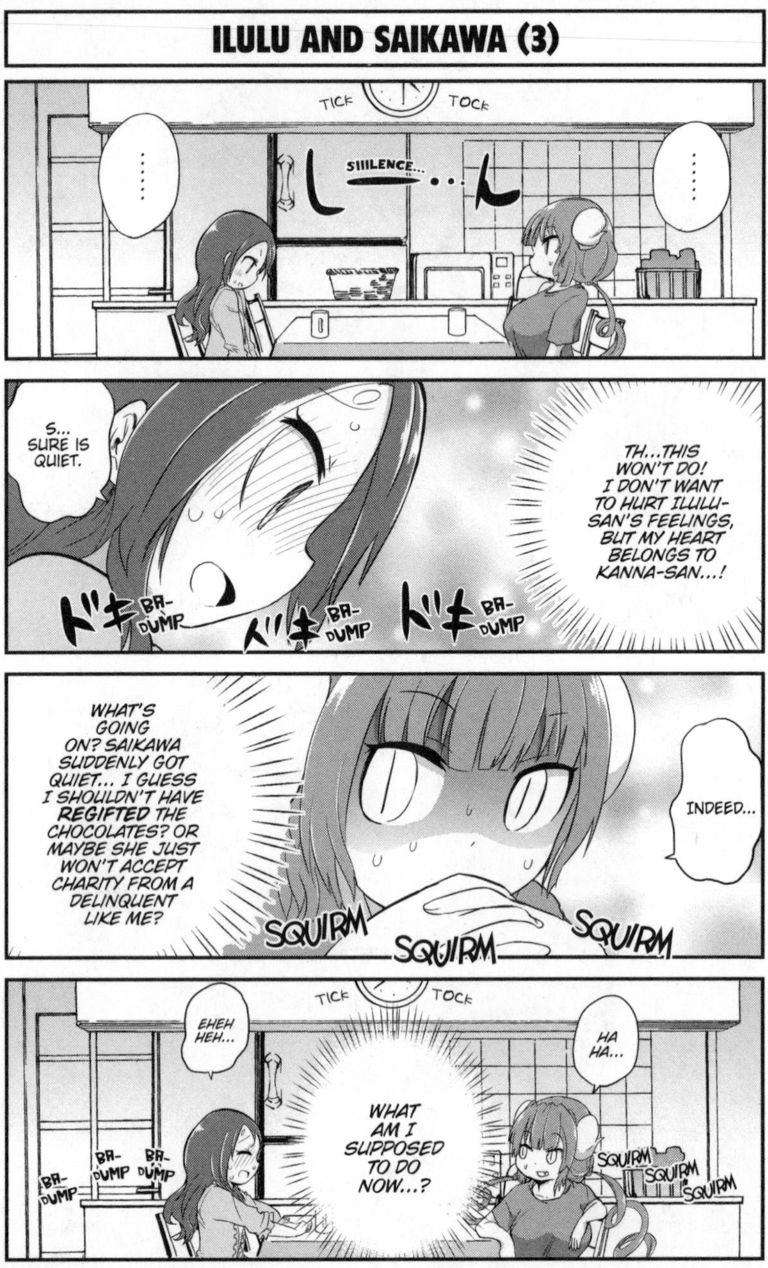
TICK TOCK
……
しーん SIIILENCE...
……
TH...THIS WON'T DO! I DON'T WANT TO HURT ILULU-SAN'S FEELINGS, BUT MY HEART BELONGS TO KANNA-SAN...!
S... SURE IS QUIET.
ドキ BA-DUMP ドキ BA-DUMP ドキ BA-DUMP
INDEED...
WHAT'S GOING ON? SAIKAWA SUDDENLY GOT QUIET... I GUESS I SHOULDN'T HAVE **REGIFTED** THE CHOCOLATES? OR MAYBE SHE JUST WON'T ACCEPT CHARITY FROM A DELINQUENT LIKE ME?
SQUIRM SQUIRM SQUIRM
TICK TOCK
HA HA...
SQUIRM SQUIRM SQUIRM
WHAT AM I SUPPOSED TO DO NOW...?
EHEH HEH...
BA-DUMP BA-DUMP BA-DUMP

MEANWHILE, KANNA...

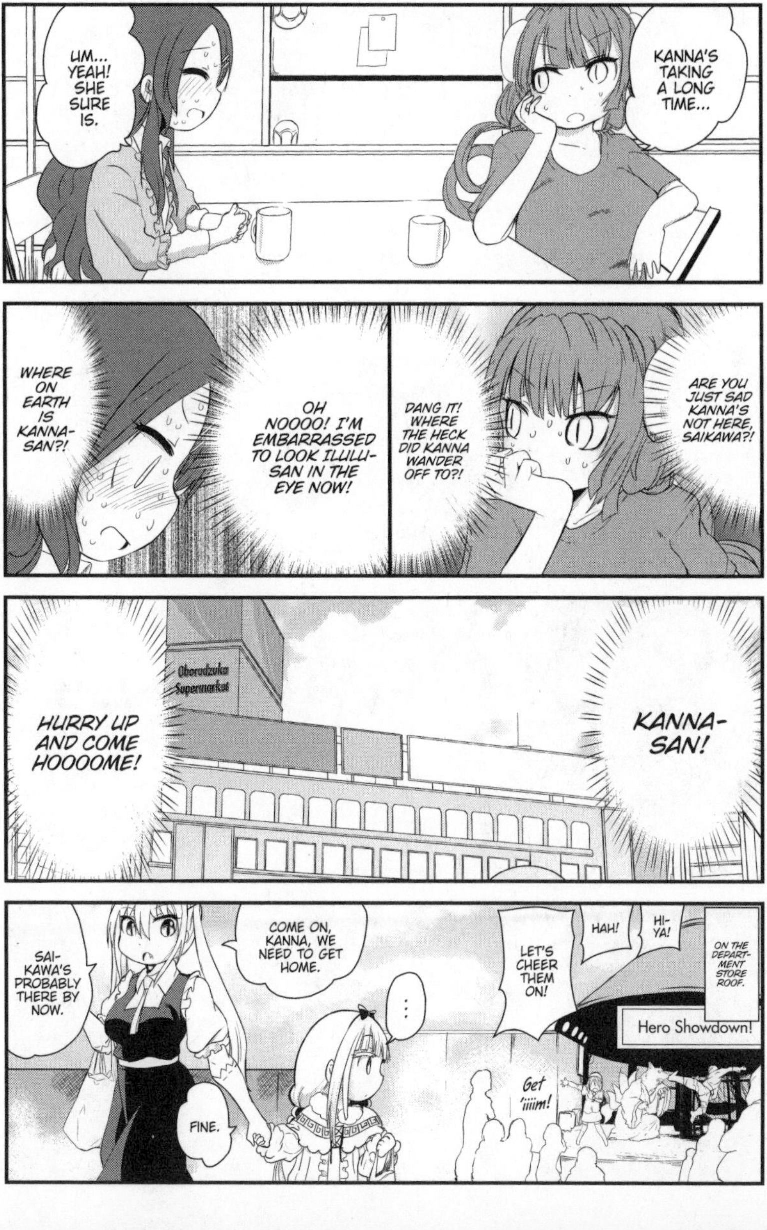
KANNA'S TAKING A LONG TIME...
UM... YEAH! SHE SURE IS.
ARE YOU JUST SAD KANNA'S NOT HERE, SAIKAWA?!
DANG IT! WHERE THE HECK DID KANNA WANDER OFF TO?!
OH NOOOO! I'M EMBARRASSED TO LOOK ILULU-SAN IN THE EYE NOW!
WHERE ON EARTH IS KANNA-SAN?!
KANNA-SAN!
Oboradzuka Supermarket
HURRY UP AND COME HOOOOME!
ON THE DEPART-MENT STORE ROOF.
Hero Showdown!
HI-YA!
HAH!
LET'S CHEER THEM ON!
Get 'iiiim!
COME ON, KANNA, WE NEED TO GET HOME.
SAI-KAWA'S PROBABLY THERE BY NOW.
...
FINE.

HANDS OFF THAT CHOCOLATE!

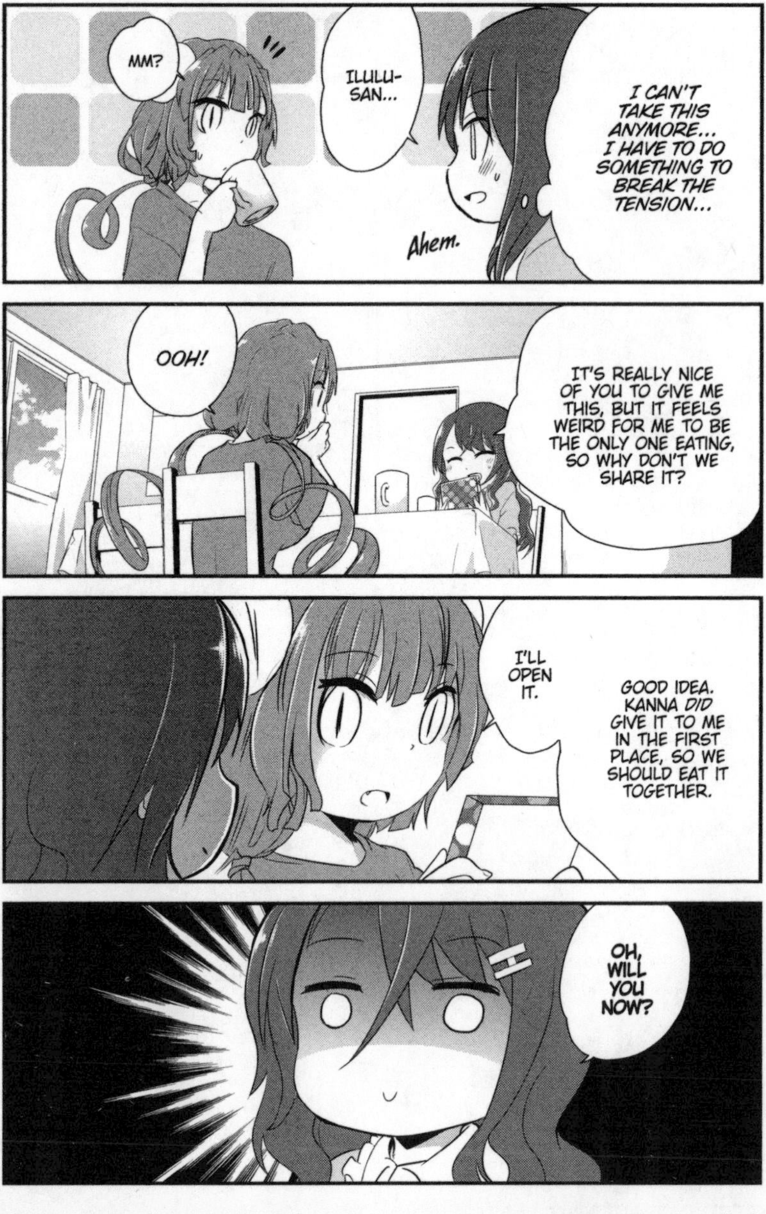
I CAN'T TAKE THIS ANYMORE... I HAVE TO DO SOMETHING TO BREAK THE TENSION...
Ahem.
ILULU-SAN...
MM?
IT'S REALLY NICE OF YOU TO GIVE ME THIS, BUT IT FEELS WEIRD FOR ME TO BE THE ONLY ONE EATING, SO WHY DON'T WE SHARE IT?
OOH!
GOOD IDEA. KANNA *DID* GIVE IT TO ME IN THE FIRST PLACE, SO WE SHOULD EAT IT TOGETHER.
I'LL OPEN IT.
OH, WILL YOU NOW?

HOW DID IT COME TO THIS?

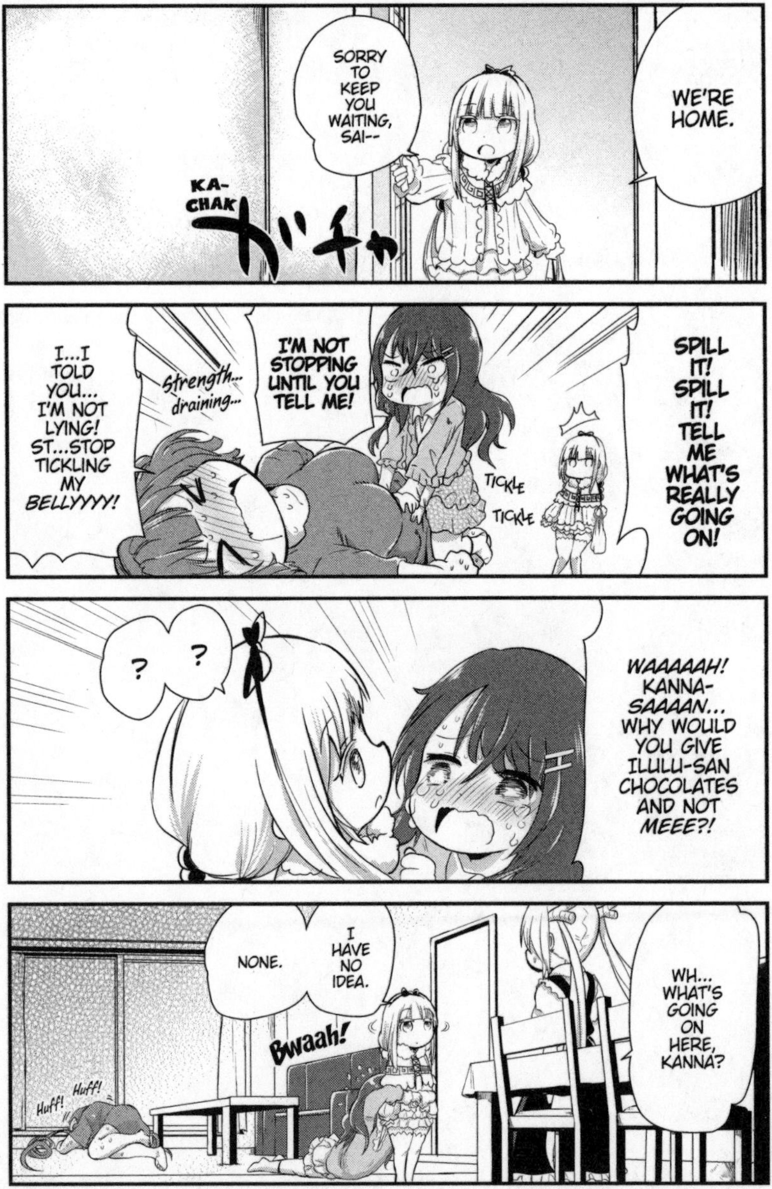
WE'RE HOME.
SORRY TO KEEP YOU WAITING, SAI--
KA-CHAK
ガチャ
SPILL IT! SPILL IT! TELL ME WHAT'S REALLY GOING ON!
TICKLE
TICKLE
I'M NOT STOPPING UNTIL YOU TELL ME!
Strength... draining...
I...I TOLD YOU... I'M NOT LYING! ST...STOP TICKLING MY BELLYYYY!
WAAAAAH! KANNA-SAAAAN... WHY WOULD YOU GIVE ILULU-SAN CHOCOLATES AND NOT MEEE?!
? ?
WH... WHAT'S GOING ON HERE, KANNA?
I HAVE NO IDEA.
NONE.
Bwaah!
Huff!
Huff!

HOW DARE YOU?!

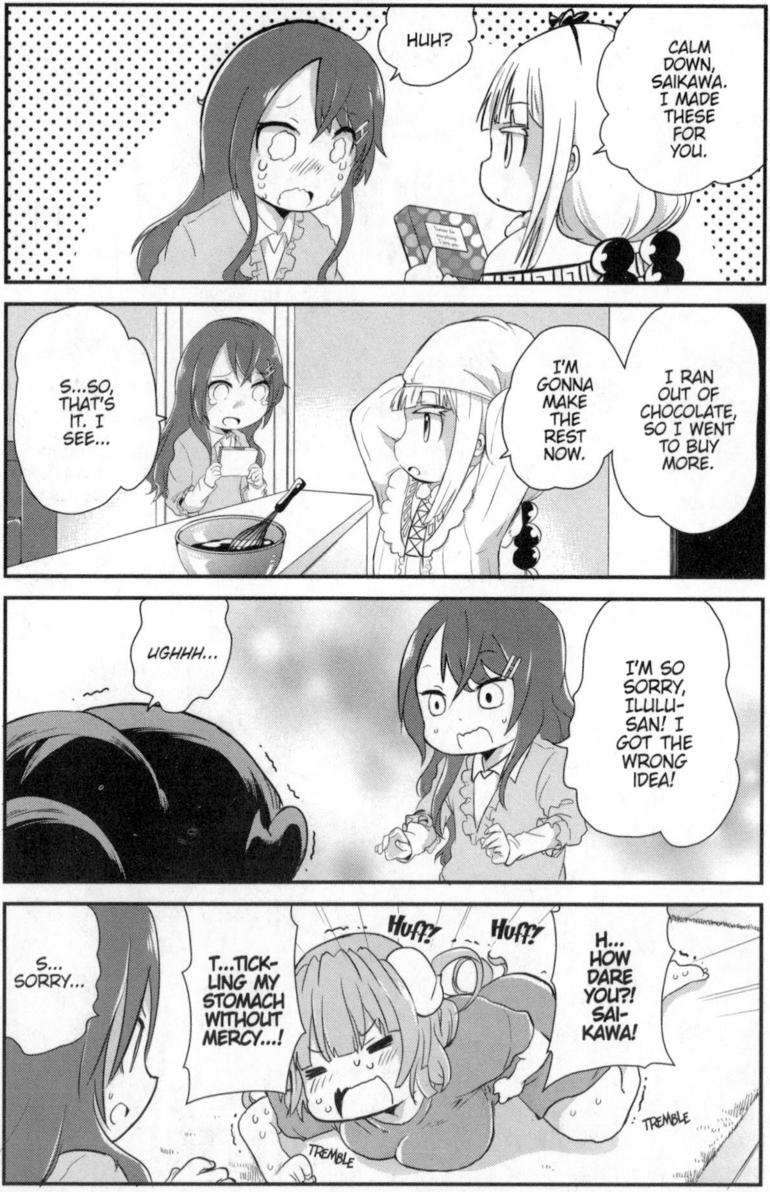
CALM DOWN, SAIKAWA. I MADE THESE FOR YOU.
HUH?
I RAN OUT OF CHOCOLATE, SO I WENT TO BUY MORE.
I'M GONNA MAKE THE REST NOW.
S...SO, THAT'S IT. I SEE...
I'M SO SORRY, ILULU-SAN! I GOT THE WRONG IDEA!
UGHHH...
H... HOW DARE YOU?! SAI-KAWA!
Huff?!
Huff?!
T...TICK-LING MY STOMACH WITHOUT MERCY...!
S... SORRY...
TREMBLE
TREMBLE

LET THE VIOLENCE BEGIN!

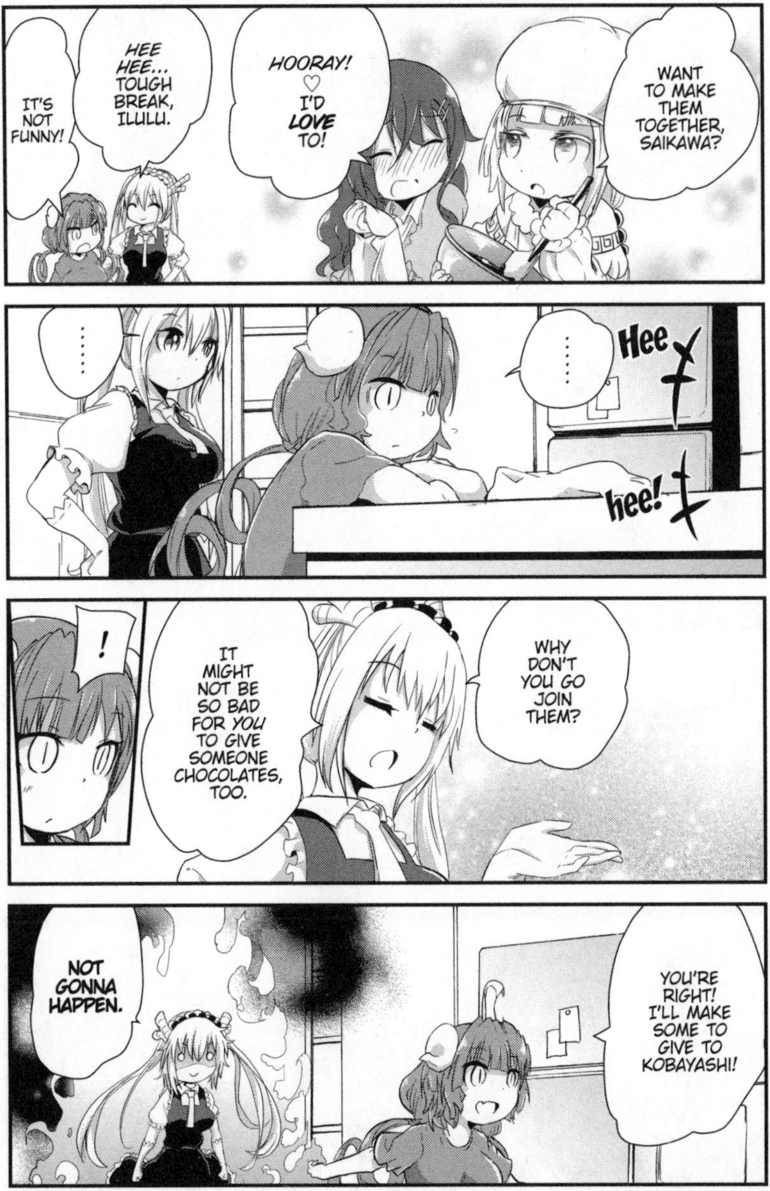
WANT TO MAKE THEM TOGETHER, SAIKAWA?
HOORAY! ♡ I'D LOVE TO!
HEE HEE... TOUGH BREAK, ILULU.
IT'S NOT FUNNY!
Hee
hee!
......
......
WHY DON'T YOU GO JOIN THEM?
IT MIGHT NOT BE SO BAD FOR YOU TO GIVE SOMEONE CHOCOLATES, TOO.
!
YOU'RE RIGHT! I'LL MAKE SOME TO GIVE TO KOBAYASHI!
NOT GONNA HAPPEN.

BITTERSWEET

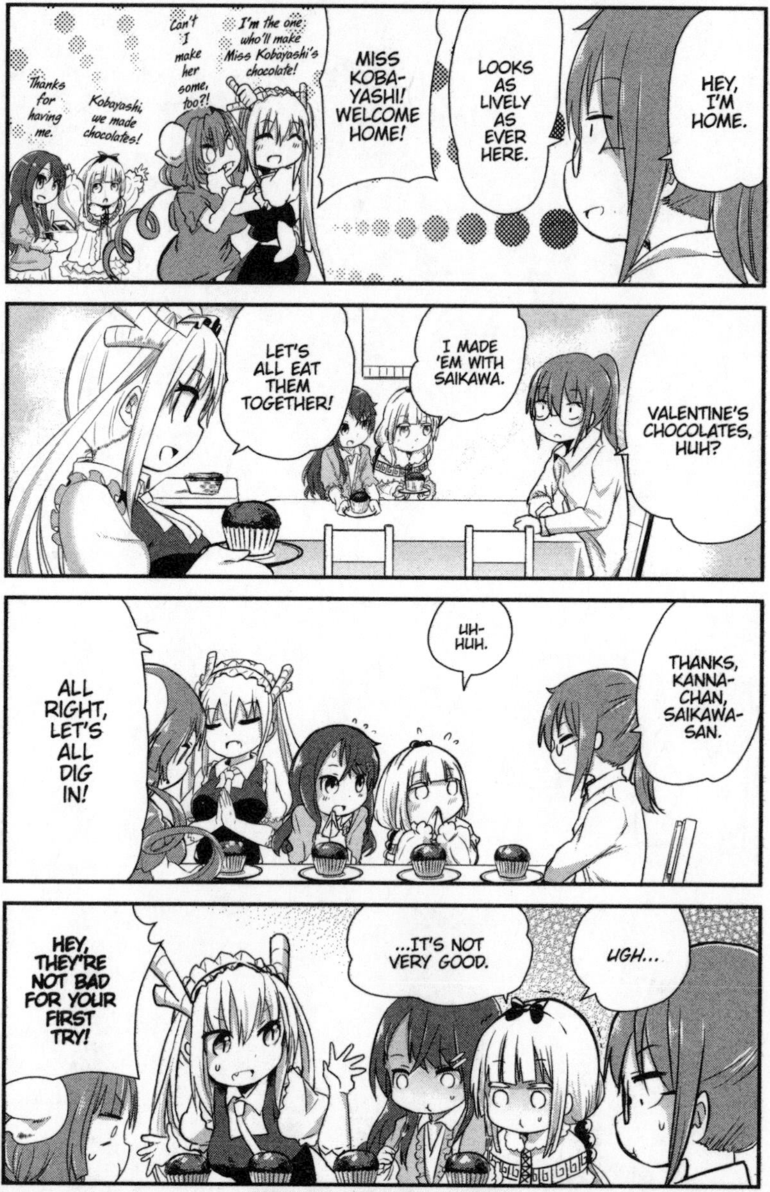
HEY, I'M HOME.
LOOKS AS LIVELY AS EVER HERE.
MISS KOBA-YASHI! WELCOME HOME!
I'm the one who'll make Miss Kobayashi's chocolate!
Can't I make her some, too?!
Kobayashi, we made chocolates!
Thanks for having me.
VALENTINE'S CHOCOLATES, HUH?
I MADE 'EM WITH SAIKAWA.
LET'S ALL EAT THEM TOGETHER!
THANKS, KANNA-CHAN, SAIKAWA-SAN.
UH-HUH.
ALL RIGHT, LET'S ALL DIG IN!
UGH...
...IT'S NOT VERY GOOD.
HEY, THEY'RE NOT BAD FOR YOUR FIRST TRY!

TIME FOR VALENTINE'S/END

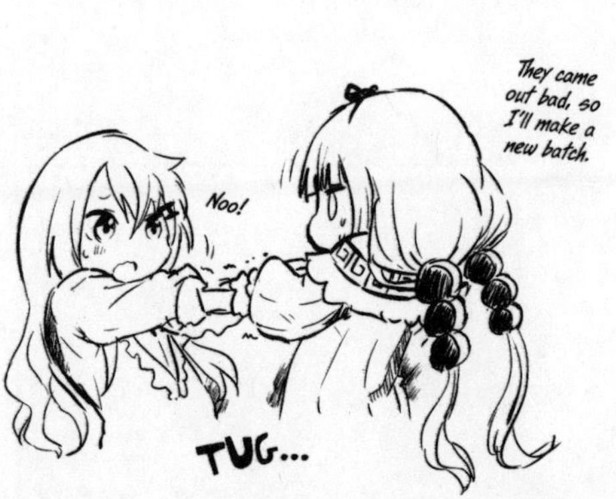
They came out bad, so I'll make a new batch.
Noo!
TUG...

Miss Kobayashi's Dragon Maid
Kanna's Daily Life

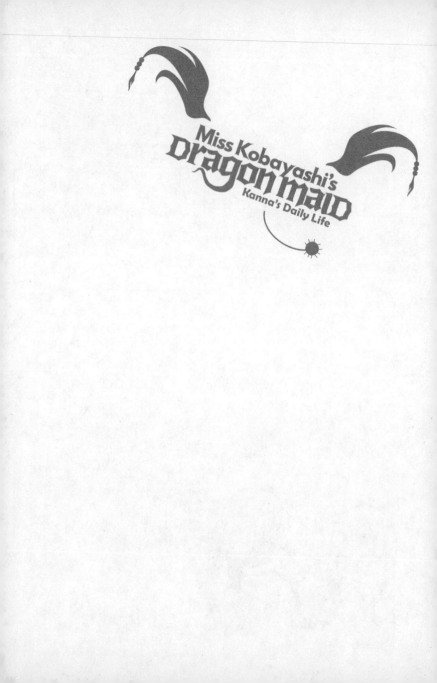

WHAT'S WRONG, SAIKAWA-SAN?!

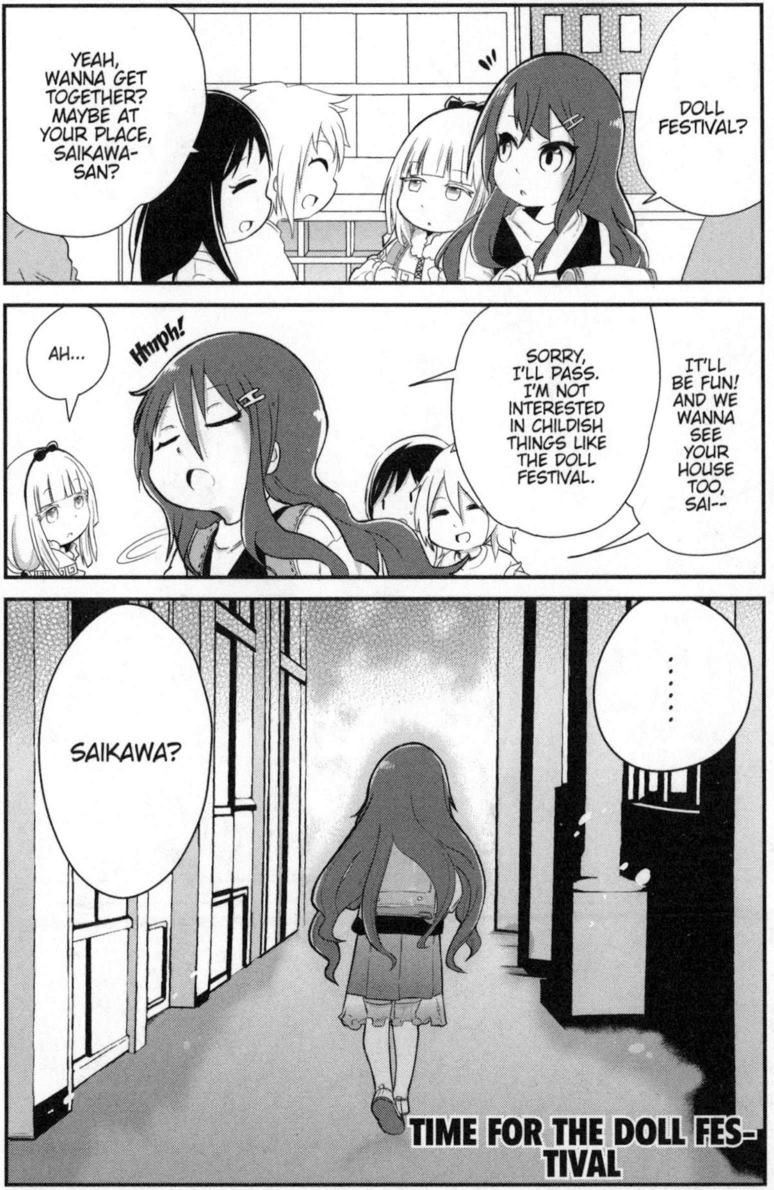
DOLL FESTIVAL?
YEAH, WANNA GET TOGETHER? MAYBE AT YOUR PLACE, SAIKAWA-SAN?
IT'LL BE FUN! AND WE WANNA SEE YOUR HOUSE TOO, SAI--
SORRY, I'LL PASS. I'M NOT INTERESTED IN CHILDISH THINGS LIKE THE DOLL FESTIVAL.
Hmph!
AH...
......
SAIKAWA?
TIME FOR THE DOLL FES-TIVAL

IT'S TOUGH BEING A KID

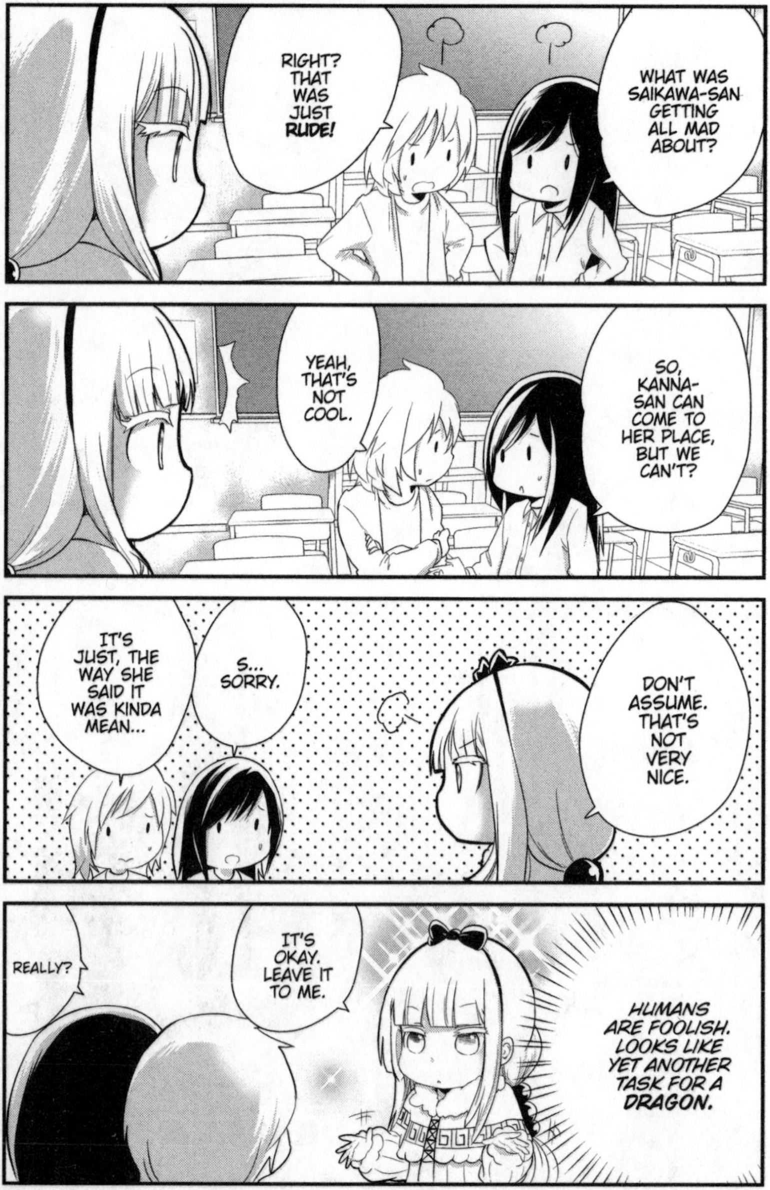
WHAT WAS SAIKAWA-SAN GETTING ALL MAD ABOUT?
RIGHT? THAT WAS JUST RUDE!
SO, KANNA-SAN CAN COME TO HER PLACE, BUT WE CAN'T?
YEAH, THAT'S NOT COOL.
DON'T ASSUME. THAT'S NOT VERY NICE.
S... SORRY.
IT'S JUST, THE WAY SHE SAID IT WAS KINDA MEAN...
HUMANS ARE FOOLISH. LOOKS LIKE YET ANOTHER TASK FOR A DRAGON.
IT'S OKAY. LEAVE IT TO ME.
REALLY?

IT'S GOOD TO BE CONFIDENT

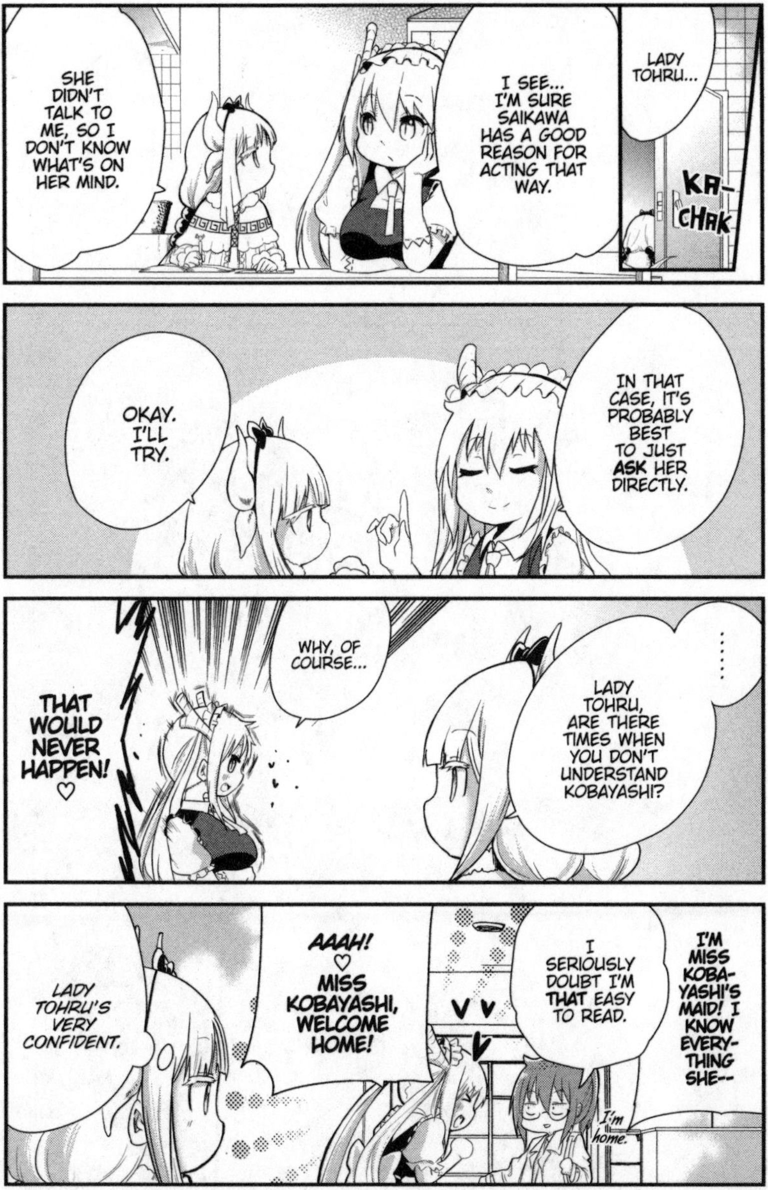
LADY TOHRU...
KA-CHAK
I SEE... I'M SURE SAIKAWA HAS A GOOD REASON FOR ACTING THAT WAY.
SHE DIDN'T TALK TO ME, SO I DON'T KNOW WHAT'S ON HER MIND.
IN THAT CASE, IT'S PROBABLY BEST TO JUST ASK HER DIRECTLY.
OKAY. I'LL TRY.
......
LADY TOHRU, ARE THERE TIMES WHEN YOU DON'T UNDERSTAND KOBAYASHI?
WHY, OF COURSE...
THAT WOULD NEVER HAPPEN! ♡
I'M MISS KOBAYASHI'S MAID! I KNOW EVERYTHING SHE--
I SERIOUSLY DOUBT I'M THAT EASY TO READ.
I'm home.
AAAH! ♡ MISS KOBAYASHI, WELCOME HOME!
LADY TOHRU'S VERY CONFIDENT.

DOLL FESTIVAL MEMORIES

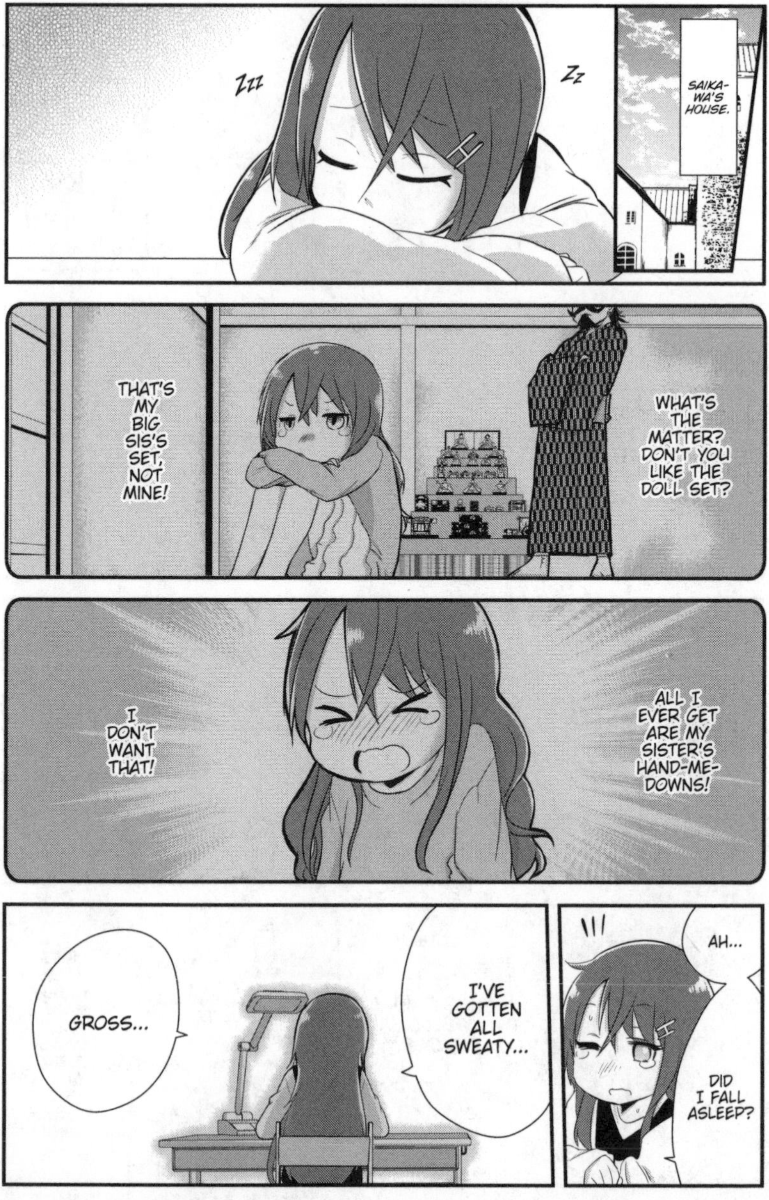

SAIKA-WA'S HOUSE.
Zz
Zzz
WHAT'S THE MATTER? DON'T YOU LIKE THE DOLL SET?
THAT'S MY BIG SIS'S SET, NOT MINE!
ALL I EVER GET ARE MY SISTER'S HAND-ME-DOWNS!
I DON'T WANT THAT!
AH...
DID I FALL ASLEEP?
I'VE GOTTEN ALL SWEATY...
GROSS...

GUESS I'LL GO HOME

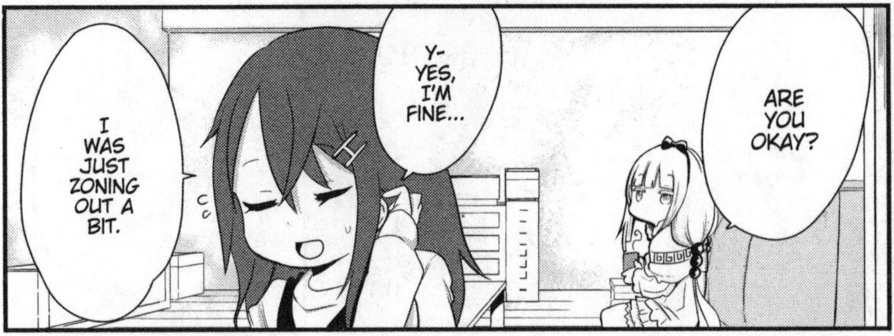
ARE YOU OKAY?
Y-YES, I'M FINE...
I WAS JUST ZONING OUT A BIT.

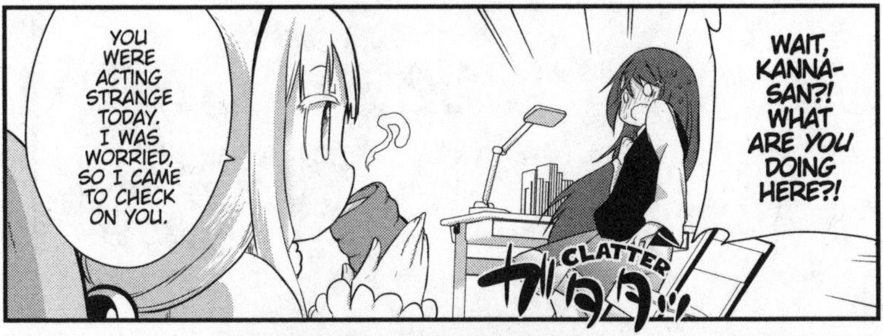
WAIT, KANNA-SAN?! WHAT ARE YOU DOING HERE?!
CLATTER
YOU WERE ACTING STRANGE TODAY. I WAS WORRIED, SO I CAME TO CHECK ON YOU.

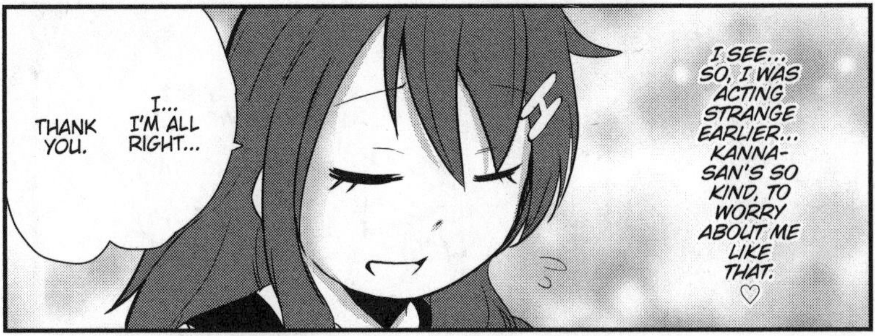
I SEE... SO, I WAS ACTING STRANGE EARLIER... KANNA-SAN'S SO KIND, TO WORRY ABOUT ME LIKE THAT. ♡
I... I'M ALL RIGHT...
THANK YOU.

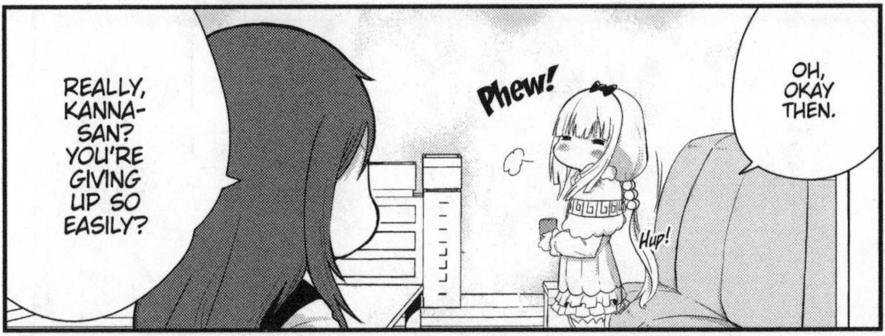
OH, OKAY THEN.
Hup!
Phew!
REALLY, KANNA-SAN? YOU'RE GIVING UP SO EASILY?

KANNA-CHAN THE POET

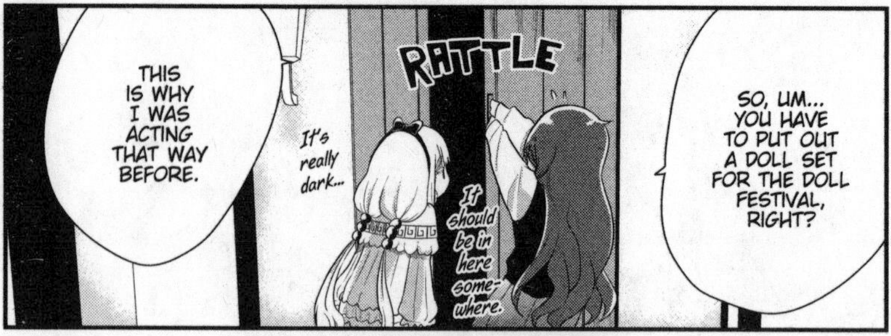
SO, UM... YOU HAVE TO PUT OUT A DOLL SET FOR THE DOLL FESTIVAL, RIGHT?
RATTLE
It should be in here some-where.
It's really dark...
THIS IS WHY I WAS ACTING THAT WAY BEFORE.

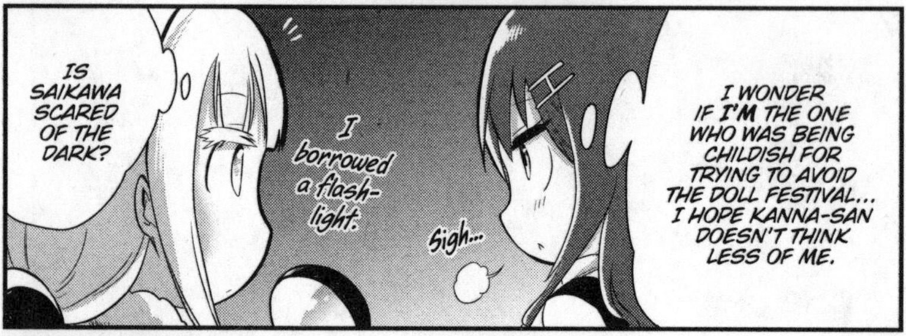
I WONDER IF I'M THE ONE WHO WAS BEING CHILDISH FOR TRYING TO AVOID THE DOLL FESTIVAL... I HOPE KANNA-SAN DOESN'T THINK LESS OF ME.
Sigh...
I borrowed a flash-light.
IS SAIKAWA SCARED OF THE DARK?

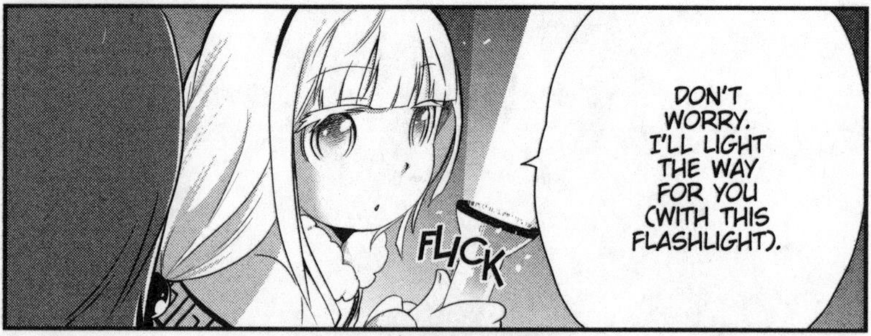
DON'T WORRY. I'LL LIGHT THE WAY FOR YOU (WITH THIS FLASHLIGHT).
FLICK

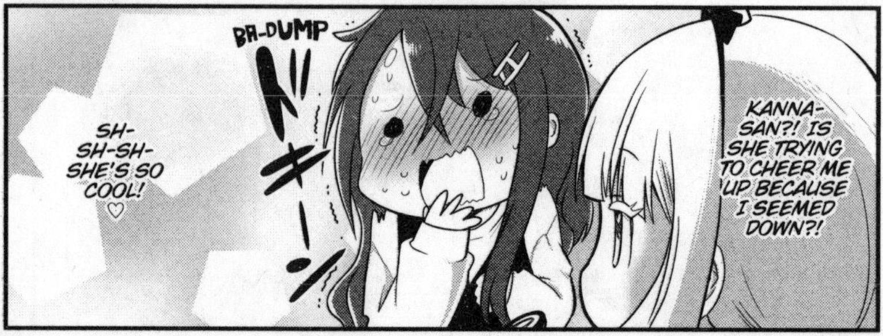
KANNA-SAN?! IS SHE TRYING TO CHEER ME UP BECAUSE I SEEMED DOWN?!
BA-DUMP
SH-SH-SH-SHE'S SO COOL! ♡

SOMEWHERE BETWEEN KINDNESS AND WILDNESS

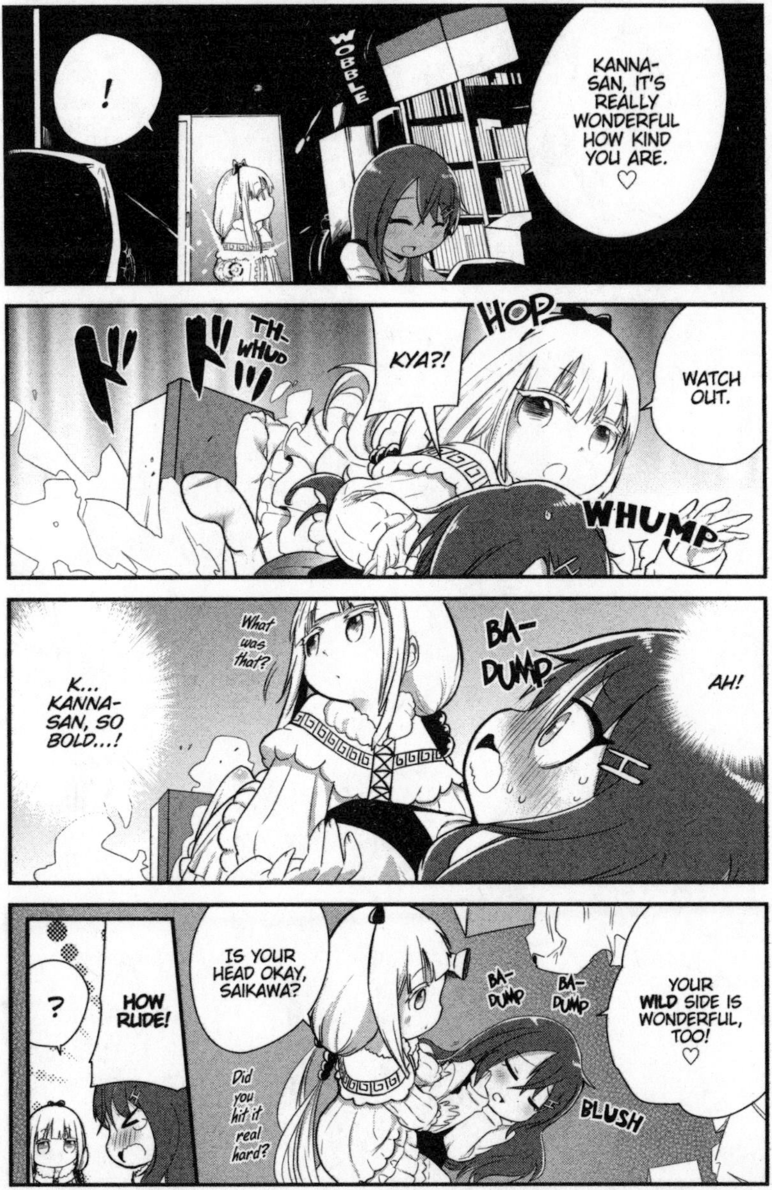
KANNA-SAN, IT'S REALLY WONDERFUL HOW KIND YOU ARE. ♡
WOBBLE
!
WATCH OUT.
HOP
KYA?!
WHUMP
TH-WHUD
AH!
BA-DUMP
What was that?
K... KANNA-SAN, SO BOLD...!
YOUR WILD SIDE IS WONDERFUL, TOO! ♡
BA-DUMP
BA-DUMP
BLUSH
IS YOUR HEAD OKAY, SAIKAWA?
Did you hit it real hard?
HOW RUDE!
?

KANNA AND SAIKAWA (1)

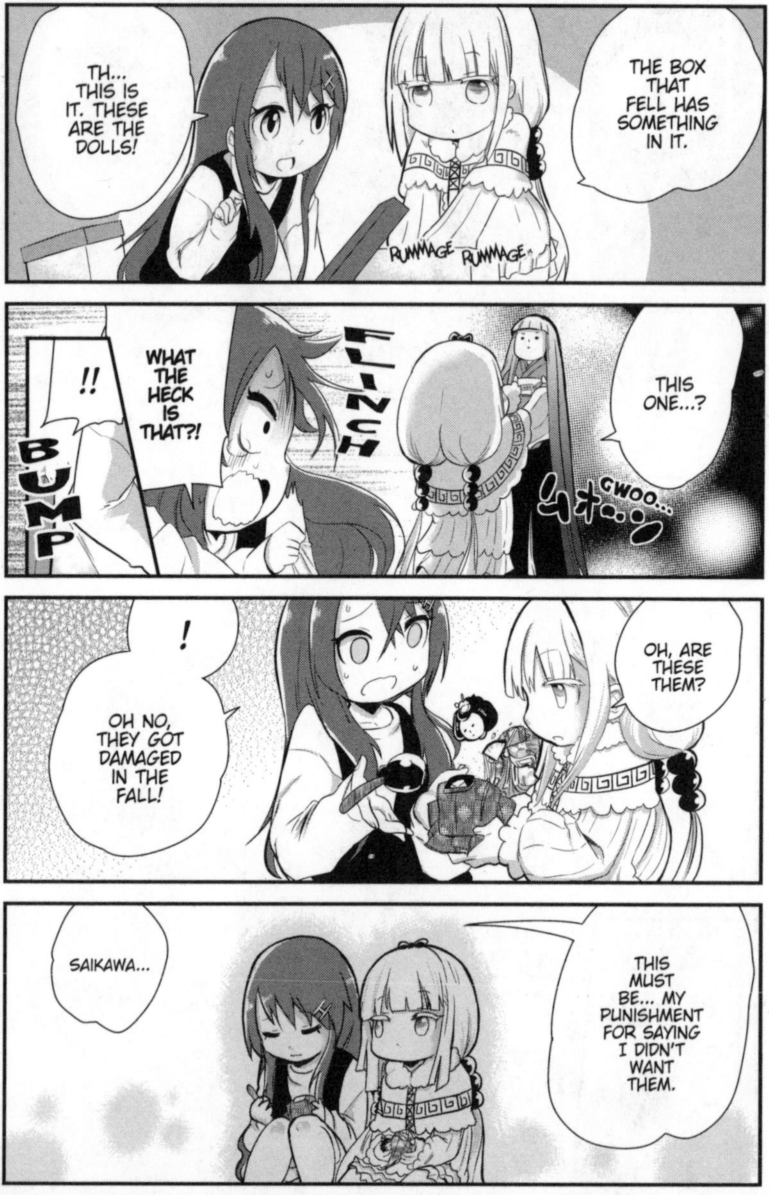
THE BOX THAT FELL HAS SOMETHING IN IT.
TH... THIS IS IT. THESE ARE THE DOLLS!
RUMMAGE RUMMAGE
THIS ONE...?
GWOO...
FLINCH
WHAT THE HECK IS THAT?!
!!
BUMP
OH, ARE THESE THEM?
!
OH NO, THEY GOT DAMAGED IN THE FALL!
THIS MUST BE... MY PUNISHMENT FOR SAYING I DIDN'T WANT THEM.
SAIKAWA...

KANNA AND SAIKAWA (2)

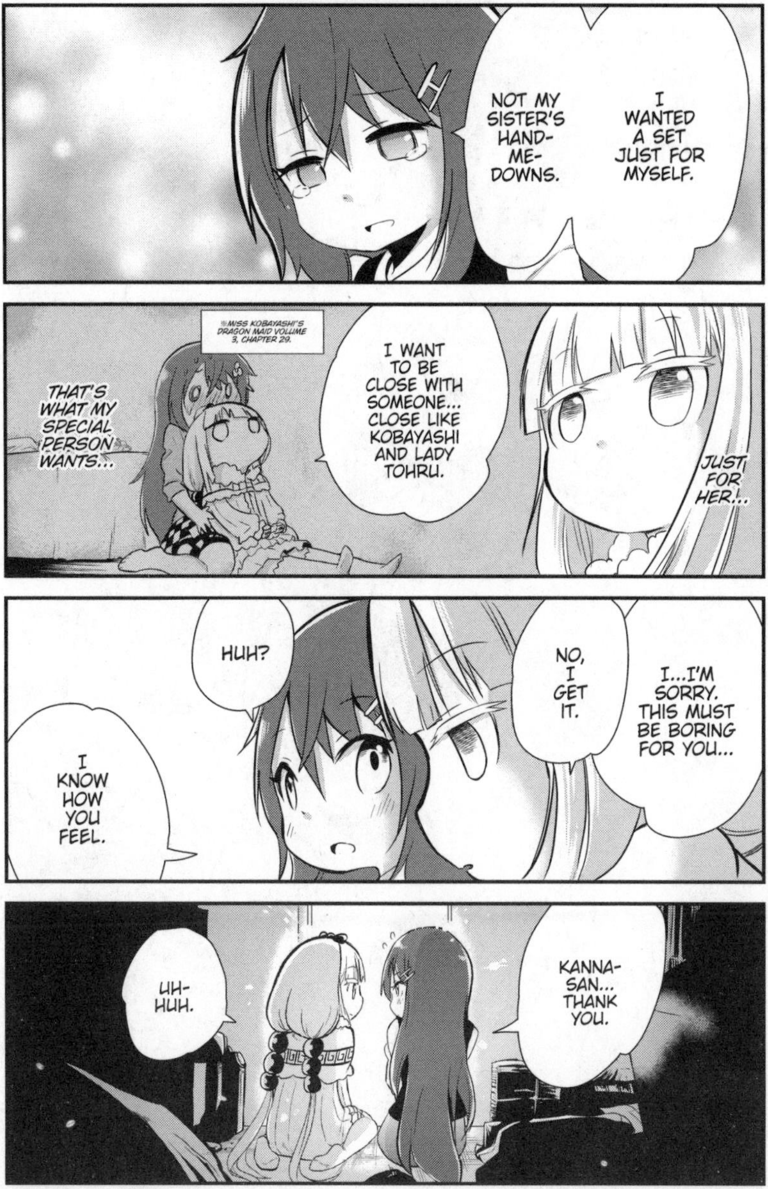
I WANTED A SET JUST FOR MYSELF.
NOT MY SISTER'S HAND-ME-DOWNS.
I WANT TO BE CLOSE WITH SOMEONE... CLOSE LIKE KOBAYASHI AND LADY TOHRU.
※MISS KOBAYASHI'S DRAGON MAID VOLUME 3, CHAPTER 29.
THAT'S WHAT MY SPECIAL PERSON WANTS...
JUST FOR HER...
I...I'M SORRY. THIS MUST BE BORING FOR YOU...
NO, I GET IT.
HUH?
I KNOW HOW YOU FEEL.
KANNA-SAN... THANK YOU.
UH-HUH.

GIRLS CAN BE STRANGELY PRAGMATIC

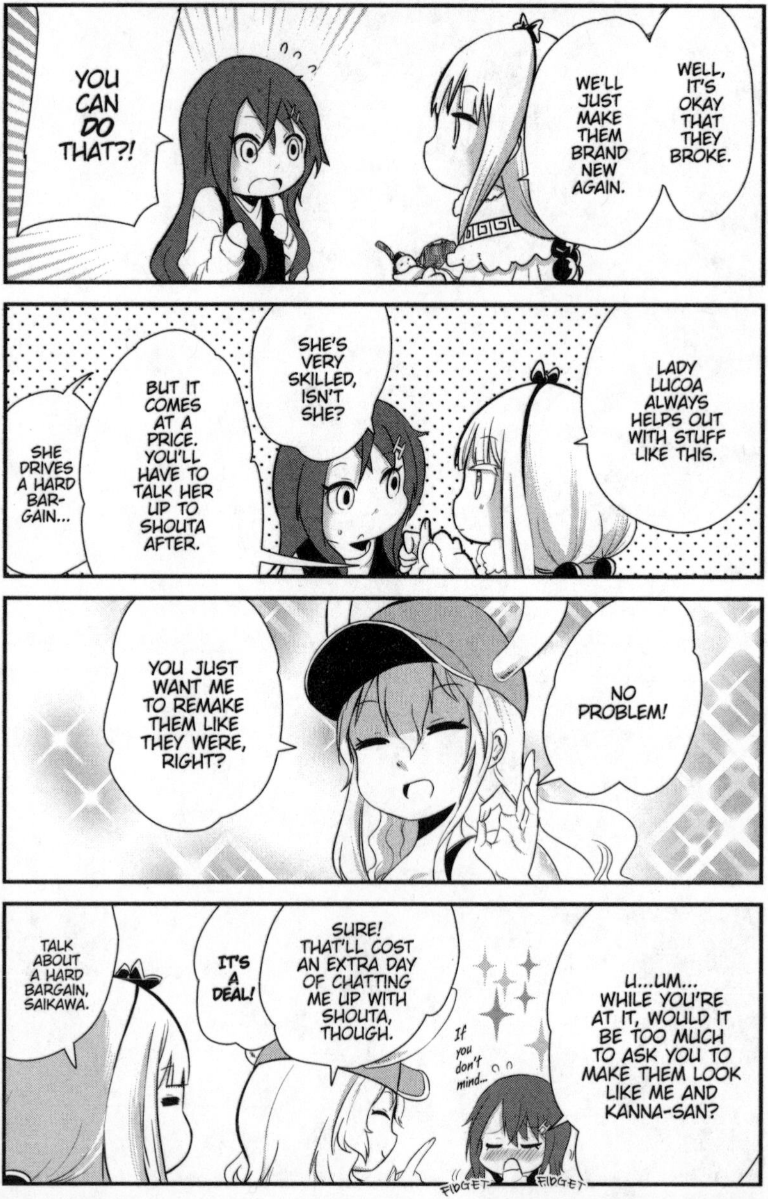

WELL, IT'S OKAY THAT THEY BROKE.
WE'LL JUST MAKE THEM BRAND NEW AGAIN.
YOU CAN DO THAT?!
LADY LUCOA ALWAYS HELPS OUT WITH STUFF LIKE THIS.
SHE'S VERY SKILLED, ISN'T SHE?
BUT IT COMES AT A PRICE. YOU'LL HAVE TO TALK HER UP TO SHOUTA AFTER.
SHE DRIVES A HARD BAR-GAIN...
NO PROBLEM!
YOU JUST WANT ME TO REMAKE THEM LIKE THEY WERE, RIGHT?
U...UM... WHILE YOU'RE AT IT, WOULD IT BE TOO MUCH TO ASK YOU TO MAKE THEM LOOK LIKE ME AND KANNA-SAN?
If you don't mind...
FIDGET FIDGET
SURE! THAT'LL COST AN EXTRA DAY OF CHATTING ME UP WITH SHOUTA, THOUGH.
IT'S A DEAL!
TALK ABOUT A HARD BARGAIN, SAIKAWA.

ONE OF A KIND

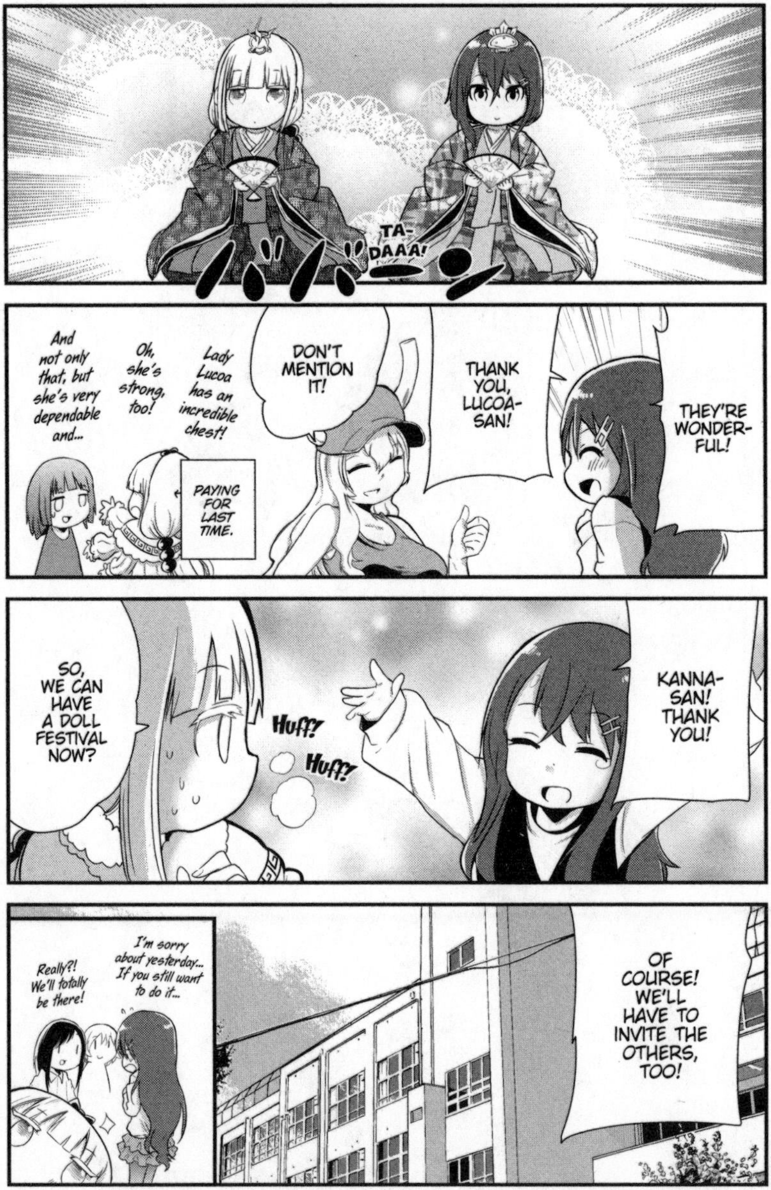
TA-DAAA!
THEY'RE WONDERFUL!
THANK YOU, LUCOA-SAN!
DON'T MENTION IT!
Lady Lucoa has an incredible chest!
PAYING FOR LAST TIME.
Oh, she's strong, too!
And not only that, but she's very dependable and...
KANNA-SAN! THANK YOU!
Huff!
Huff!
SO, WE CAN HAVE A DOLL FESTIVAL NOW?
OF COURSE! WE'LL HAVE TO INVITE THE OTHERS, TOO!
I'm sorry about yesterday... If you still want to do it...
Really?! We'll totally be there!

THE MAIN EVENT

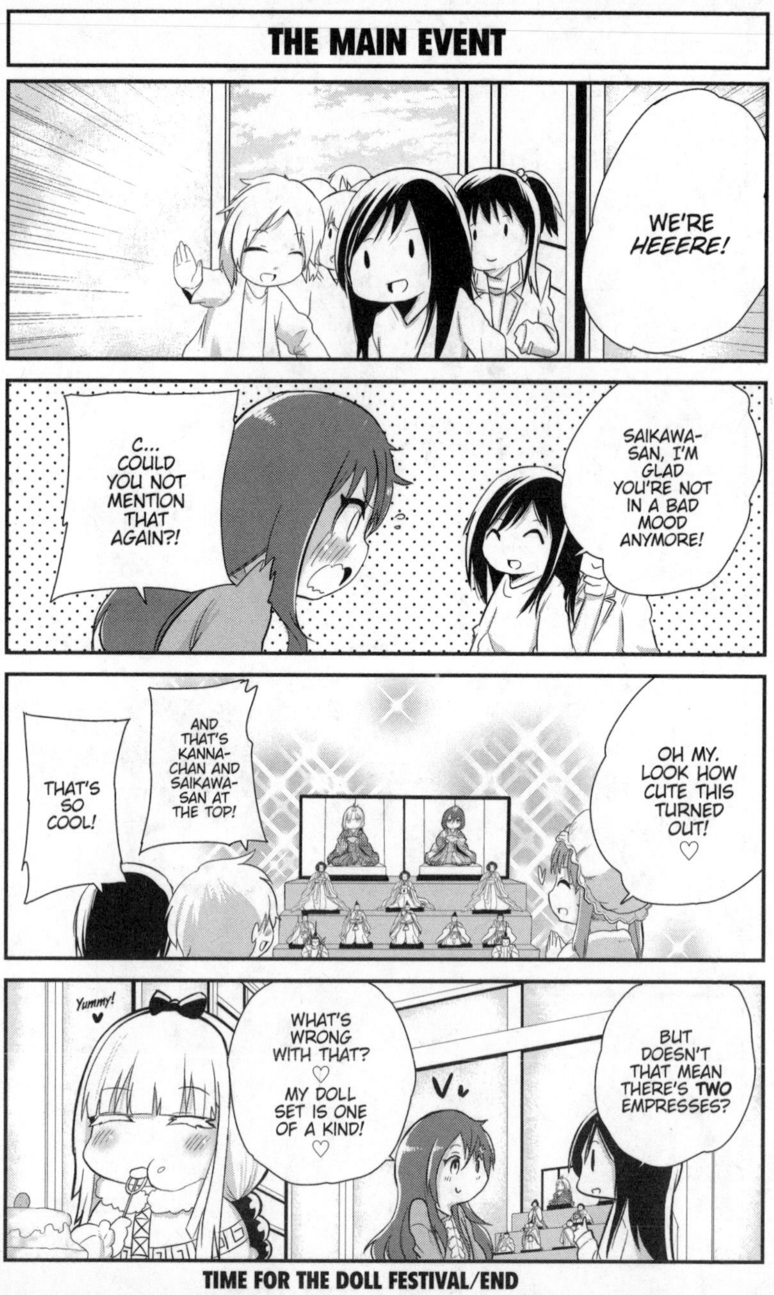

WE'RE HEEERE!
SAIKAWA-SAN, I'M GLAD YOU'RE NOT IN A BAD MOOD ANYMORE!
C... COULD YOU NOT MENTION THAT AGAIN?!
OH MY. LOOK HOW CUTE THIS TURNED OUT! ♡
AND THAT'S KANNA-CHAN AND SAIKAWA-SAN AT THE TOP!
THAT'S SO COOL!
BUT DOESN'T THAT MEAN THERE'S **TWO** EMPRESSES?
WHAT'S WRONG WITH THAT? ♡ MY DOLL SET IS ONE OF A KIND! ♡
Yummy! ♥

TIME FOR THE DOLL FESTIVAL/END

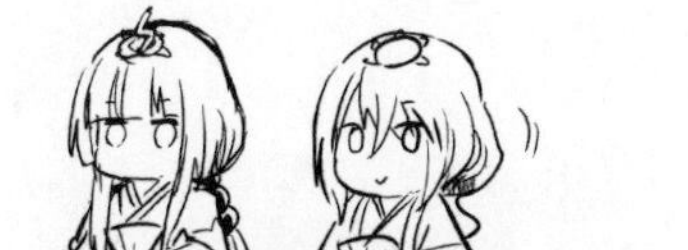
SLIDE...
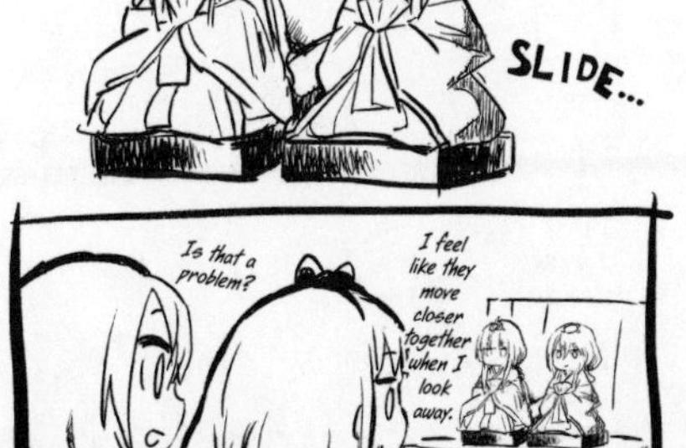
I feel like they move closer together when I look away.
Is that a problem?

Miss Kobayashi's Dragon Maid
Kanna's Daily Life

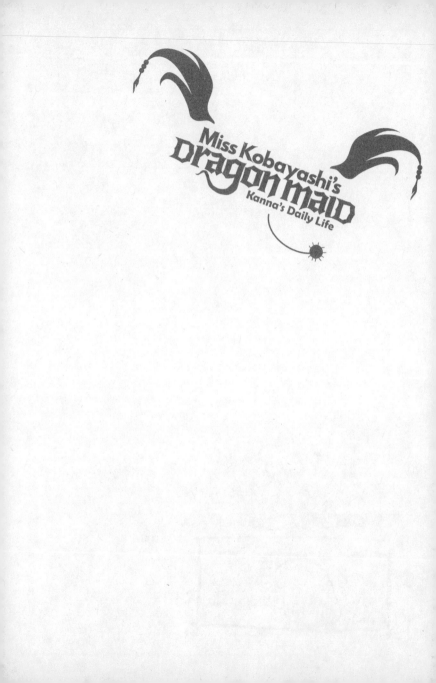

KANNA'S TEST OF COURAGE

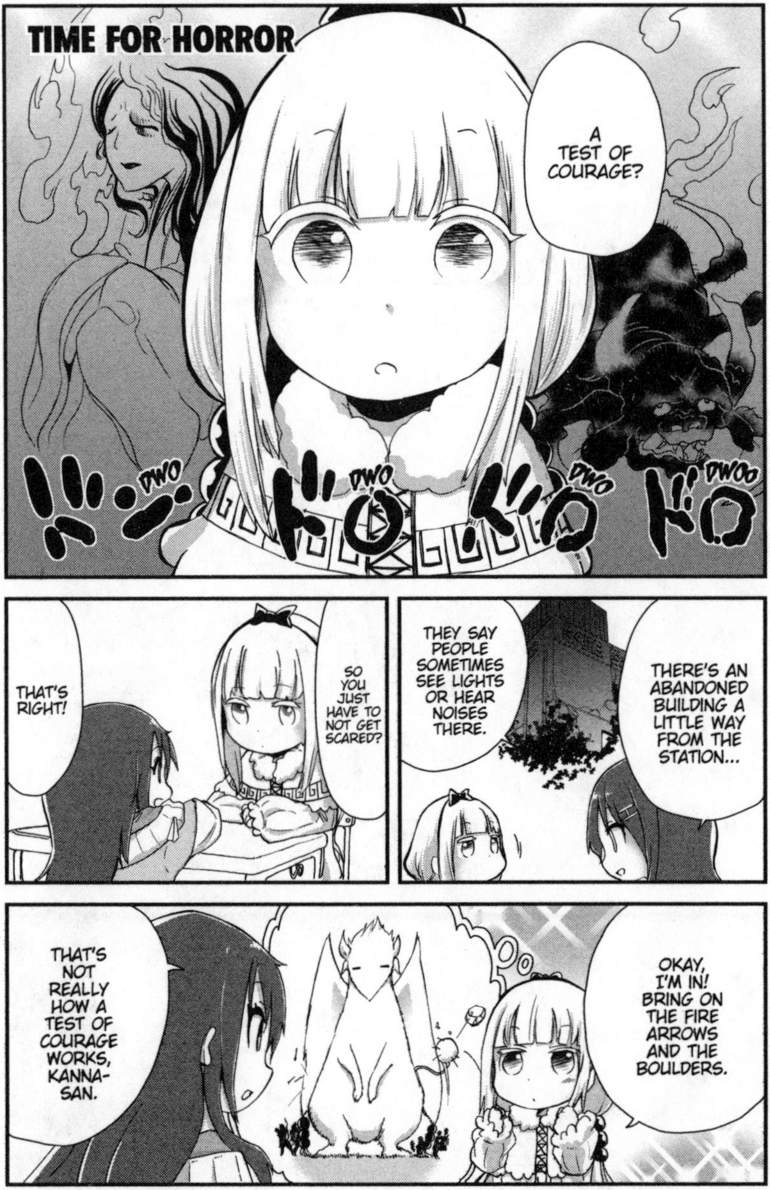
TIME FOR HORROR
A TEST OF COURAGE?
DWO DWO DWO DWOO
THERE'S AN ABANDONED BUILDING A LITTLE WAY FROM THE STATION...
THEY SAY PEOPLE SOMETIMES SEE LIGHTS OR HEAR NOISES THERE.
SO YOU JUST HAVE TO NOT GET SCARED?
THAT'S RIGHT!
OKAY, I'M IN! BRING ON THE FIRE ARROWS AND THE BOULDERS.
THAT'S NOT REALLY HOW A TEST OF COURAGE WORKS, KANNA-SAN.

WAS IT JUST...AN AFTERIMAGE?!

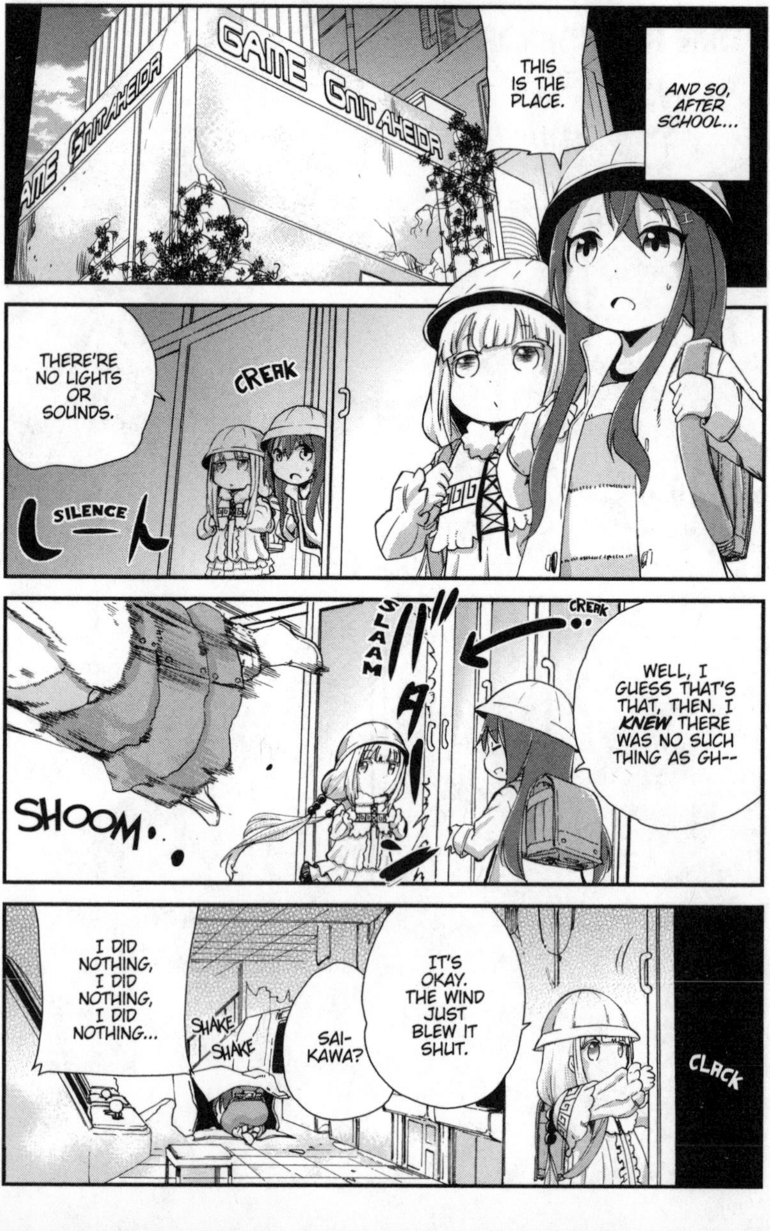
AND SO, AFTER SCHOOL...
THIS IS THE PLACE.
GAME GNITAHEIDA
CREAK
THERE'RE NO LIGHTS OR SOUNDS.
SILENCE
CREAK
WELL, I GUESS THAT'S THAT, THEN. I *KNEW* THERE WAS NO SUCH THING AS GH--
SLAAAM
SHOOM
CLACK
IT'S OKAY. THE WIND JUST BLEW IT SHUT.
SAI-KAWA?
SHAKE
SHAKE
I DID NOTHING, I DID NOTHING, I DID NOTHING...

RETRO MASTER KANNA

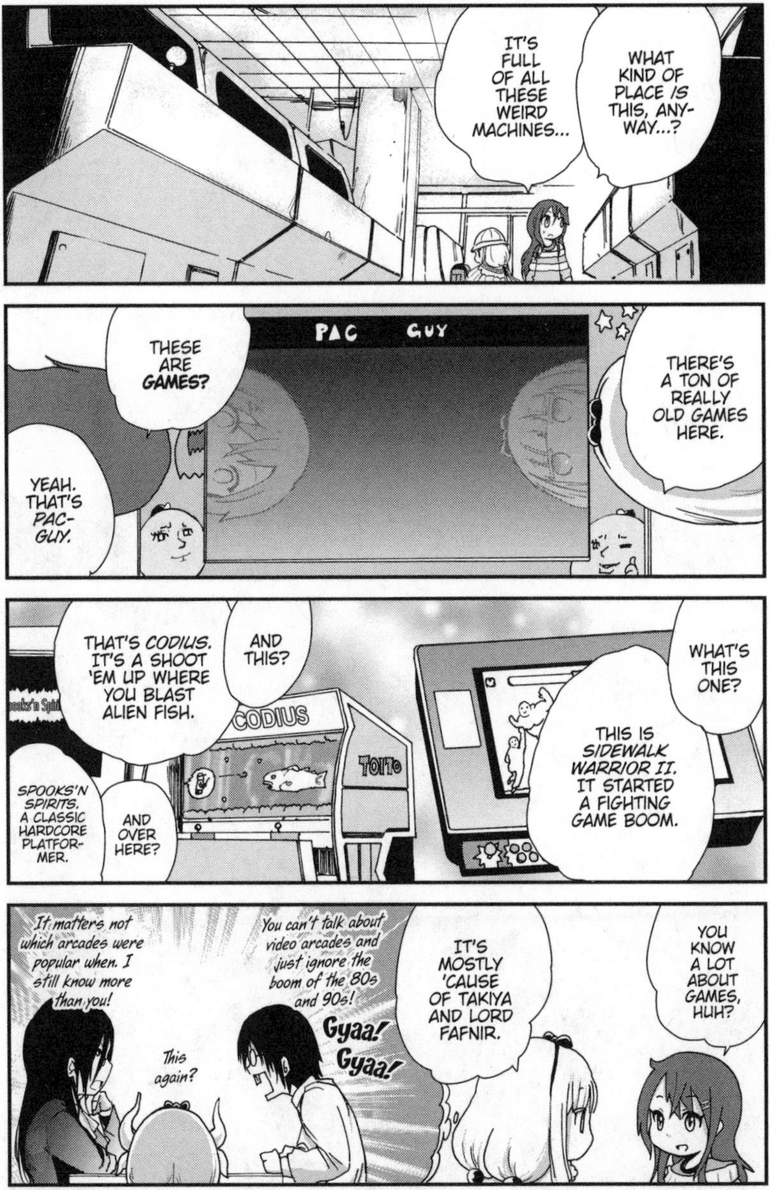
WHAT KIND OF PLACE *IS* THIS, ANYWAY...?
IT'S FULL OF ALL THESE WEIRD MACHINES...
PAC GUY
THERE'S A TON OF REALLY OLD GAMES HERE.
THESE ARE **GAMES?**
YEAH. THAT'S *PAC-GUY.*
WHAT'S THIS ONE?
THIS IS *SIDEWALK WARRIOR II.* IT STARTED A FIGHTING GAME BOOM.
AND THIS?
THAT'S *CODIUS.* IT'S A SHOOT 'EM UP WHERE YOU BLAST ALIEN FISH.
CODIUS
TOITO
AND OVER HERE?
SPOOKS'N SPIRITS. A CLASSIC HARDCORE PLATFORMER.
YOU KNOW A LOT ABOUT GAMES, HUH?
IT'S MOSTLY 'CAUSE OF TAKIYA AND LORD FAFNIR.
You can't talk about video arcades and just ignore the boom of the 80s and 90s!
Gyaa! Gyaa!
It matters not which arcades were popular when. I still know more than you!
This again?

GAMER GIRLS

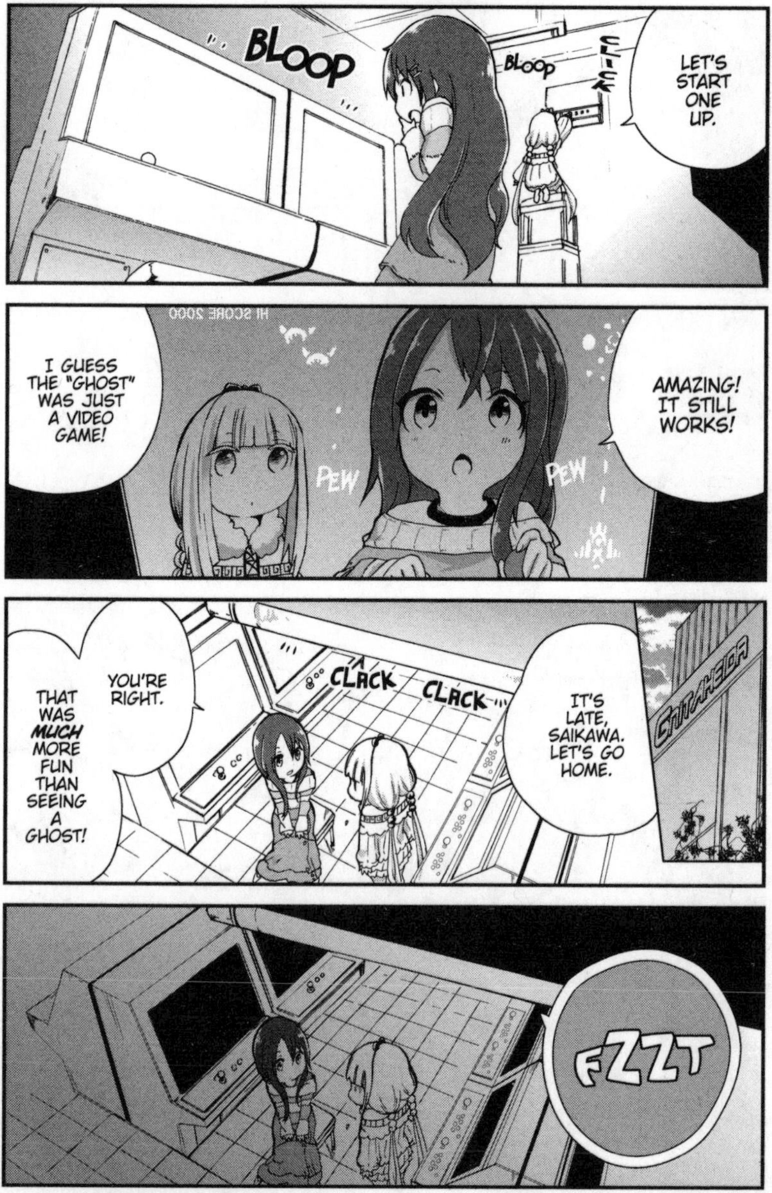
LET'S START ONE UP.
CLICK
BLOOP
BLOOP
AMAZING! IT STILL WORKS!
HI SCORE 2000
PEW
PEW
I GUESS THE "GHOST" WAS JUST A VIDEO GAME!
IT'S LATE, SAIKAWA. LET'S GO HOME.
CLACK
CLACK
YOU'RE RIGHT.
THAT WAS *MUCH* MORE FUN THAN SEEING A GHOST!
FZZT

SOMETHING'S THERE!

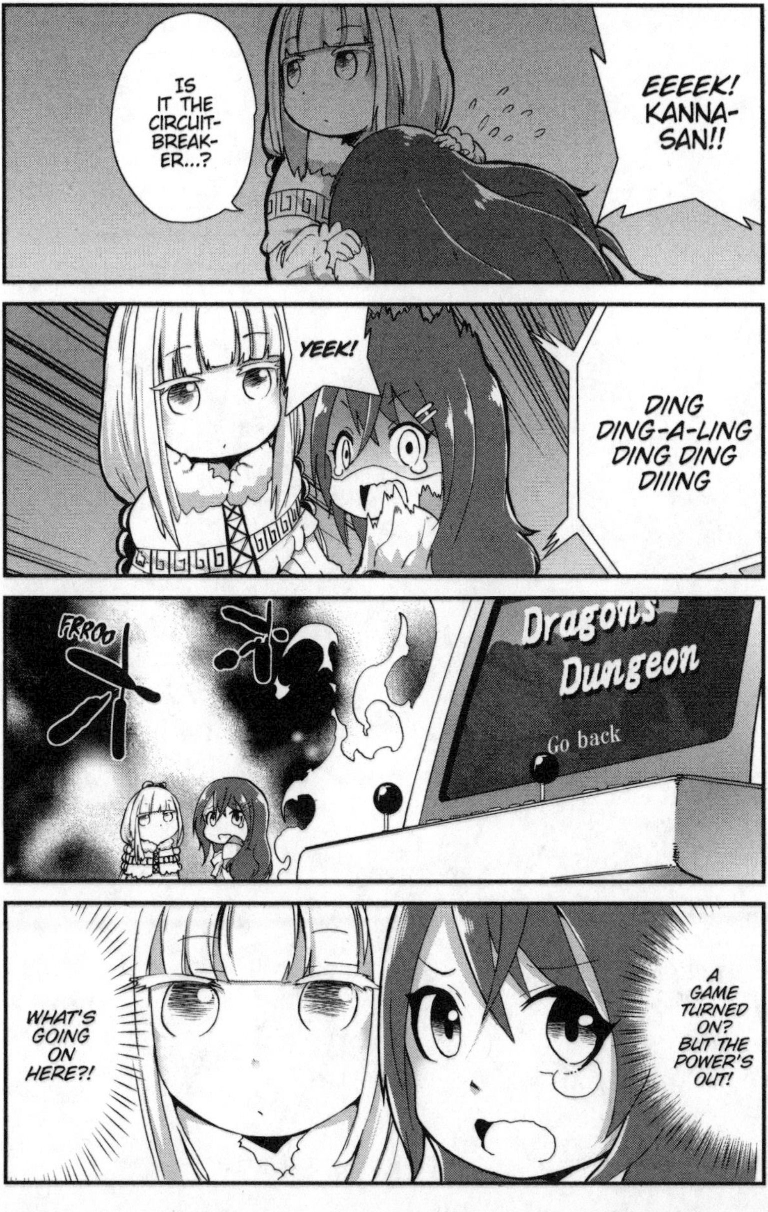
EEEEK! KANNA-SAN!!
IS IT THE CIRCUIT-BREAKER...?
DING DING-A-LING DING DING DIIING
YEEK!
Dragons Dungeon
Go back
FRROO
A GAME TURNED ON? BUT THE POWER'S OUT!
WHAT'S GOING ON HERE?!

KANNA THE BRAVE

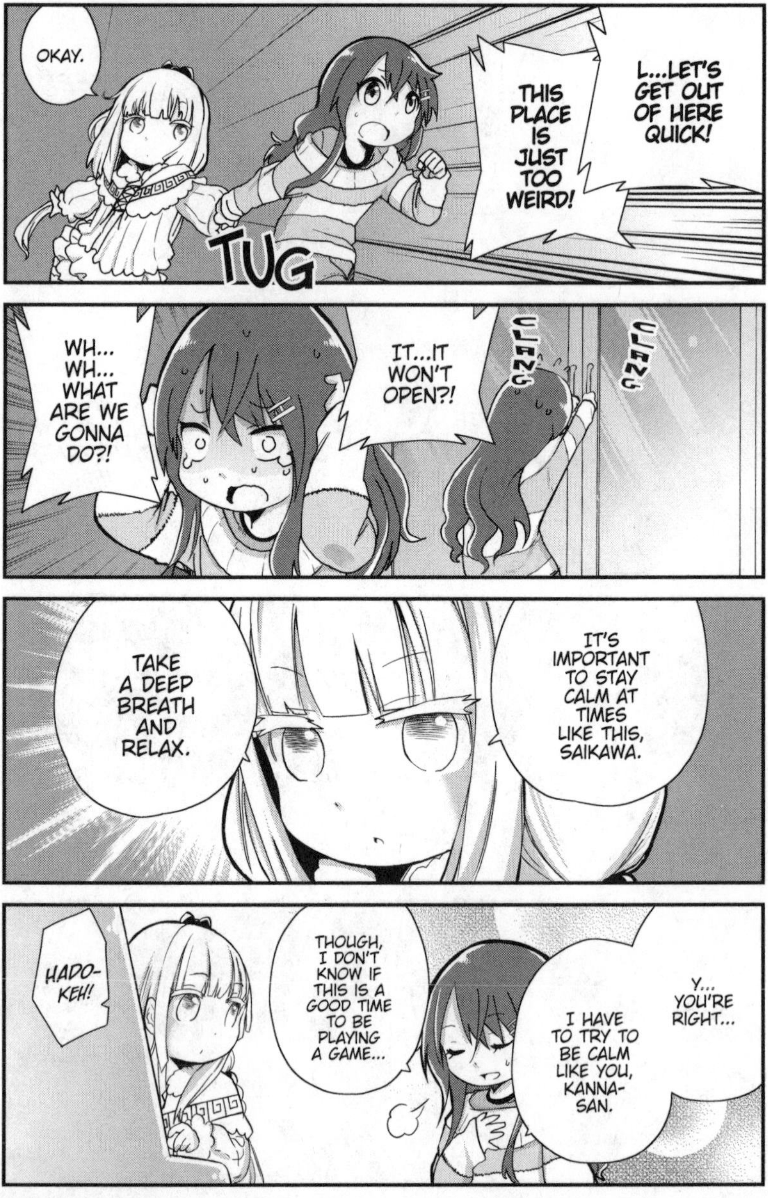
L...LET'S GET OUT OF HERE QUICK!
THIS PLACE IS JUST TOO WEIRD!
OKAY.
TUG
CLANG
CLANG
IT...IT WON'T OPEN?!
WH... WH... WHAT ARE WE GONNA DO?!
IT'S IMPORTANT TO STAY CALM AT TIMES LIKE THIS, SAIKAWA.
TAKE A DEEP BREATH AND RELAX.
Y... YOU'RE RIGHT...
I HAVE TO TRY TO BE CALM LIKE YOU, KANNA-SAN.
THOUGH, I DON'T KNOW IF THIS IS A GOOD TIME TO BE PLAYING A GAME...
HADO-KEH!

GATOR PANIC

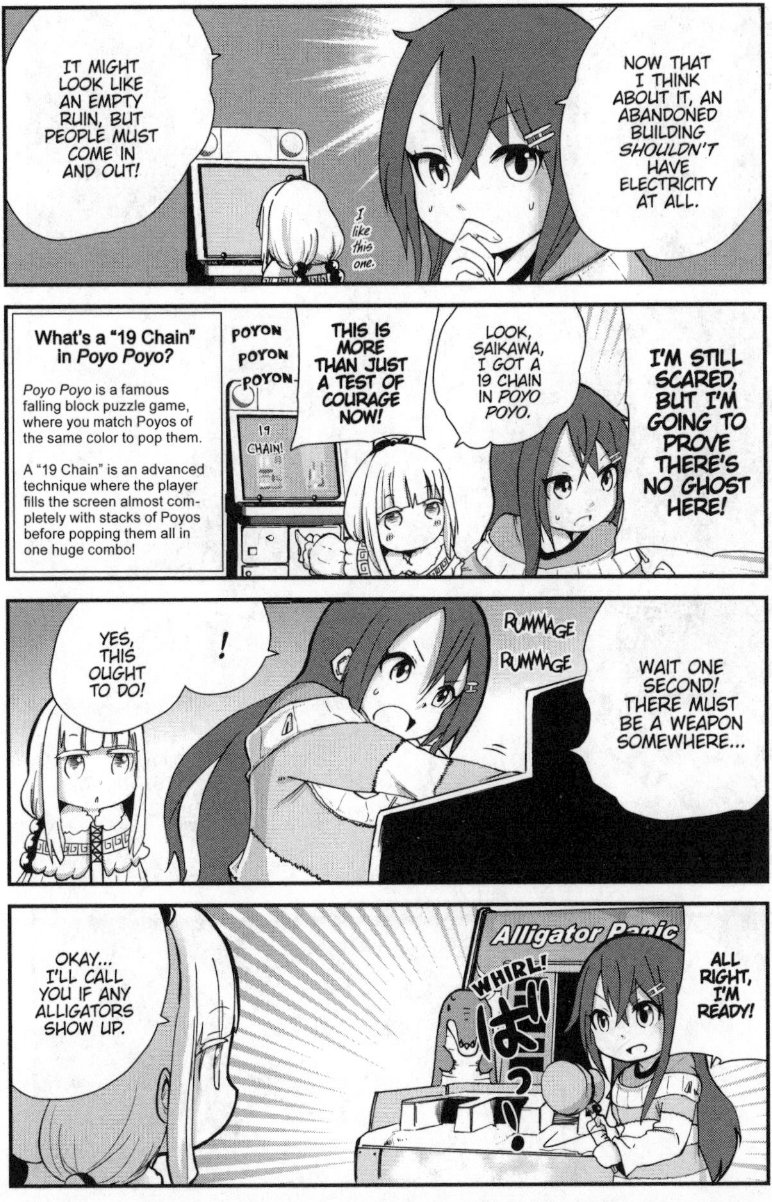
NOW THAT I THINK ABOUT IT, AN ABANDONED BUILDING *SHOULDN'T* HAVE ELECTRICITY AT ALL.
I like this one.
IT MIGHT LOOK LIKE AN EMPTY RUIN, BUT PEOPLE MUST COME IN AND OUT!
I'M STILL SCARED, BUT I'M GOING TO PROVE THERE'S NO GHOST HERE!
LOOK, SAIKAWA, I GOT A 19 CHAIN IN *POYO POYO*.
THIS IS MORE THAN JUST A TEST OF COURAGE NOW!
POYON POYON POYON
19 CHAIN!
What's a "19 Chain" in *Poyo Poyo?*
Poyo Poyo is a famous falling block puzzle game, where you match Poyos of the same color to pop them.
A "19 Chain" is an advanced technique where the player fills the screen almost completely with stacks of Poyos before popping them all in one huge combo!
WAIT ONE SECOND! THERE MUST BE A WEAPON SOMEWHERE...
RUMMAGE RUMMAGE
!
YES, THIS OUGHT TO DO!
ALL RIGHT, I'M READY!
Alligator Panic
WHIRL!
OKAY... I'LL CALL YOU IF ANY ALLIGATORS SHOW UP.

DON'T LOOK AT ME LIKE THAT (IT'S SCARY)

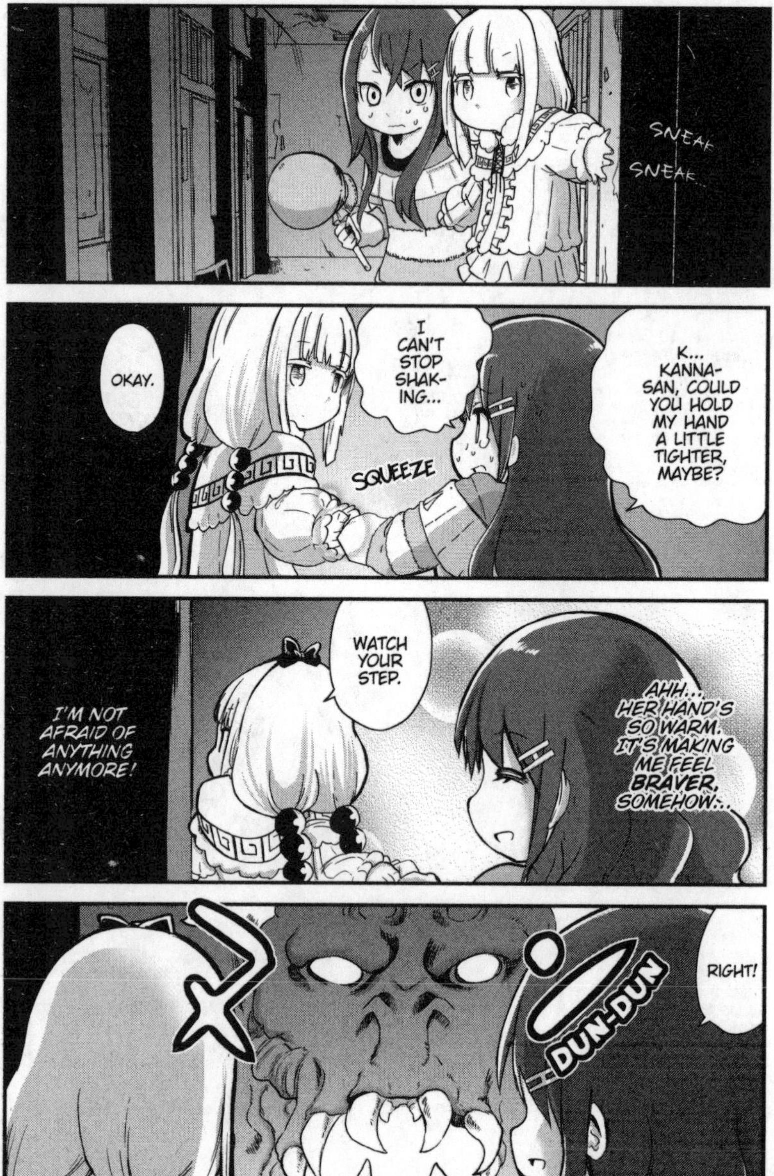
SNEAK
SNEAK...
K... KANNA-SAN, COULD YOU HOLD MY HAND A LITTLE TIGHTER, MAYBE?
SQUEEZE
I CAN'T STOP SHAKING...
OKAY.
AHH... HER HAND'S SO WARM. IT'S MAKING ME FEEL BRAVER, SOMEHOW...
WATCH YOUR STEP.
I'M NOT AFRAID OF ANYTHING ANYMORE!
RIGHT!
DUN-DUN

FAFNIR OBJECTS

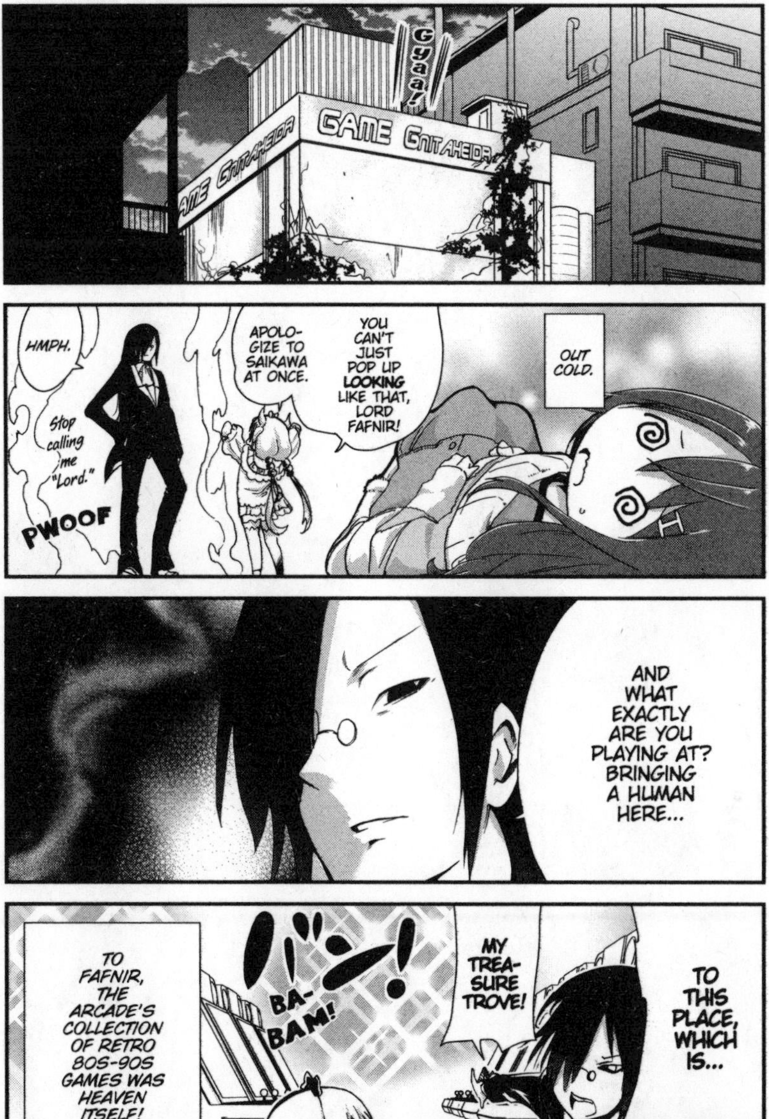
Gyaa!
GAME GNITAHEIDA
GAME GNITAHEIDA
OUT COLD.
YOU CAN'T JUST POP UP LOOKING LIKE THAT, LORD FAFNIR!
APOLO-GIZE TO SAIKAWA AT ONCE.
HMPH.
Stop calling me "Lord."
PWOOF
AND WHAT EXACTLY ARE YOU PLAYING AT? BRINGING A HUMAN HERE...
TO THIS PLACE, WHICH IS...
MY TREA-SURE TROVE!
BA-BAM!
Mrr...
TO FAFNIR, THE ARCADE'S COLLECTION OF RETRO 80S-90S GAMES WAS HEAVEN ITSELF!

FAFNIR IS FORGIVEN

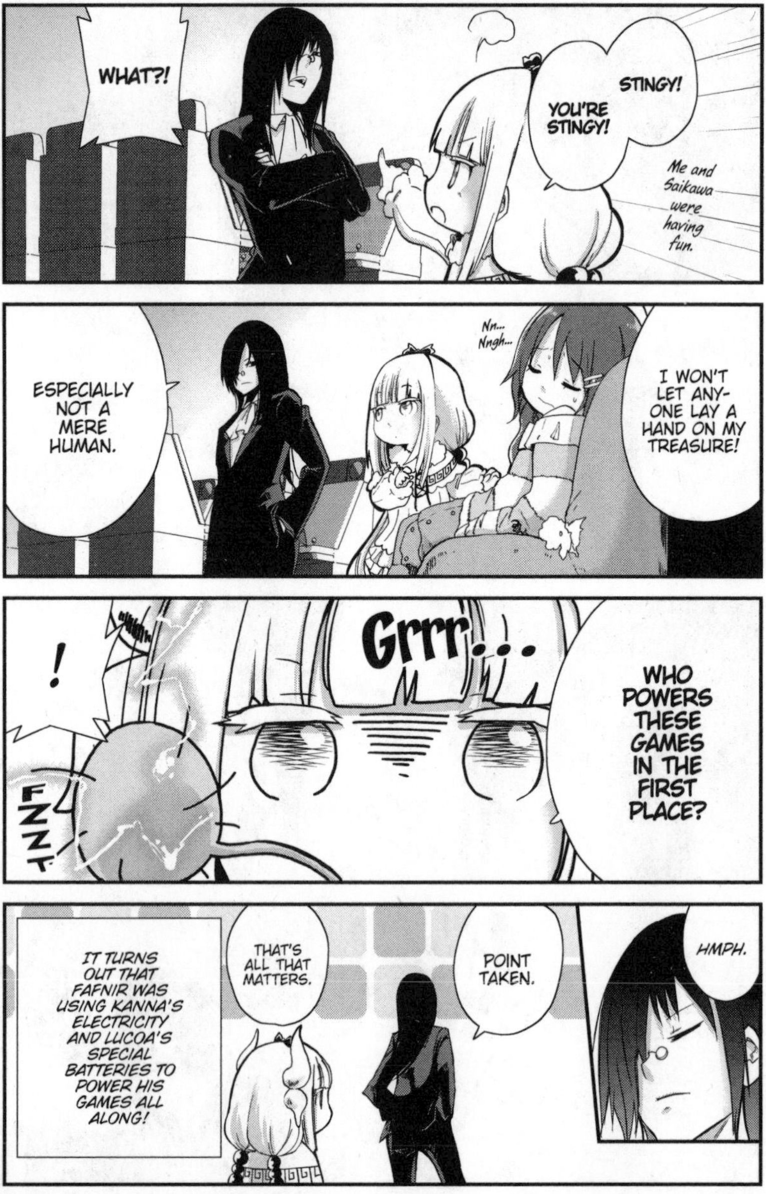
STINGY!
YOU'RE STINGY!
Me and Saikawa were having fun.
WHAT?!
I WON'T LET ANYONE LAY A HAND ON MY TREASURE!
Nn... Nngh...
ESPECIALLY NOT A MERE HUMAN.
WHO POWERS THESE GAMES IN THE FIRST PLACE?
Grrr...
!
FZZT
HMPH.
POINT TAKEN.
THAT'S ALL THAT MATTERS.
IT TURNS OUT THAT FAFNIR WAS USING KANNA'S ELECTRICITY AND LUCOA'S SPECIAL BATTERIES TO POWER HIS GAMES ALL ALONG!

FAFNIR IS FRIENDLY?

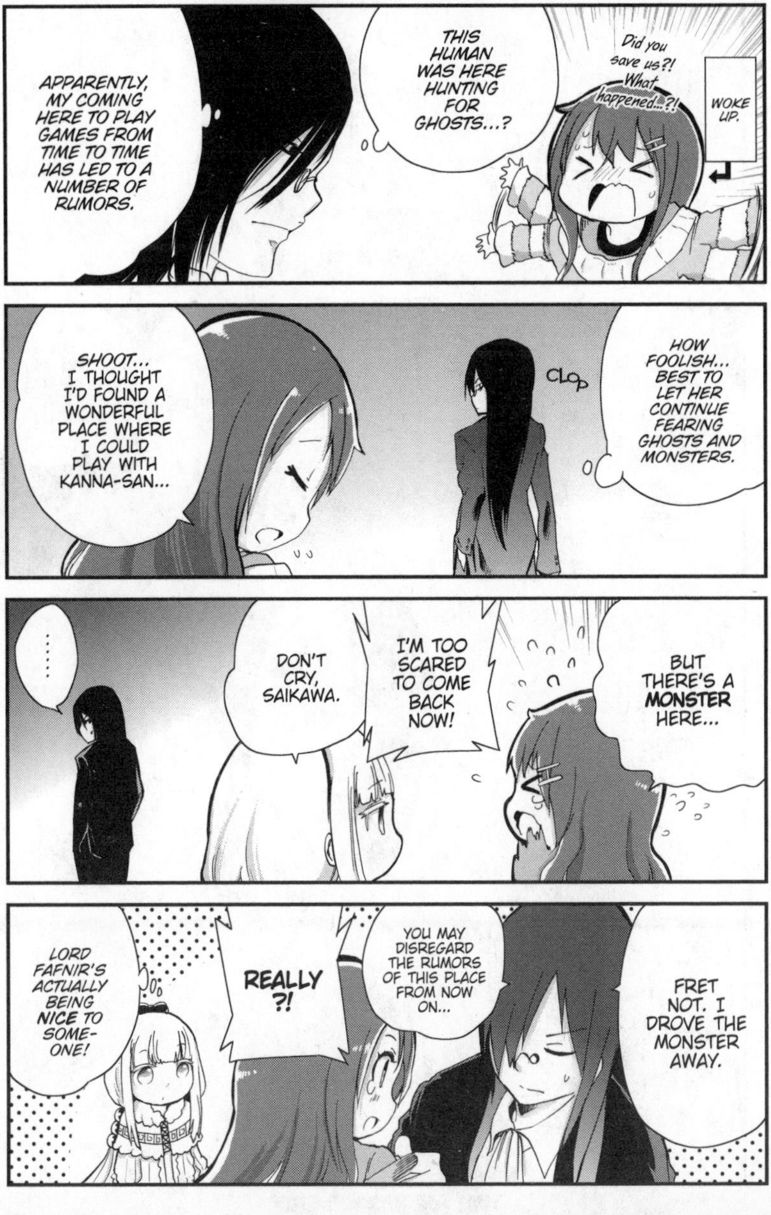
WOKE UP.
Did you save us?! What happened...?!
THIS HUMAN WAS HERE HUNTING FOR GHOSTS...?
APPARENTLY, MY COMING HERE TO PLAY GAMES FROM TIME TO TIME HAS LED TO A NUMBER OF RUMORS.
HOW FOOLISH... BEST TO LET HER CONTINUE FEARING GHOSTS AND MONSTERS.
CLOP
SHOOT... I THOUGHT I'D FOUND A WONDERFUL PLACE WHERE I COULD PLAY WITH KANNA-SAN...
BUT THERE'S A MONSTER HERE...
I'M TOO SCARED TO COME BACK NOW!
DON'T CRY, SAIKAWA.
......
FRET NOT. I DROVE THE MONSTER AWAY.
YOU MAY DISREGARD THE RUMORS OF THIS PLACE FROM NOW ON...
REALLY?!
LORD FAFNIR'S ACTUALLY BEING NICE TO SOME-ONE!

KANNA AND FAFNIR

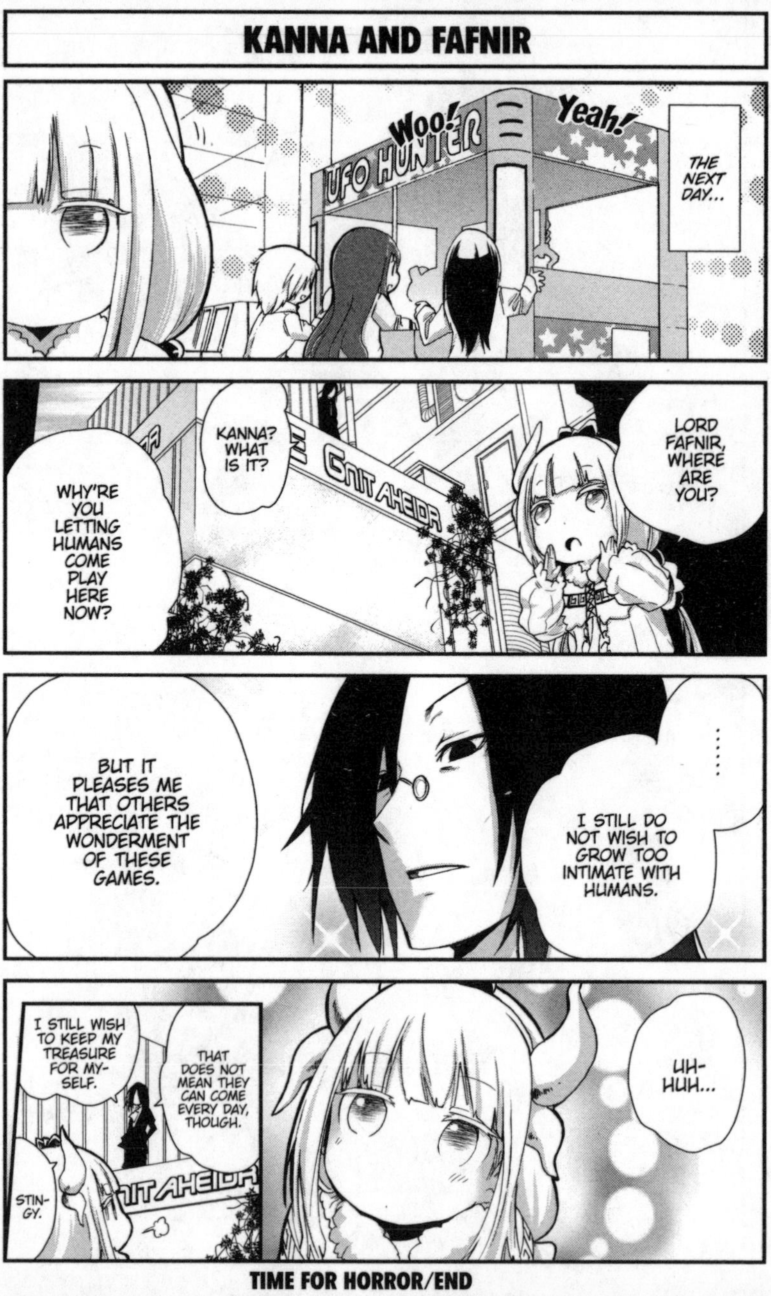
THE NEXT DAY...
Yeah!
Woo!
UFO HUNTER
LORD FAFNIR, WHERE ARE YOU?
KANNA? WHAT IS IT?
WHY'RE YOU LETTING HUMANS COME PLAY HERE NOW?
......
I STILL DO NOT WISH TO GROW TOO INTIMATE WITH HUMANS.
BUT IT PLEASES ME THAT OTHERS APPRECIATE THE WONDERMENT OF THESE GAMES.
UH-HUH...
THAT DOES NOT MEAN THEY CAN COME EVERY DAY, THOUGH.
I STILL WISH TO KEEP MY TREASURE FOR MY-SELF.
STIN-GY.

TIME FOR HORROR/END

KANNA'S LATE-NIGHT DISCOVERY

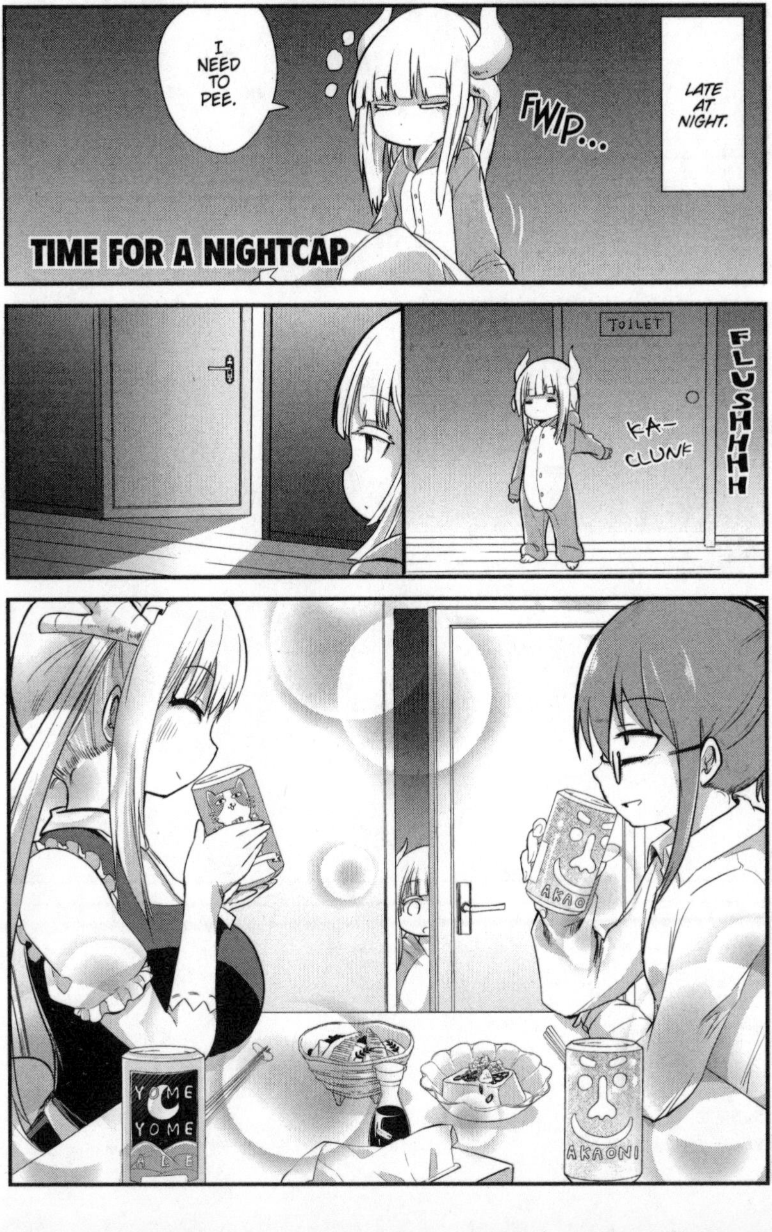
LATE AT NIGHT.
FWIP...
I NEED TO PEE.
TIME FOR A NIGHTCAP
FLUSHHHH
TOILET
KA-CLUNK
AKAONI
AKAONI
YOME YOME ALE

IS IT REALLY THAT GREAT?!

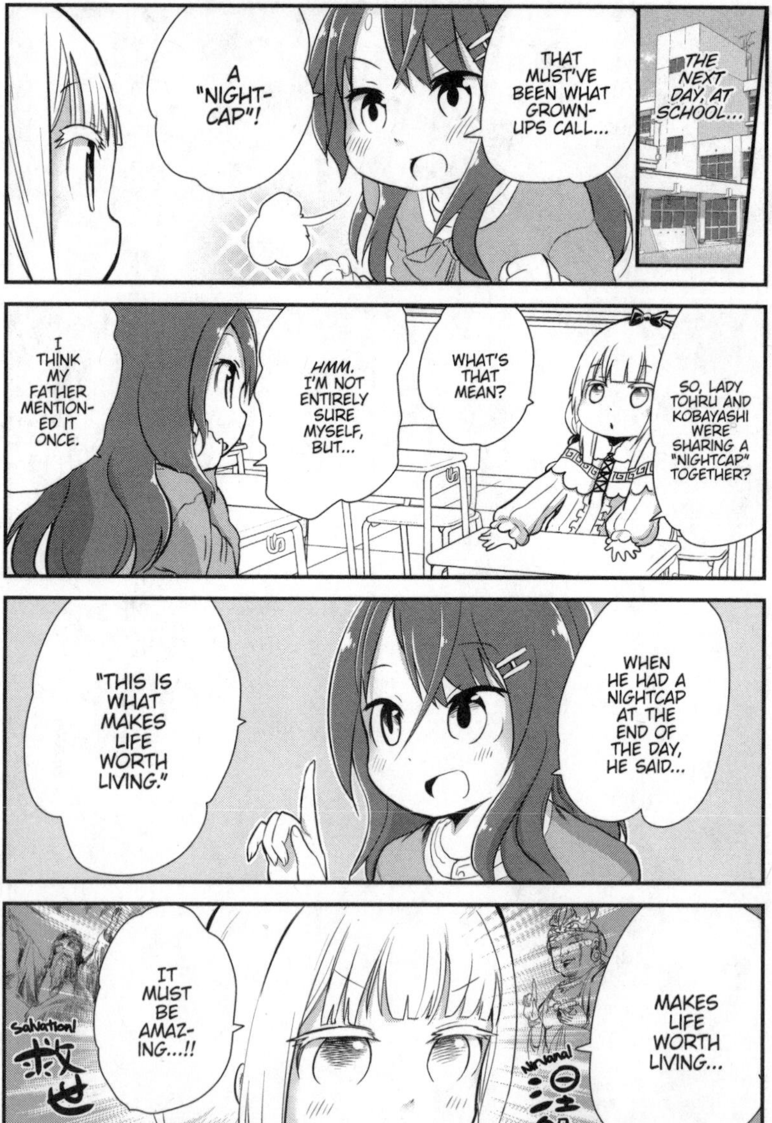
THE NEXT DAY, AT SCHOOL...
THAT MUST'VE BEEN WHAT GROWN-UPS CALL...
A "NIGHT-CAP"!
SO, LADY TOHRU AND KOBAYASHI WERE SHARING A "NIGHTCAP" TOGETHER?
WHAT'S THAT MEAN?
HMM. I'M NOT ENTIRELY SURE MYSELF, BUT...
I THINK MY FATHER MENTION-ED IT ONCE.
WHEN HE HAD A NIGHTCAP AT THE END OF THE DAY, HE SAID...
"THIS IS WHAT MAKES LIFE WORTH LIVING."
MAKES LIFE WORTH LIVING...
Nirvana!
涅槃
IT MUST BE AMAZ-ING...!!
Salvation!
救世

NOT VERY CONVINCING!

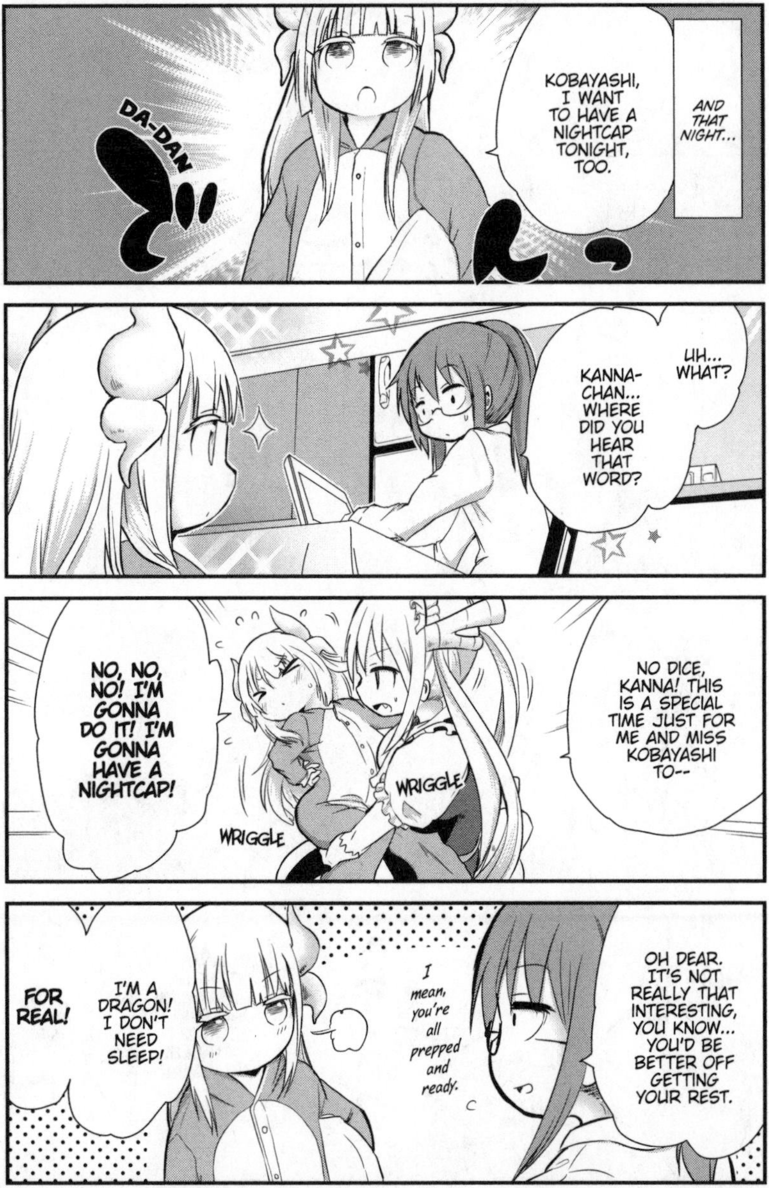
AND THAT NIGHT...
KOBAYASHI, I WANT TO HAVE A NIGHTCAP TONIGHT, TOO.
DA-DAN
UH... WHAT?
KANNA-CHAN... WHERE DID YOU HEAR THAT WORD?
NO DICE, KANNA! THIS IS A SPECIAL TIME JUST FOR ME AND MISS KOBAYASHI TO--
WRIGGLE
NO, NO, NO! I'M GONNA DO IT! I'M GONNA HAVE A NIGHTCAP!
WRIGGLE
OH DEAR. IT'S NOT REALLY THAT INTERESTING, YOU KNOW... YOU'D BE BETTER OFF GETTING YOUR REST.
I mean, you're all prepped and ready.
I'M A DRAGON! I DON'T NEED SLEEP!
FOR REAL!

DRAGON-SIZED TEMPER TANTRUMS

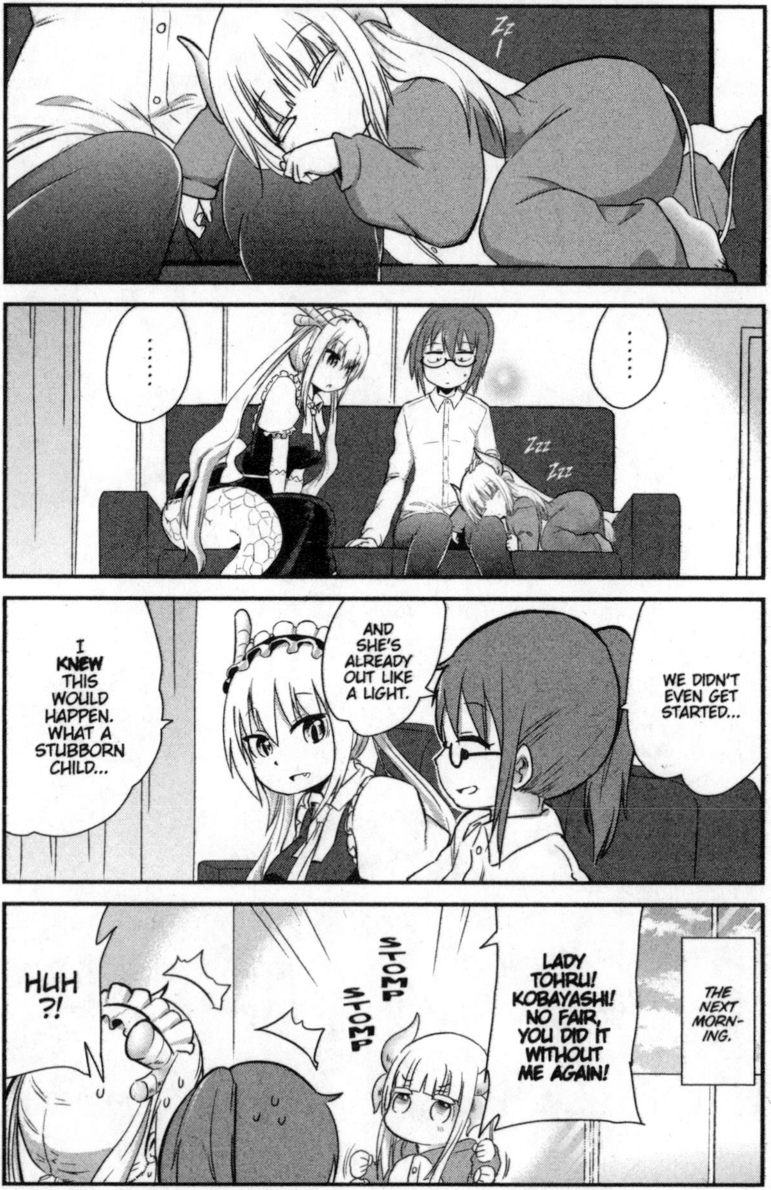
Zz
......
......
Zzz
Zzz
WE DIDN'T EVEN GET STARTED...
AND SHE'S ALREADY OUT LIKE A LIGHT.
I KNEW THIS WOULD HAPPEN. WHAT A STUBBORN CHILD...
THE NEXT MORNING.
LADY TOHRU! KOBAYASHI! NO FAIR, YOU DID IT WITHOUT ME AGAIN!
STOMP
STOMP
HUH ?!

NECTAR OF THE GODS

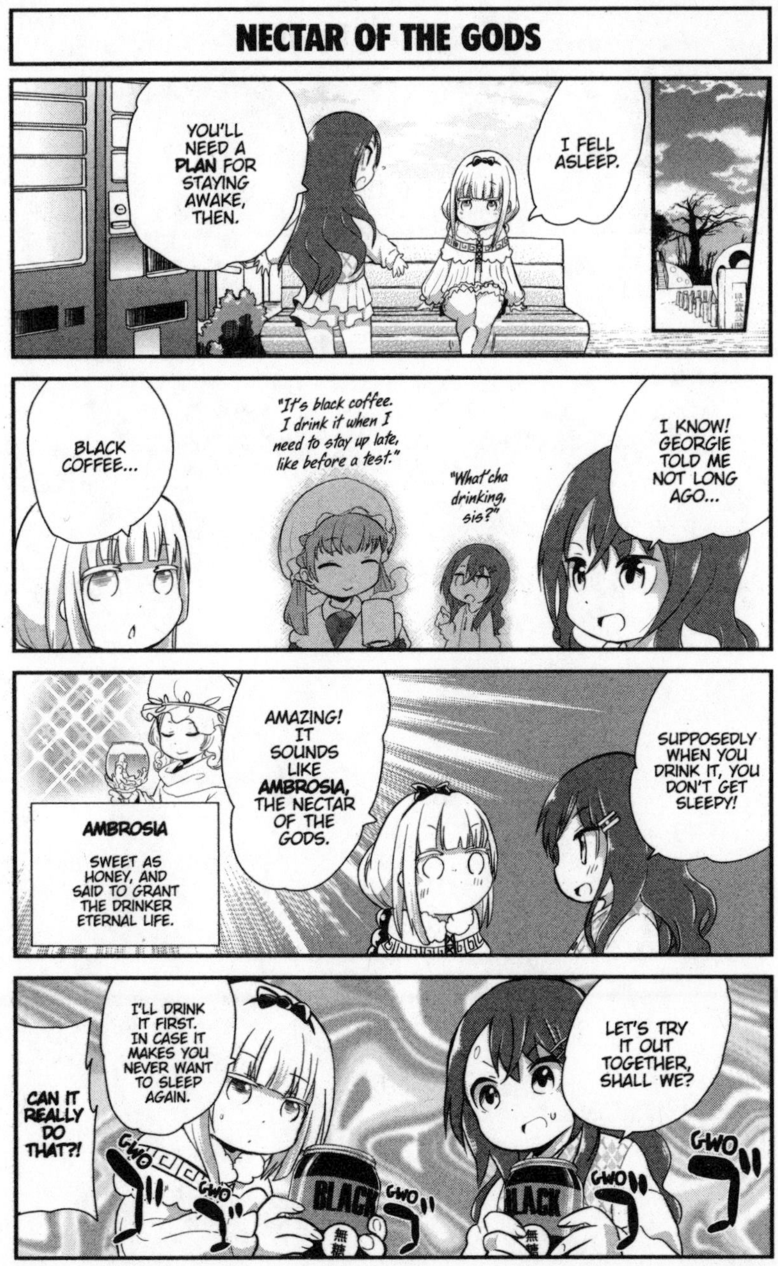
I FELL ASLEEP.
YOU'LL NEED A PLAN FOR STAYING AWAKE, THEN.
I KNOW! GEORGIE TOLD ME NOT LONG AGO...
"What'cha drinking, sis?"
"It's black coffee. I drink it when I need to stay up late, like before a test."
BLACK COFFEE...
SUPPOSEDLY WHEN YOU DRINK IT, YOU DON'T GET SLEEPY!
AMAZING! IT SOUNDS LIKE AMBROSIA, THE NECTAR OF THE GODS.
AMBROSIA
SWEET AS HONEY, AND SAID TO GRANT THE DRINKER ETERNAL LIFE.
LET'S TRY IT OUT TOGETHER, SHALL WE?
GWO
GWO
BLACK
無糖
I'LL DRINK IT FIRST. IN CASE IT MAKES YOU NEVER WANT TO SLEEP AGAIN.
GWO
GWO
GWO
BLACK
無糖
CAN IT REALLY DO THAT?!

ACQUIRED TASTE

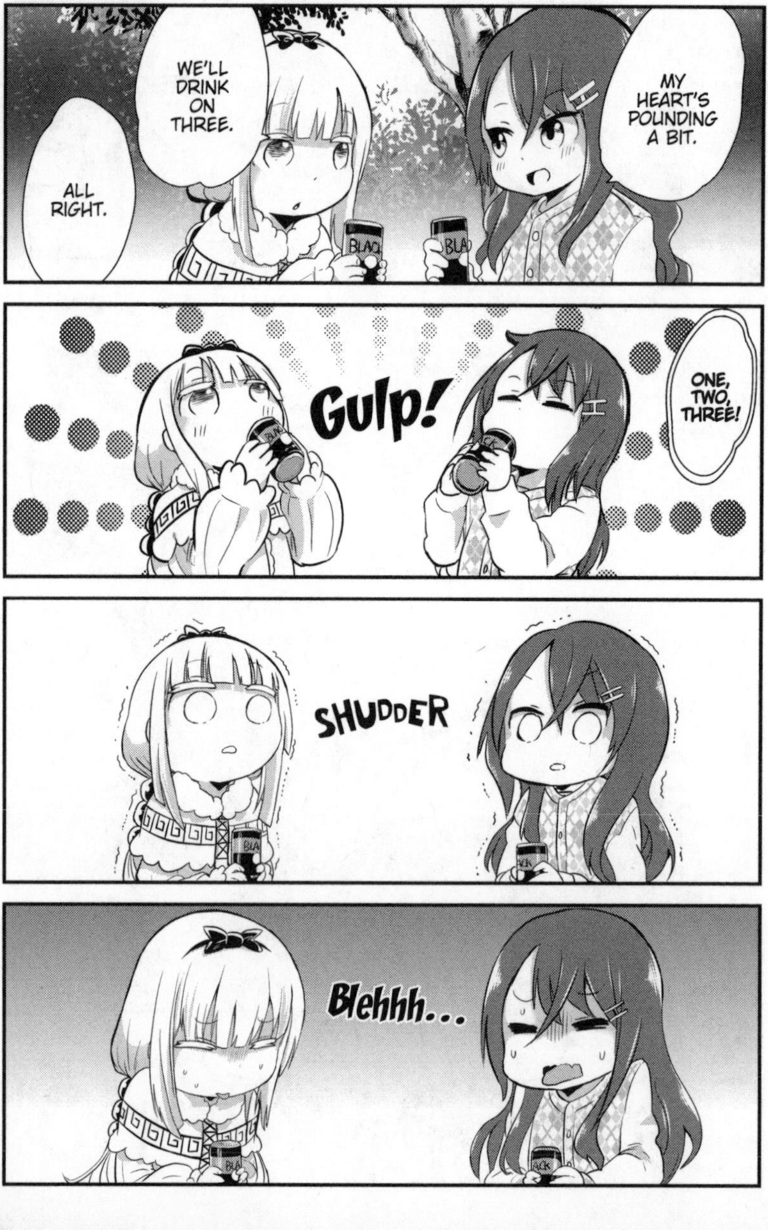
MY HEART'S POUNDING A BIT.
WE'LL DRINK ON THREE.
ALL RIGHT.
ONE, TWO, THREE!
Gulp!
SHUDDER
Blehhh...

KIDS PLAY TIL THEY DROP

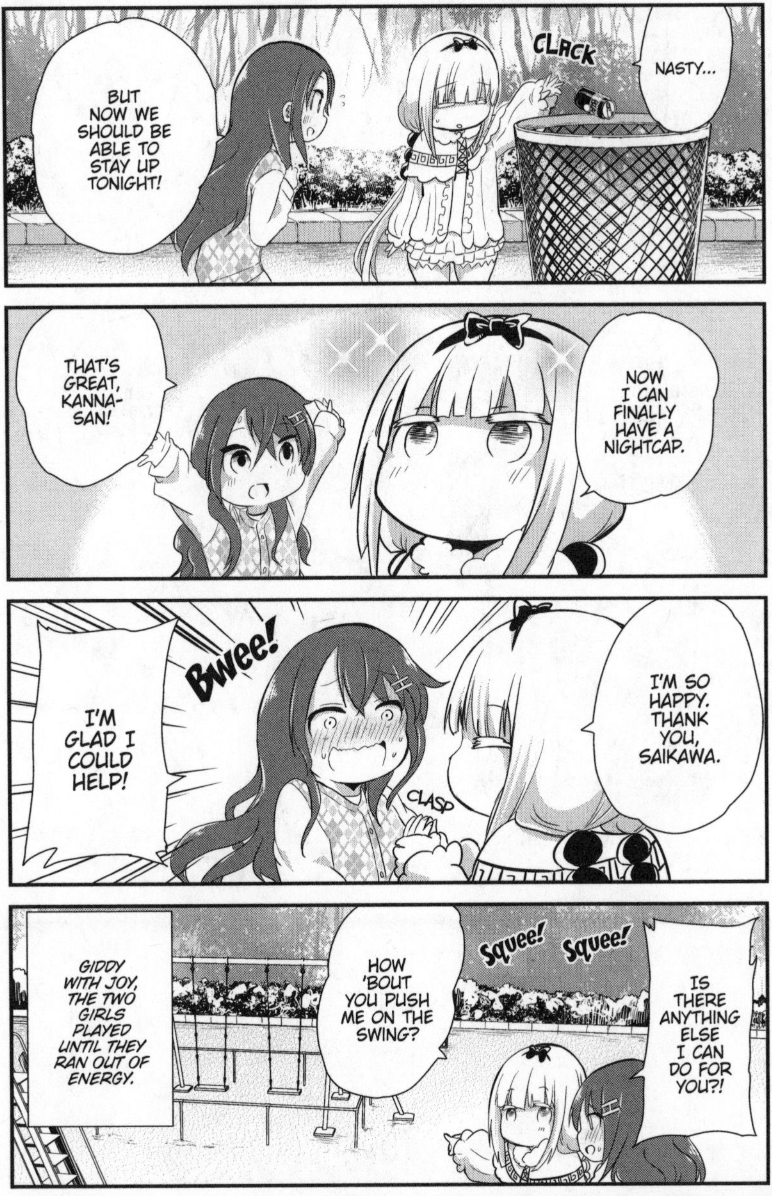
CLACK
NASTY...
BUT NOW WE SHOULD BE ABLE TO STAY UP TONIGHT!
NOW I CAN FINALLY HAVE A NIGHTCAP.
THAT'S GREAT, KANNA-SAN!
I'M SO HAPPY. THANK YOU, SAIKAWA.
CLASP
Bwee!
I'M GLAD I COULD HELP!
IS THERE ANYTHING ELSE I CAN DO FOR YOU?!
Squee!
Squee!
HOW 'BOUT YOU PUSH ME ON THE SWING?
GIDDY WITH JOY, THE TWO GIRLS PLAYED UNTIL THEY RAN OUT OF ENERGY.

SWEET DREAMS?

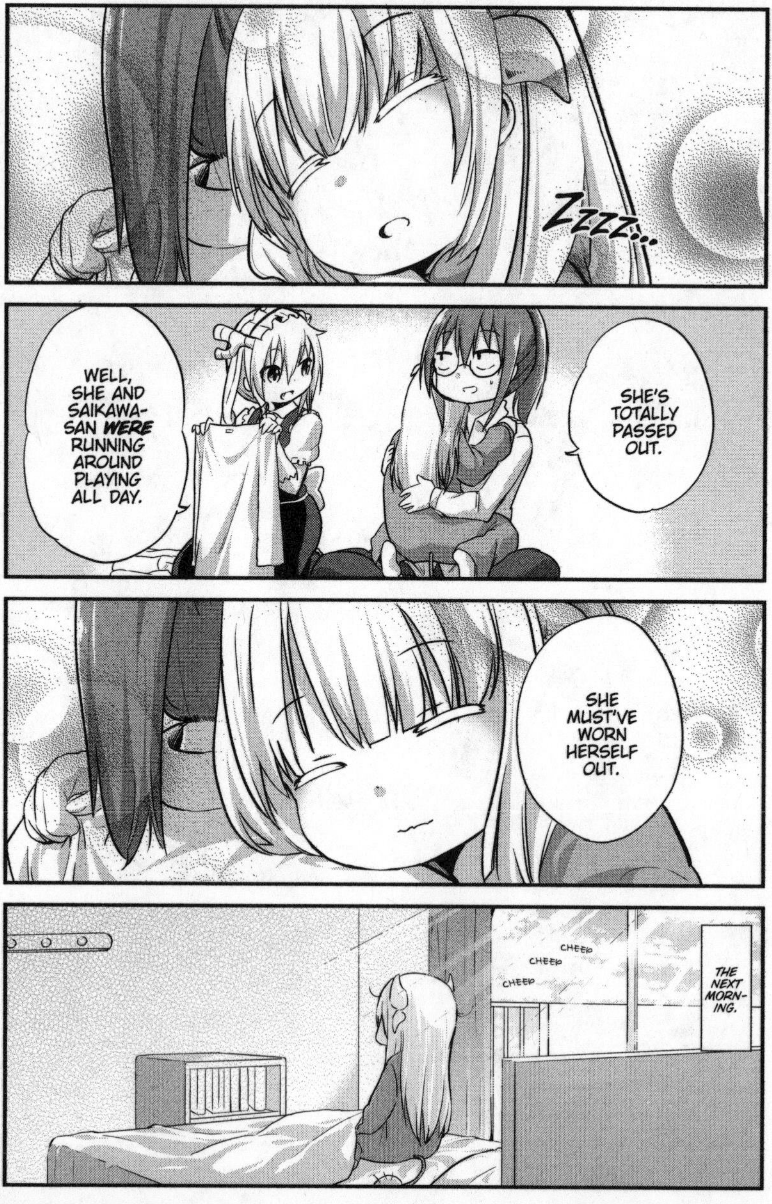
Zzzz...
SHE'S TOTALLY PASSED OUT.
WELL, SHE AND SAIKAWA-SAN *WERE* RUNNING AROUND PLAYING ALL DAY.
SHE MUST'VE WORN HERSELF OUT.
THE NEXT MORNING.
CHEEP
CHEEP
CHEEP

KANNA'S TANTRUM OF RAGE

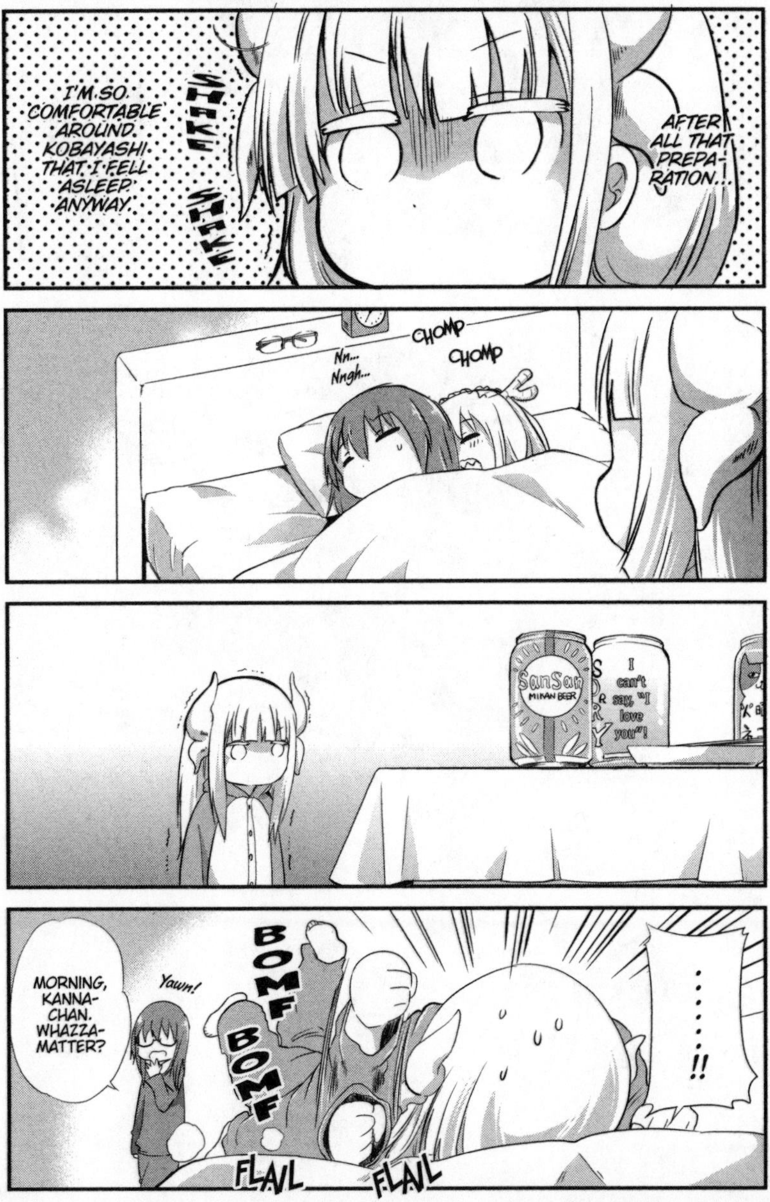
AFTER ALL THAT PREPARATION...
SHAKE SHAKE
I'M SO COMFORTABLE AROUND KOBAYASHI THAT I FELL ASLEEP ANYWAY.
CHOMP
CHOMP
Nn... Nngh...
SanSan MIKAN BEER
I can't say, "I love you"!
......!!
FLAIL FLAIL
BOMF BOMF
Yawn!
MORNING, KANNA-CHAN. WHAZZA-MATTER?

LEND ME YOUR STRENGTH!

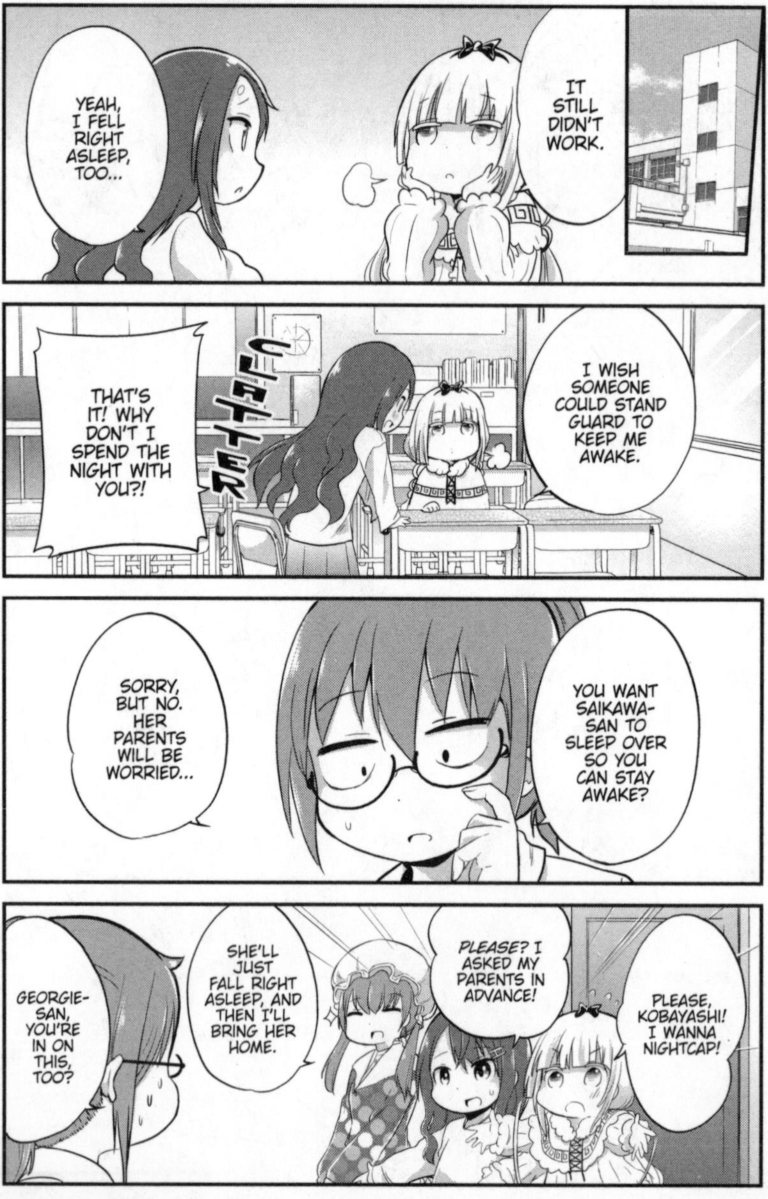
IT STILL DIDN'T WORK.
YEAH, I FELL RIGHT ASLEEP, TOO...
I WISH SOMEONE COULD STAND GUARD TO KEEP ME AWAKE.
CLATTER
THAT'S IT! WHY DON'T I SPEND THE NIGHT WITH YOU?!
YOU WANT SAIKAWA-SAN TO SLEEP OVER SO YOU CAN STAY AWAKE?
SORRY, BUT NO. HER PARENTS WILL BE WORRIED...
PLEASE, KOBAYASHI! I WANNA NIGHTCAP!
PLEASE? I ASKED MY PARENTS IN ADVANCE!
SHE'LL JUST FALL RIGHT ASLEEP, AND THEN I'LL BRING HER HOME.
GEORGIE-SAN, YOU'RE IN ON THIS, TOO?

AT THE END OF THE DAY

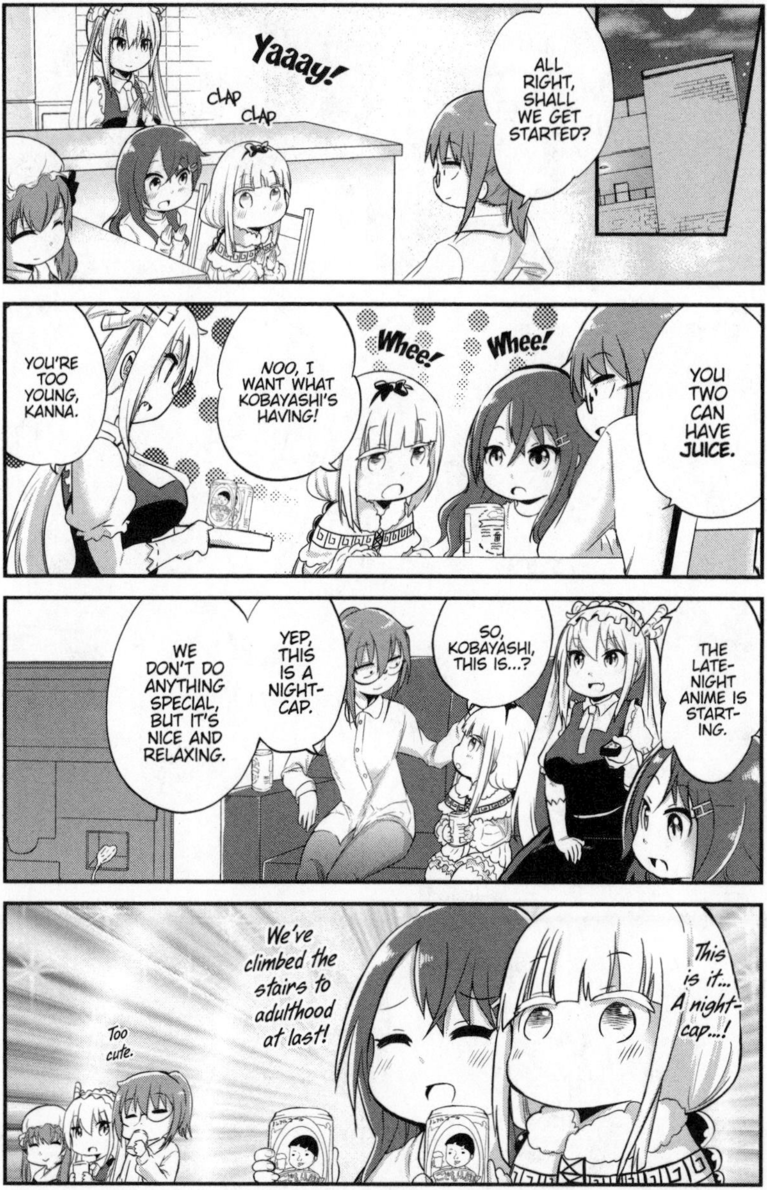
ALL RIGHT, SHALL WE GET STARTED?
Yaaay!
CLAP CLAP
YOU TWO CAN HAVE JUICE.
Whee!
Whee!
NOO, I WANT WHAT KOBAYASHI'S HAVING!
YOU'RE TOO YOUNG, KANNA.
THE LATE-NIGHT ANIME IS STARTING.
SO, KOBAYASHI, THIS IS...?
YEP, THIS IS A NIGHT-CAP.
WE DON'T DO ANYTHING SPECIAL, BUT IT'S NICE AND RELAXING.
This is it... A night-cap...!
We've climbed the stairs to adulthood at last!
Too cute.

THEY FELL ASLEEP RIGHT AFTER THIS

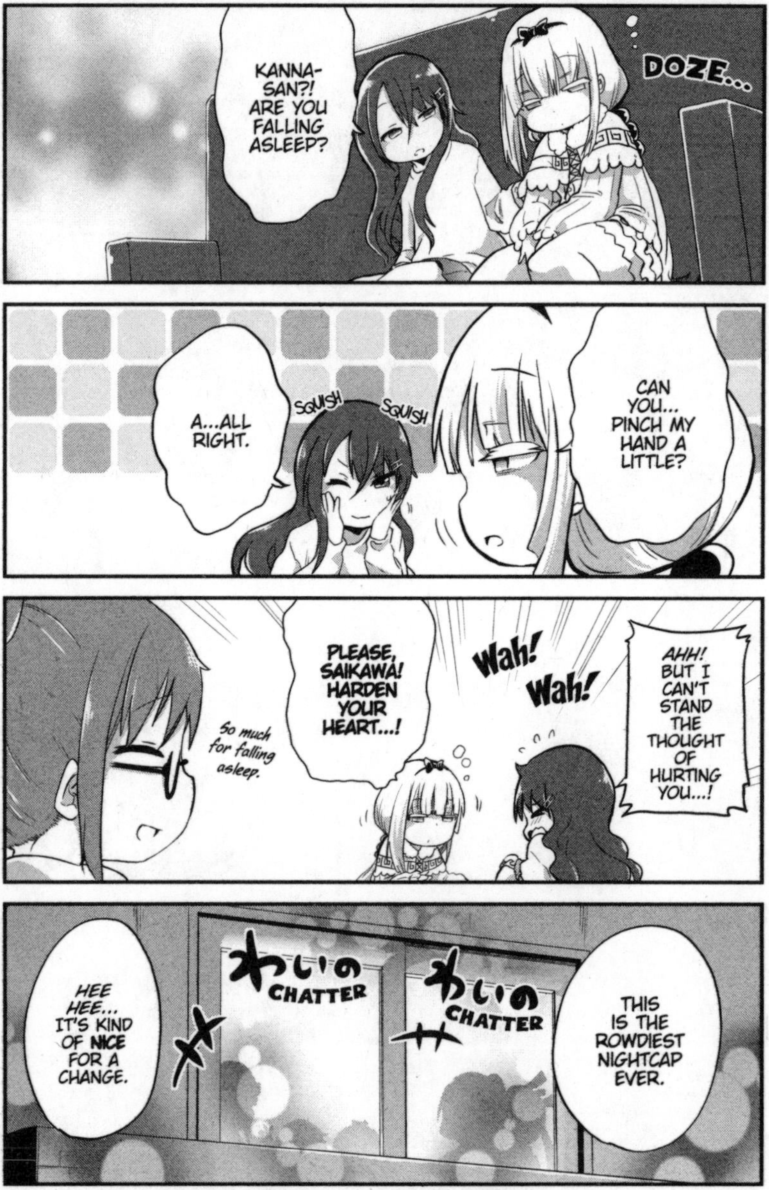

TIME FOR A NIGHTCAP/END

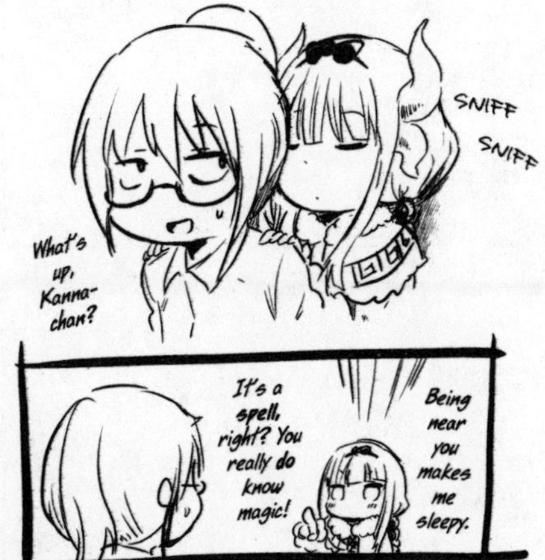
SNIFF
SNIFF
What's up, Kanna-chan?
Being near you makes me sleepy.
It's a spell, right? You really do know magic!

Miss Kobayashi's Dragon Maid
Kanna's Daily Life

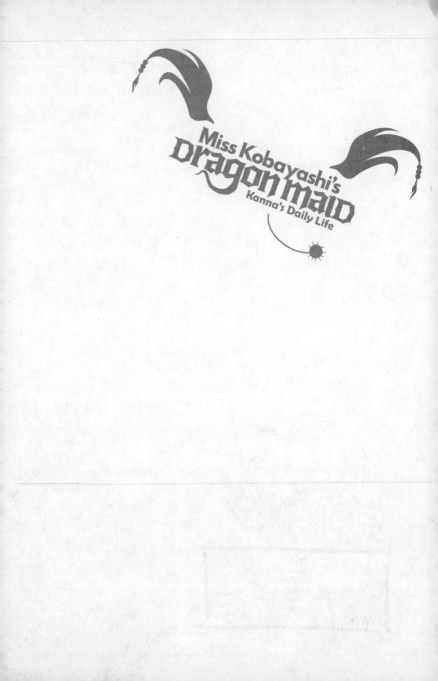

I CAN DO IT MYSELF!

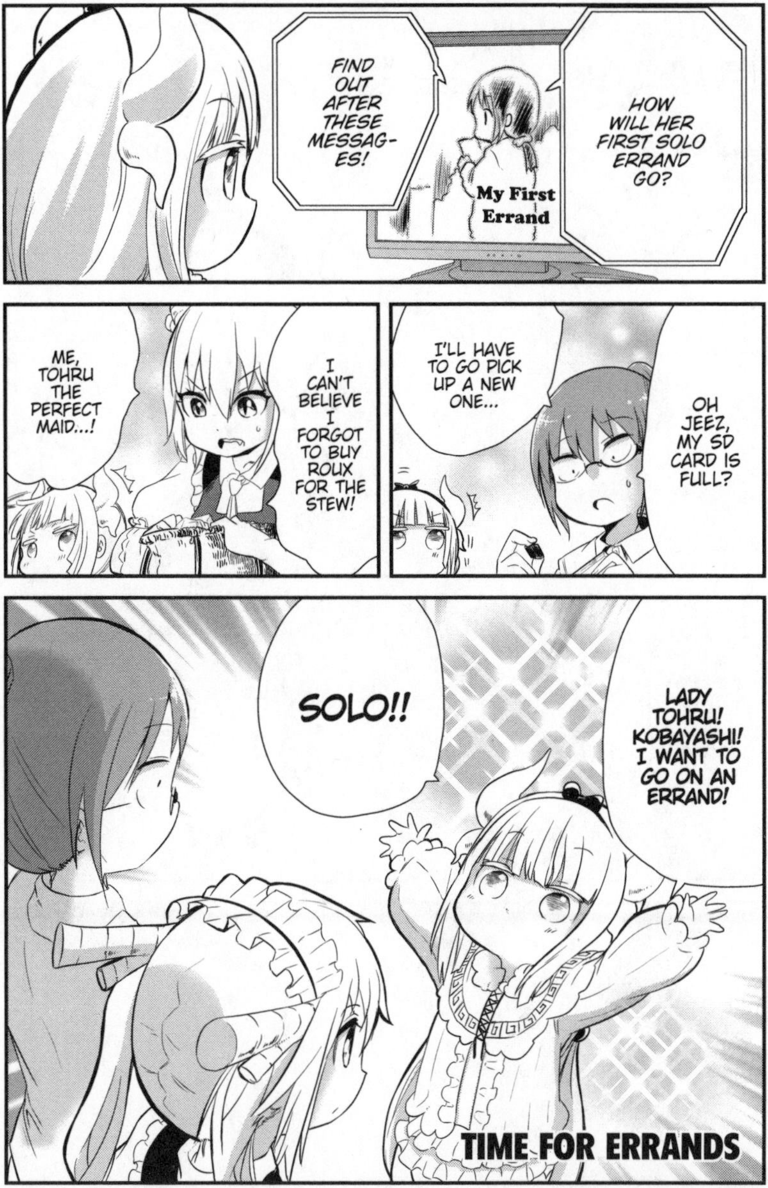
HOW WILL HER FIRST SOLO ERRAND GO?
FIND OUT AFTER THESE MESSAG-ES!
My First Errand
OH JEEZ, MY SD CARD IS FULL?
I'LL HAVE TO GO PICK UP A NEW ONE...
I CAN'T BELIEVE I FORGOT TO BUY ROUX FOR THE STEW!
ME, TOHRU THE PERFECT MAID...!
LADY TOHRU! KOBAYASHI! I WANT TO GO ON AN ERRAND!
SOLO!!
TIME FOR ERRANDS

JUST FELT LIKE TAKING A WALK

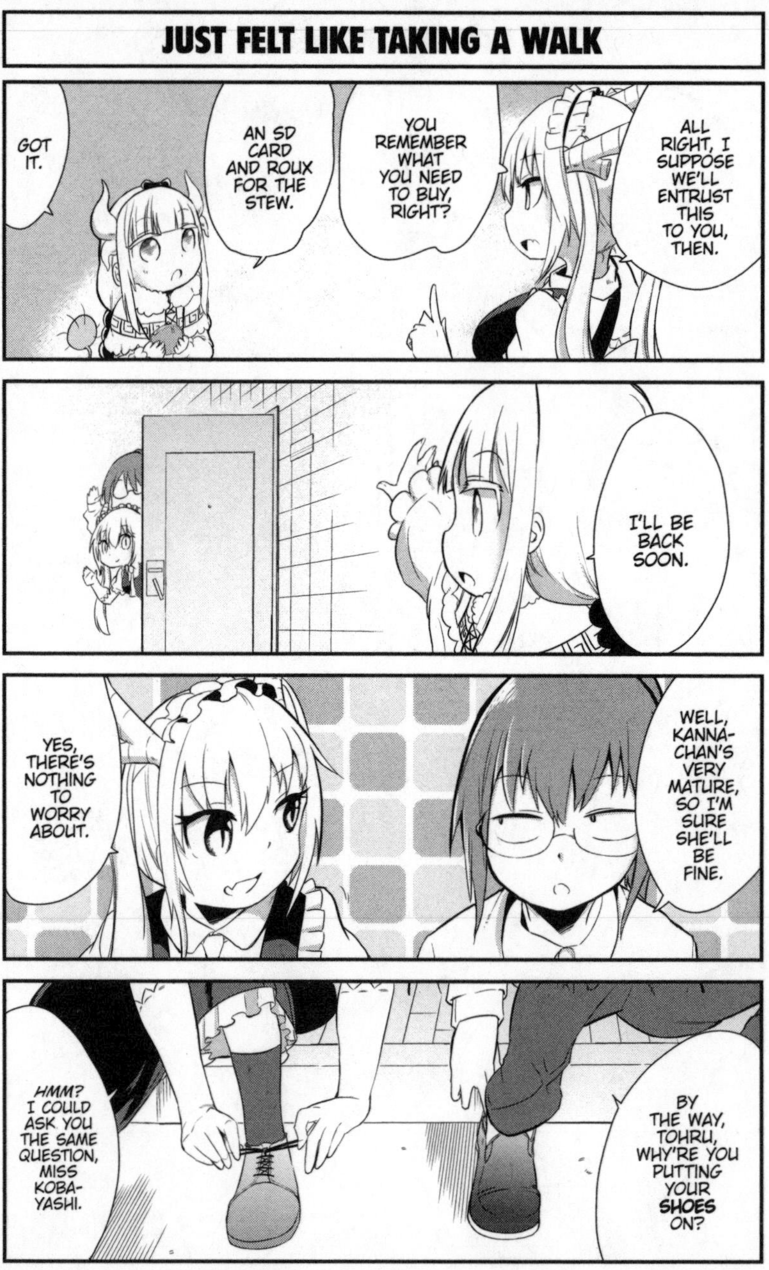
ALL RIGHT, I SUPPOSE WE'LL ENTRUST THIS TO YOU, THEN.
YOU REMEMBER WHAT YOU NEED TO BUY, RIGHT?
AN SD CARD AND ROUX FOR THE STEW.
GOT IT.
I'LL BE BACK SOON.
WELL, KANNA-CHAN'S VERY MATURE, SO I'M SURE SHE'LL BE FINE.
YES, THERE'S NOTHING TO WORRY ABOUT.
BY THE WAY, TOHRU, WHY'RE YOU PUTTING YOUR **SHOES** ON?
HMM? I COULD ASK YOU THE SAME QUESTION, MISS KOBAYASHI.

BUSTED...

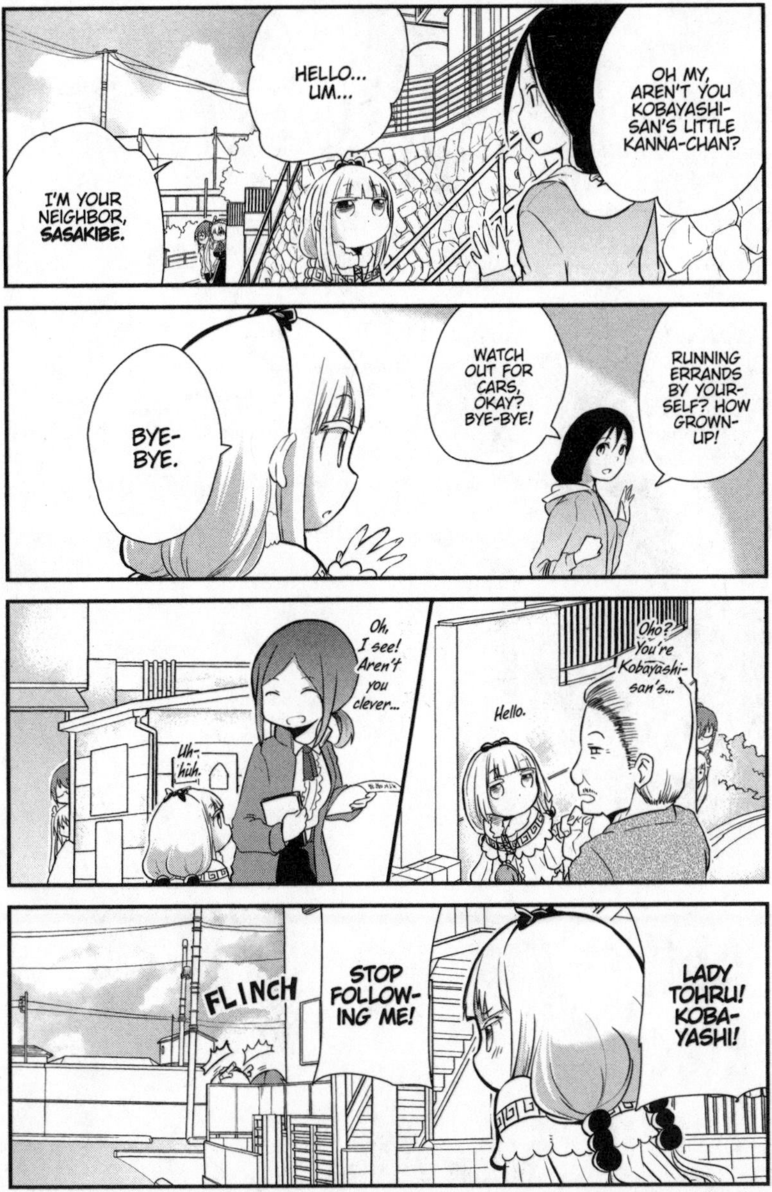
OH MY, AREN'T YOU KOBAYASHI-SAN'S LITTLE KANNA-CHAN?
HELLO... UM...
I'M YOUR NEIGHBOR, SASAKIBE.
RUNNING ERRANDS BY YOURSELF? HOW GROWN-UP!
WATCH OUT FOR CARS, OKAY? BYE-BYE!
BYE-BYE.
Oho? You're Kobayashi-san's...
Hello.
Oh, I see! Aren't you clever...
Uh-huh.
LADY TOHRU! KOBAYASHI!
STOP FOLLOWING ME!
FLINCH

PURISTS

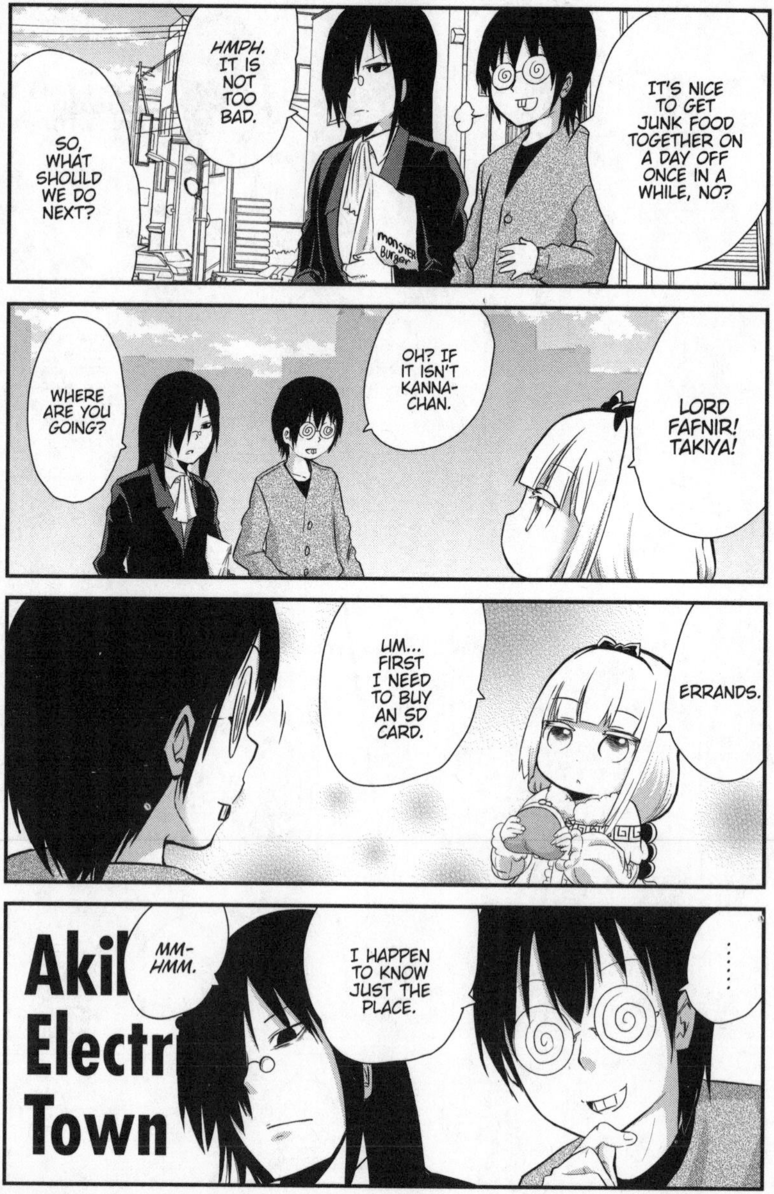
IT'S NICE TO GET JUNK FOOD TOGETHER ON A DAY OFF ONCE IN A WHILE, NO?
HMPH. IT IS NOT TOO BAD.
monster Burger
SO, WHAT SHOULD WE DO NEXT?
LORD FAFNIR! TAKIYA!
OH? IF IT ISN'T KANNA-CHAN.
WHERE ARE YOU GOING?
ERRANDS.
UM... FIRST I NEED TO BUY AN SD CARD.
......
I HAPPEN TO KNOW JUST THE PLACE.
MM-HMM.
Town

THEY...DISAPPEARED...?

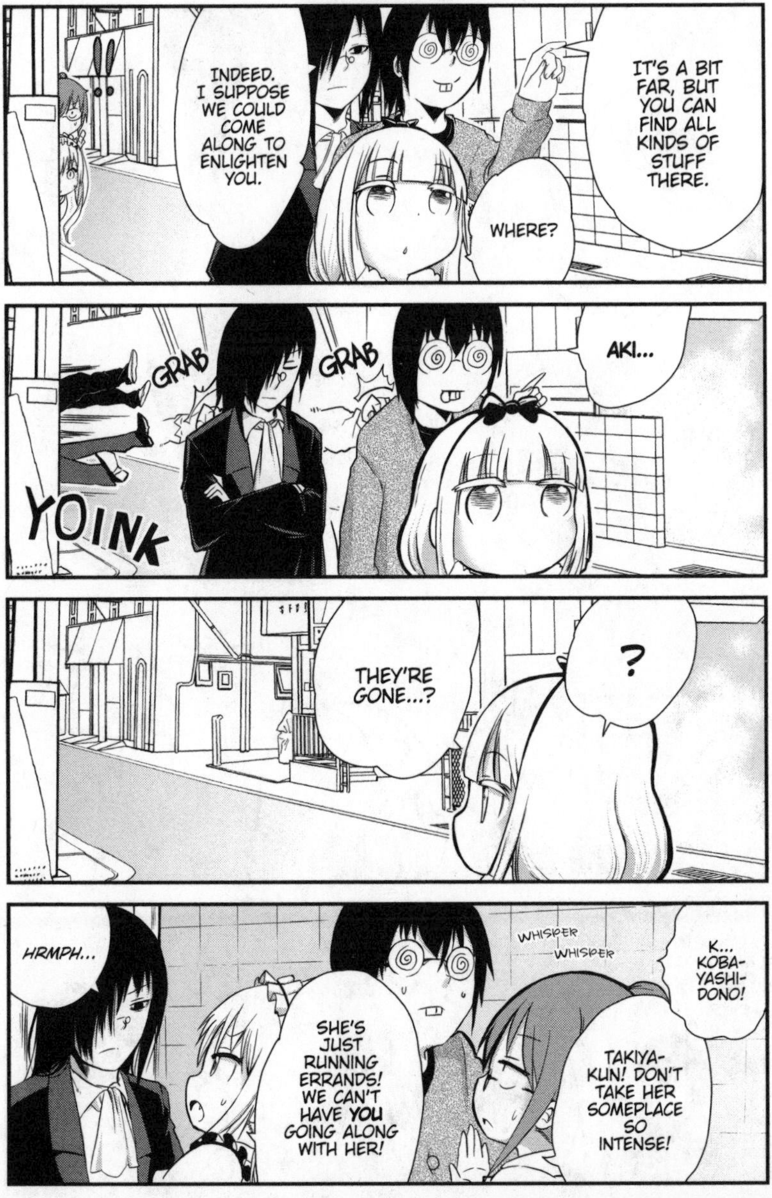
IT'S A BIT FAR, BUT YOU CAN FIND ALL KINDS OF STUFF THERE.
WHERE?
INDEED. I SUPPOSE WE COULD COME ALONG TO ENLIGHTEN YOU.
AKI...
GRAB
GRAB
YOINK
?
THEY'RE GONE...?
K... KOBAYASHI-DONO!
TAKIYA-KUN! DON'T TAKE HER SOMEPLACE SO INTENSE!
WHISPER
WHISPER
SHE'S JUST RUNNING ERRANDS! WE CAN'T HAVE **YOU** GOING ALONG WITH HER!
HRMPH...

WE'RE ALWAYS WATCHING

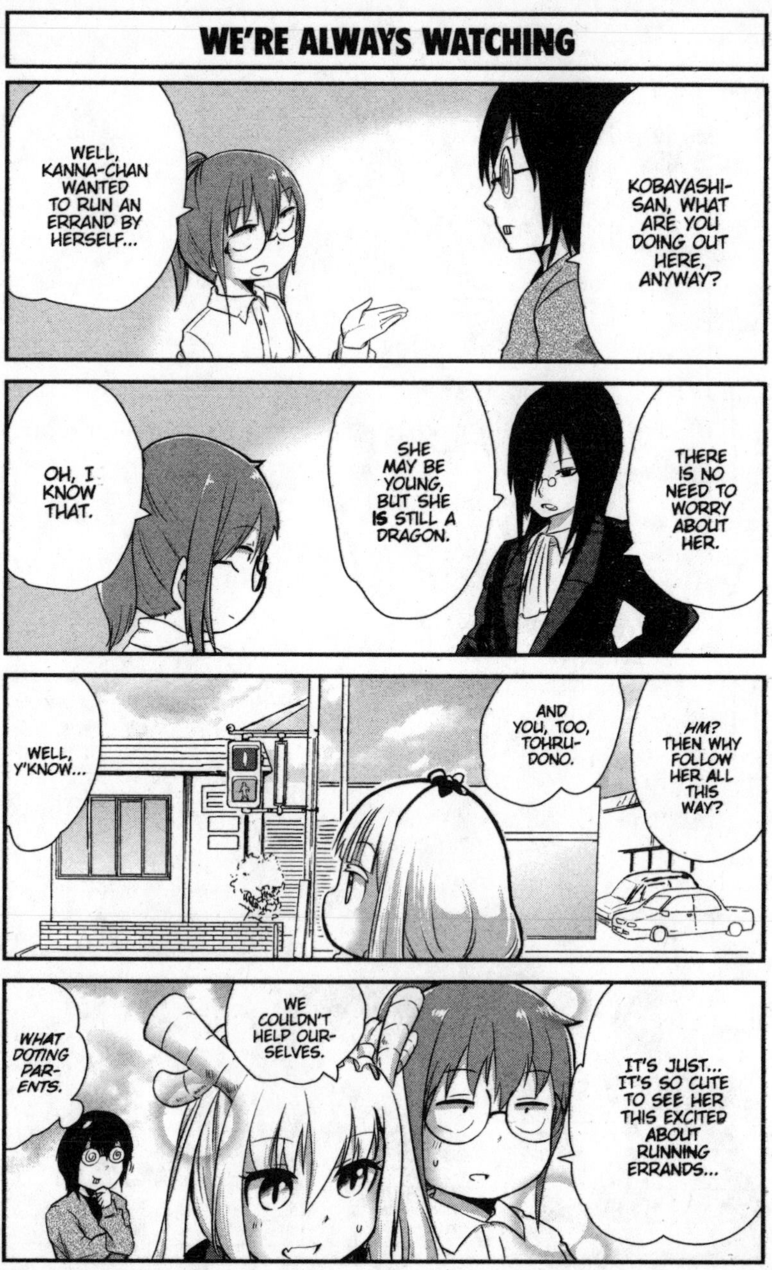
KOBAYASHI-SAN, WHAT ARE YOU DOING OUT HERE, ANYWAY?
WELL, KANNA-CHAN WANTED TO RUN AN ERRAND BY HERSELF...
THERE IS NO NEED TO WORRY ABOUT HER.
SHE MAY BE YOUNG, BUT SHE **IS** STILL A DRAGON.
OH, I KNOW THAT.
HM? THEN WHY FOLLOW HER ALL THIS WAY?
AND YOU, TOO, TOHRU-DONO.
WELL, Y'KNOW...
IT'S JUST... IT'S SO CUTE TO SEE HER THIS EXCITED ABOUT RUNNING ERRANDS...
WE COULDN'T HELP OUR-SELVES.
WHAT DOTING PAR-ENTS.

TAKE THIS! THE CAR-STOPPING POSE!

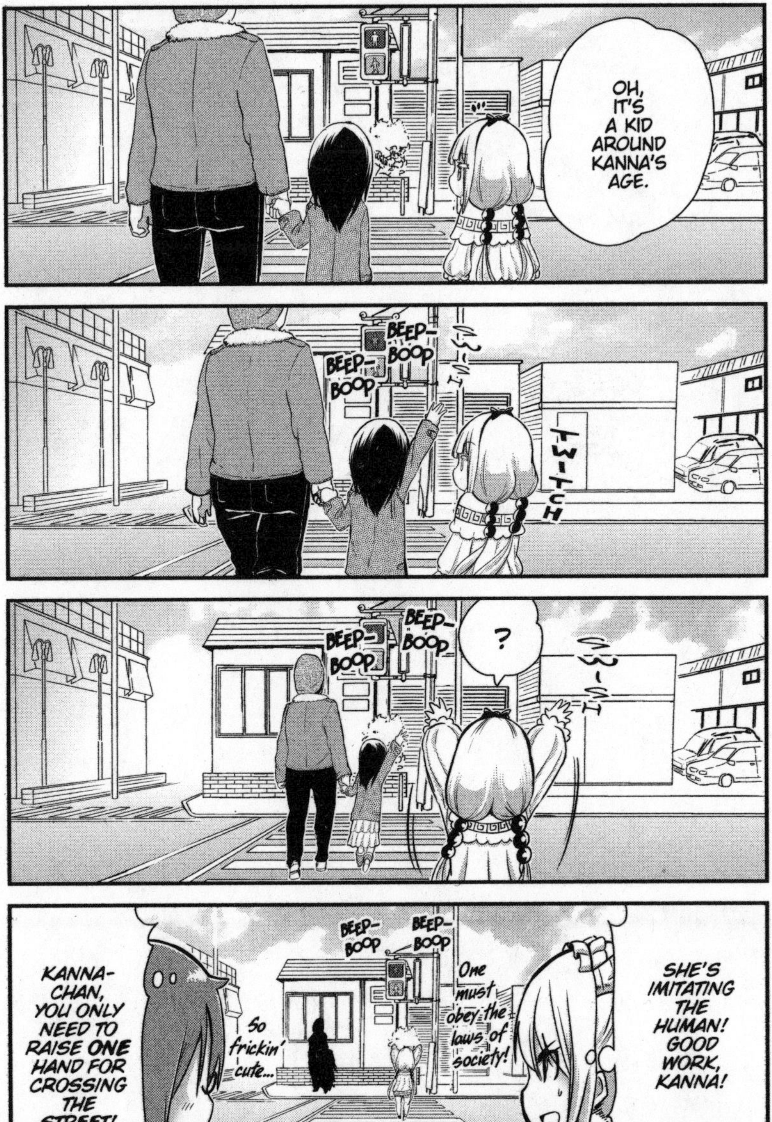
OH, IT'S A KID AROUND KANNA'S AGE.
TWITCH
BEEP-BOOP
BEEP-BOOP
?
BEEP-BOOP
BEEP-BOOP
SHE'S IMITATING THE HUMAN! GOOD WORK, KANNA!
One must obey the laws of society!
BEEP-BOOP
BEEP-BOOP
So frickin' cute...
KANNA-CHAN, YOU ONLY NEED TO RAISE ONE HAND FOR CROSSING THE STREET!

NATURAL COURSE OF ACTION

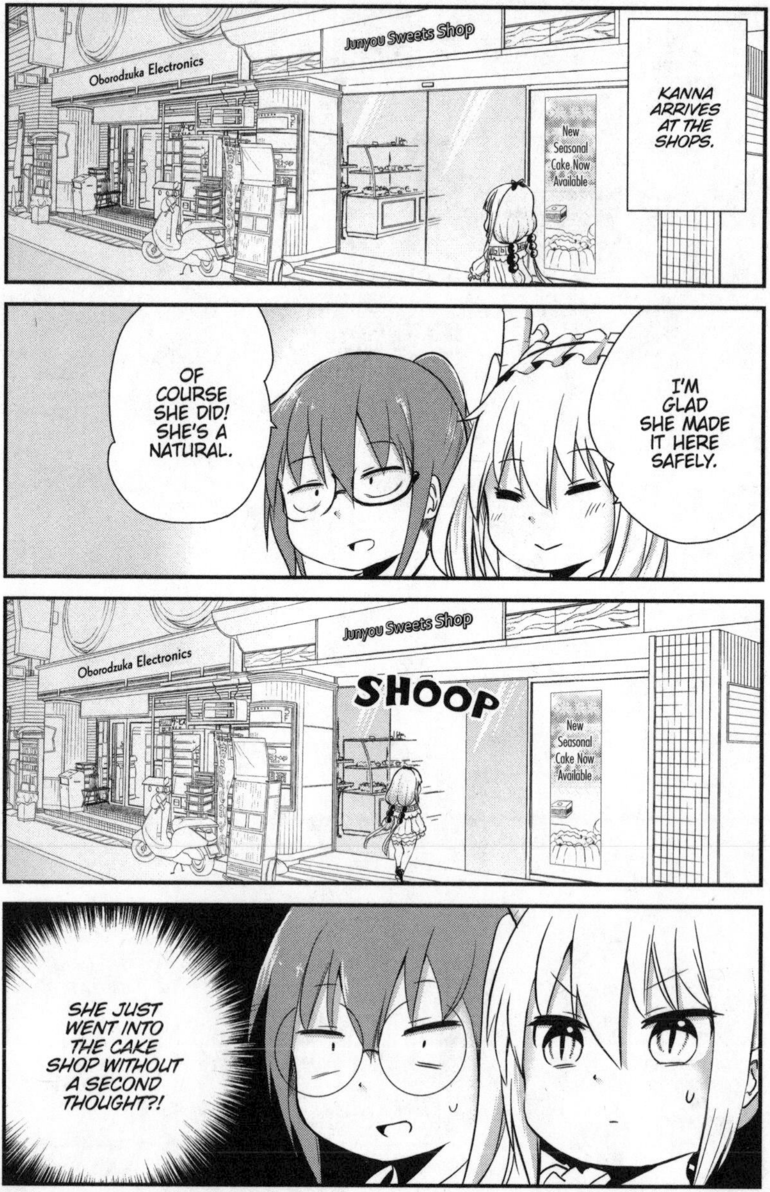
KANNA ARRIVES AT THE SHOPS.
Junyou Sweets Shop
Oborodzuka Electronics
New Seasonal Cake Now Available
I'M GLAD SHE MADE IT HERE SAFELY.
OF COURSE SHE DID! SHE'S A NATURAL.
Junyou Sweets Shop
Oborodzuka Electronics
SHOOP
New Seasonal Cake Now Available
SHE JUST WENT INTO THE CAKE SHOP WITHOUT A SECOND THOUGHT?!

KANNA-CHAN LOVES CHOCOLATE CAKE

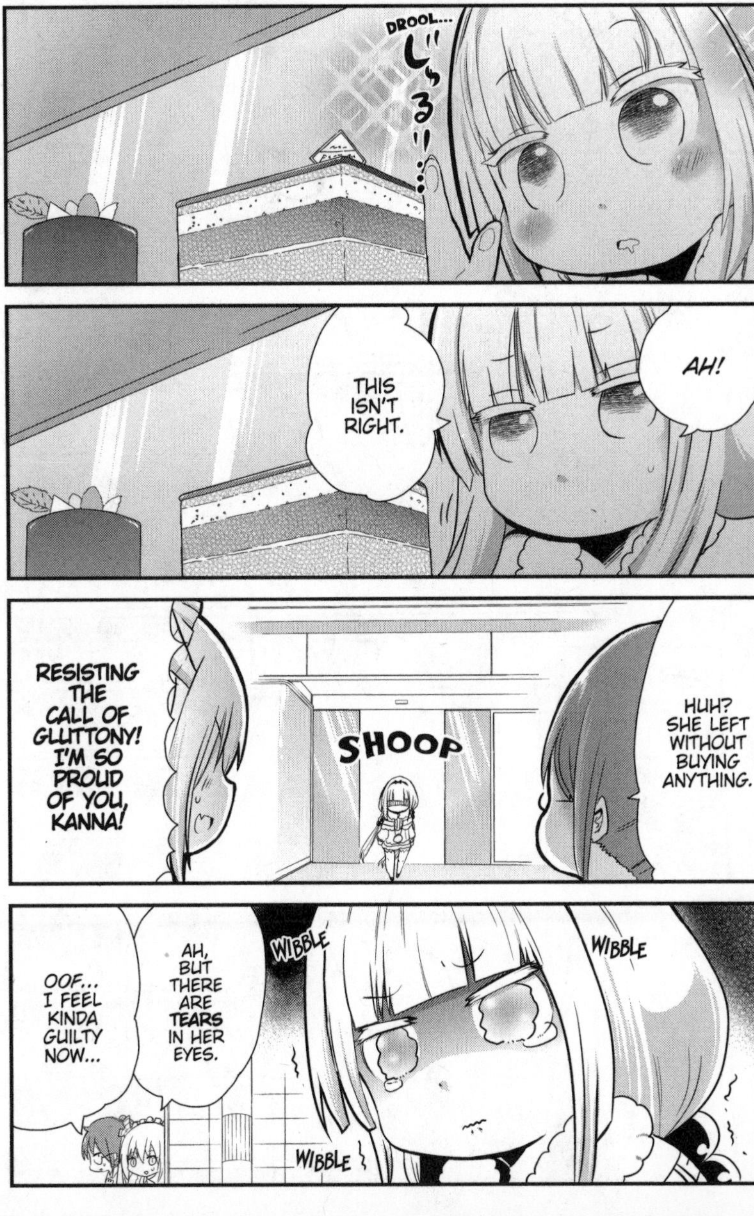
DROOL...
じゅるり!!
AH!
THIS ISN'T RIGHT.
HUH? SHE LEFT WITHOUT BUYING ANYTHING.
SHOOP
RESISTING THE CALL OF GLUTTONY! I'M SO PROUD OF YOU, KANNA!
WIBBLE
WIBBLE
WIBBLE
AH, BUT THERE ARE **TEARS** IN HER EYES.
OOF... I FEEL KINDA GUILTY NOW...

SO CLOSE

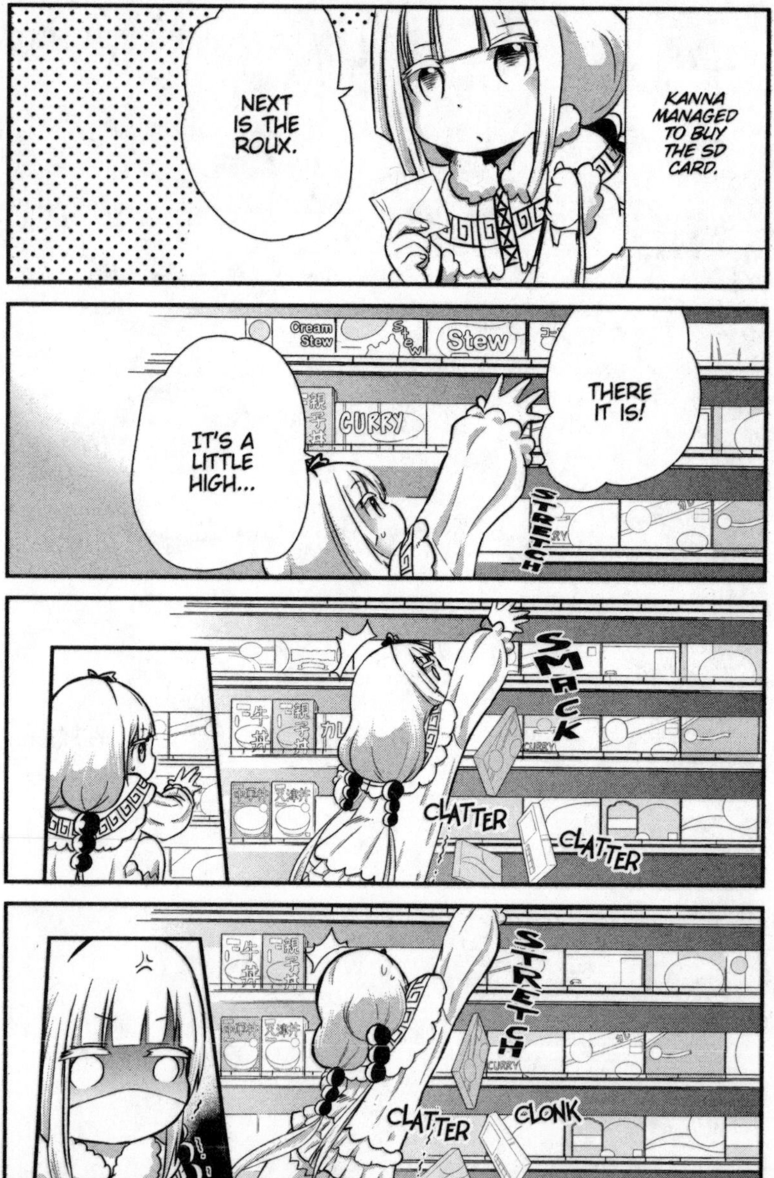
KANNA MANAGED TO BUY THE SD CARD.
NEXT IS THE ROUX.
Cream Stew
Stew
Stew
CURRY
THERE IT IS!
IT'S A LITTLE HIGH...
STRETCH
SMACK
CLATTER
CLATTER
STRETCH
CLONK
CLATTER

CLEVER KANNA-CHAN

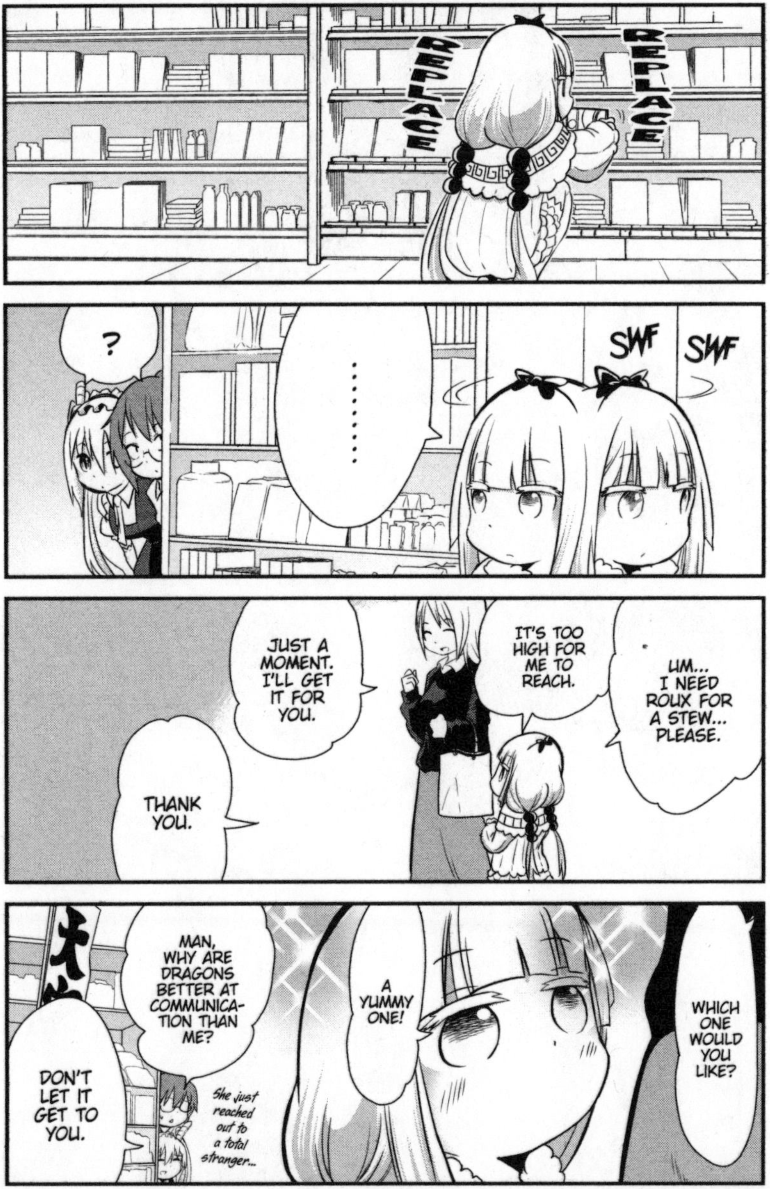
REPLACE
REPLACE
SWF
SWF
......
?
UM... I NEED ROUX FOR A STEW... PLEASE.
IT'S TOO HIGH FOR ME TO REACH.
JUST A MOMENT. I'LL GET IT FOR YOU.
THANK YOU.
WHICH ONE WOULD YOU LIKE?
A YUMMY ONE!
MAN, WHY ARE DRAGONS BETTER AT COMMUNICATION THAN ME?
She just reached out to a total stranger...
DON'T LET IT GET TO YOU.

LET'S GO HOME

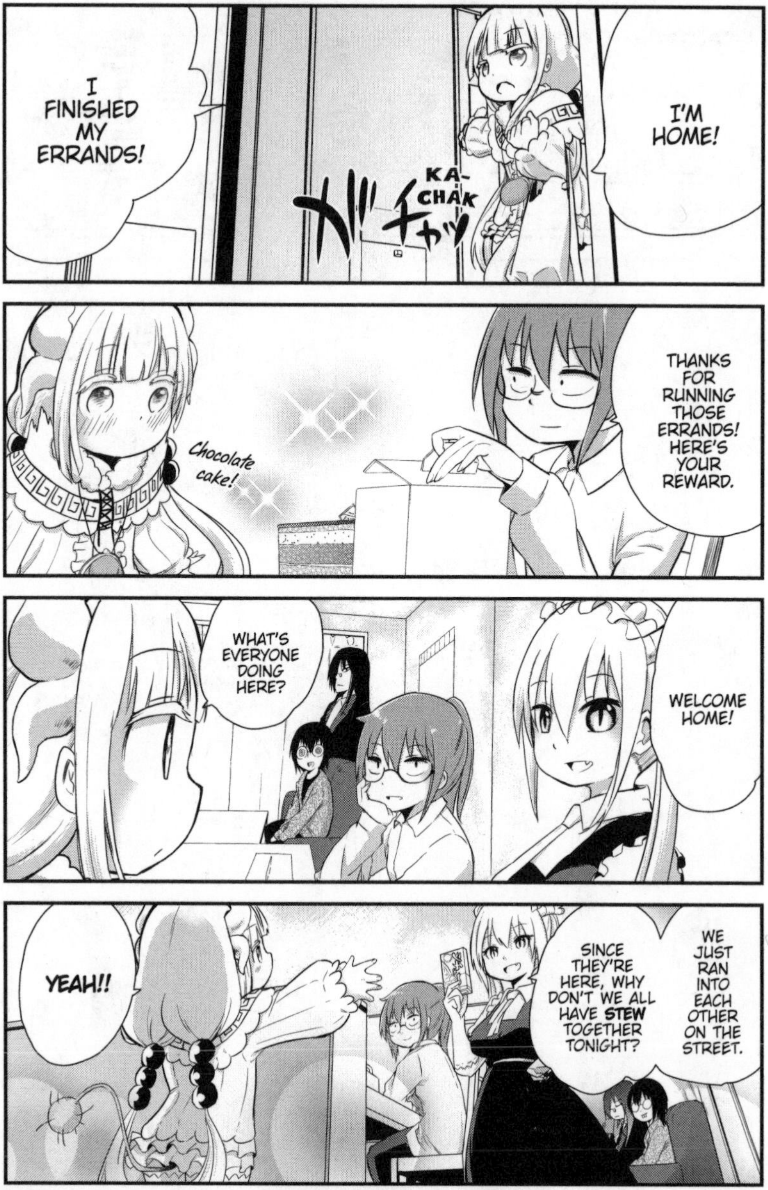
I'M HOME!
KA-CHAK
ガチャッ
I FINISHED MY ERRANDS!
THANKS FOR RUNNING THOSE ERRANDS! HERE'S YOUR REWARD.
Chocolate cake!
WELCOME HOME!
WHAT'S EVERYONE DOING HERE?
WE JUST RAN INTO EACH OTHER ON THE STREET.
SINCE THEY'RE HERE, WHY DON'T WE ALL HAVE **STEW** TOGETHER TONIGHT?
YEAH!!

TIME FOR ERRANDS/END

Thanks for the food!

Afterword Manga!

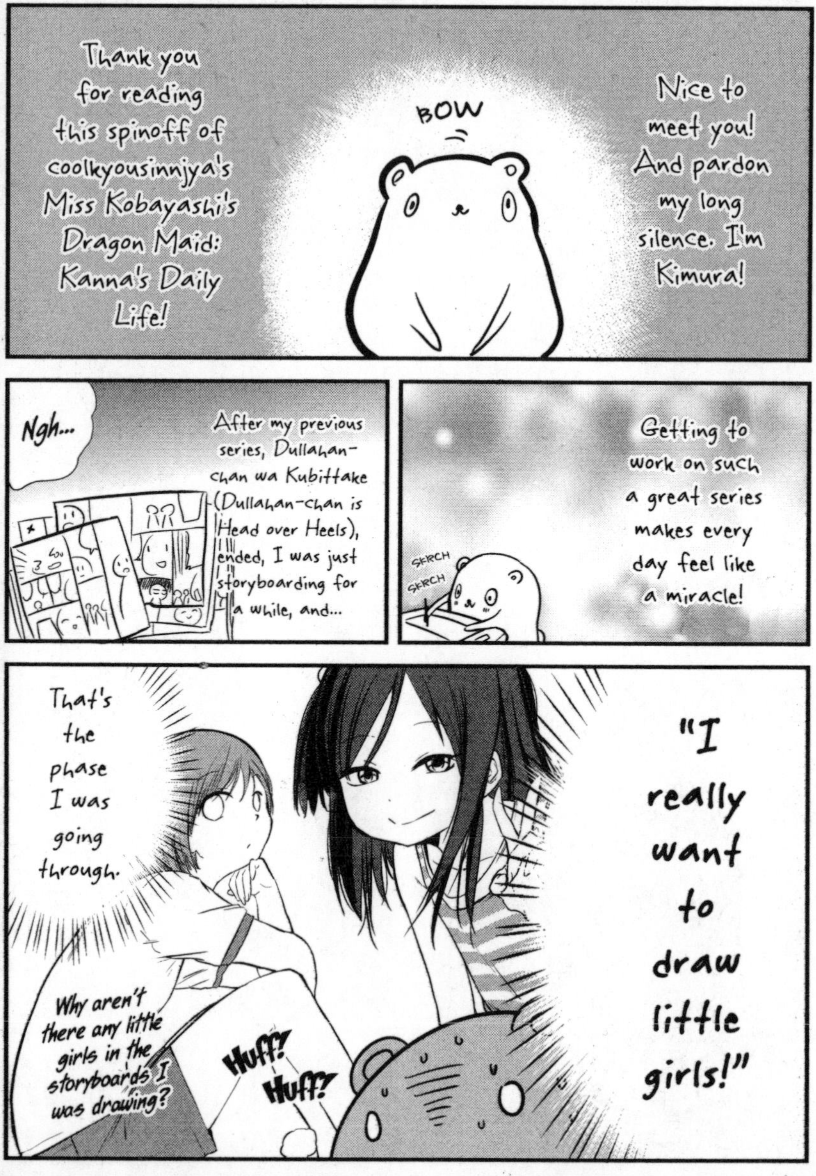
Nice to meet you! And pardon my long silence. I'm Kimura!
BOW
Thank you for reading this spinoff of coolkyousinnjya's Miss Kobayashi's Dragon Maid: Kanna's Daily Life!
Getting to work on such a great series makes every day feel like a miracle!
SKRCH
SKRCH
After my previous series, Dullahan-chan wa Kubittake (Dullahan-chan is Head over Heels), ended, I was just storyboarding for a while, and...
Ngh...
"I really want to draw little girls!"
That's the phase I was going through.
HUFF!
HUFF!
Why aren't there any little girls in the storyboards I was drawing?

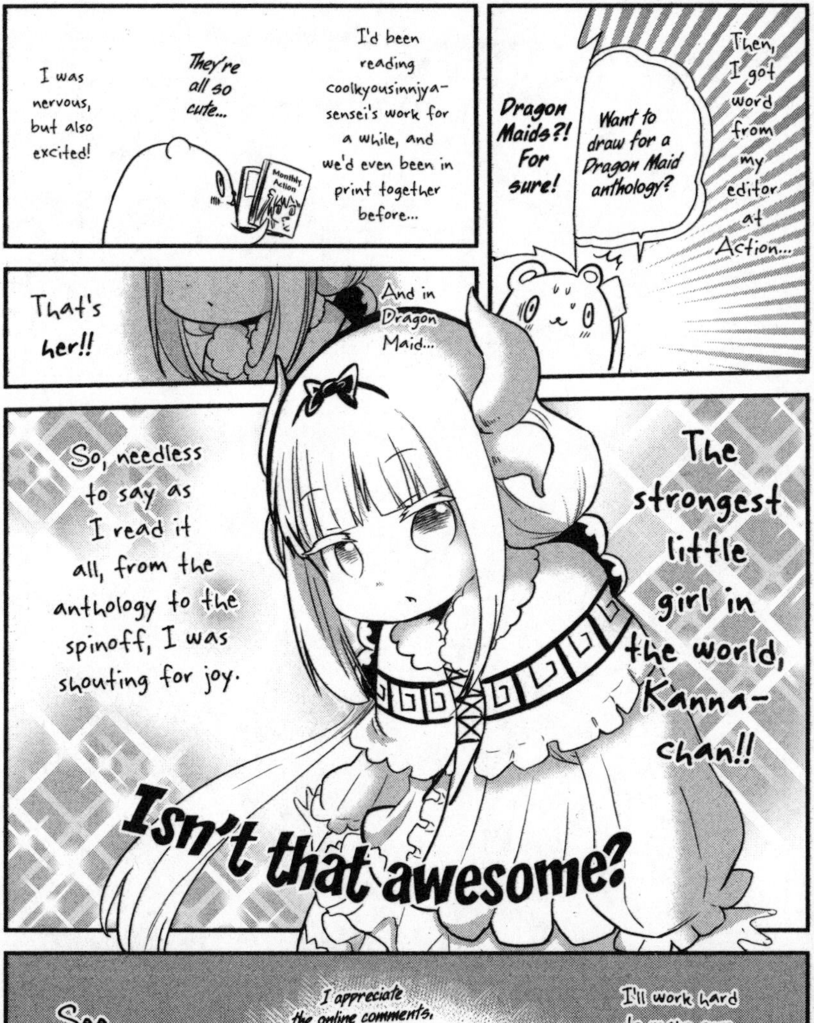

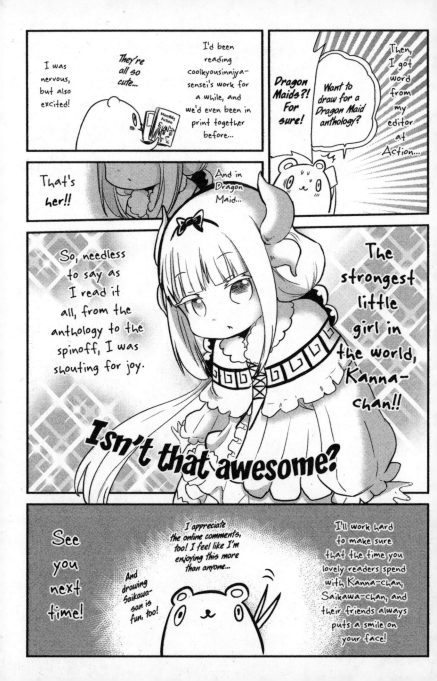

Then, I got word from my editor at Action...
Want to draw for a Dragon Maid anthology?
Dragon Maids?! For sure!
I'd been reading coolkyousinnjya-sensei's work for a while, and we'd even been in print together before...
They're all so cute...
Monthly Action
I was nervous, but also excited!
And in Dragon Maid...
That's her!!
The strongest little girl in the world, Kanna-chan!!
So, needless to say as I read it all, from the anthology to the spinoff, I was shouting for joy.
Isn't that awesome?
I'll work hard to make sure that the time you lovely readers spend with Kanna-chan, Saikawa-chan, and their friends always puts a smile on your face!
I appreciate the online comments, too! I feel like I'm enjoying this more than anyone...
And drawing Saikawa-san is fun, too!
See you next time!

Miss Kobayashi's Dragon Maid

Kanna's Daily Life

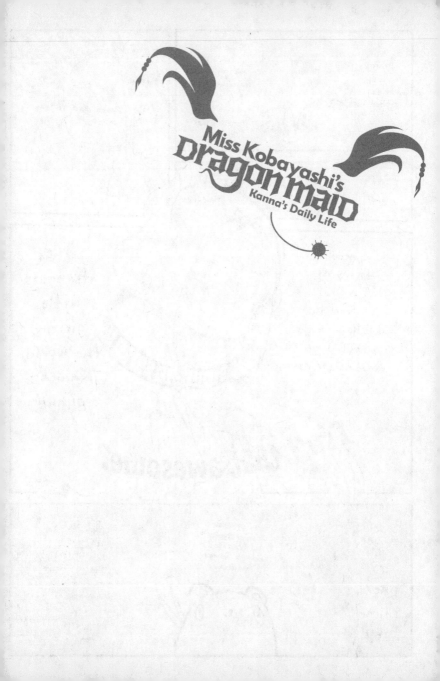

COOLKYOUSINNJYA

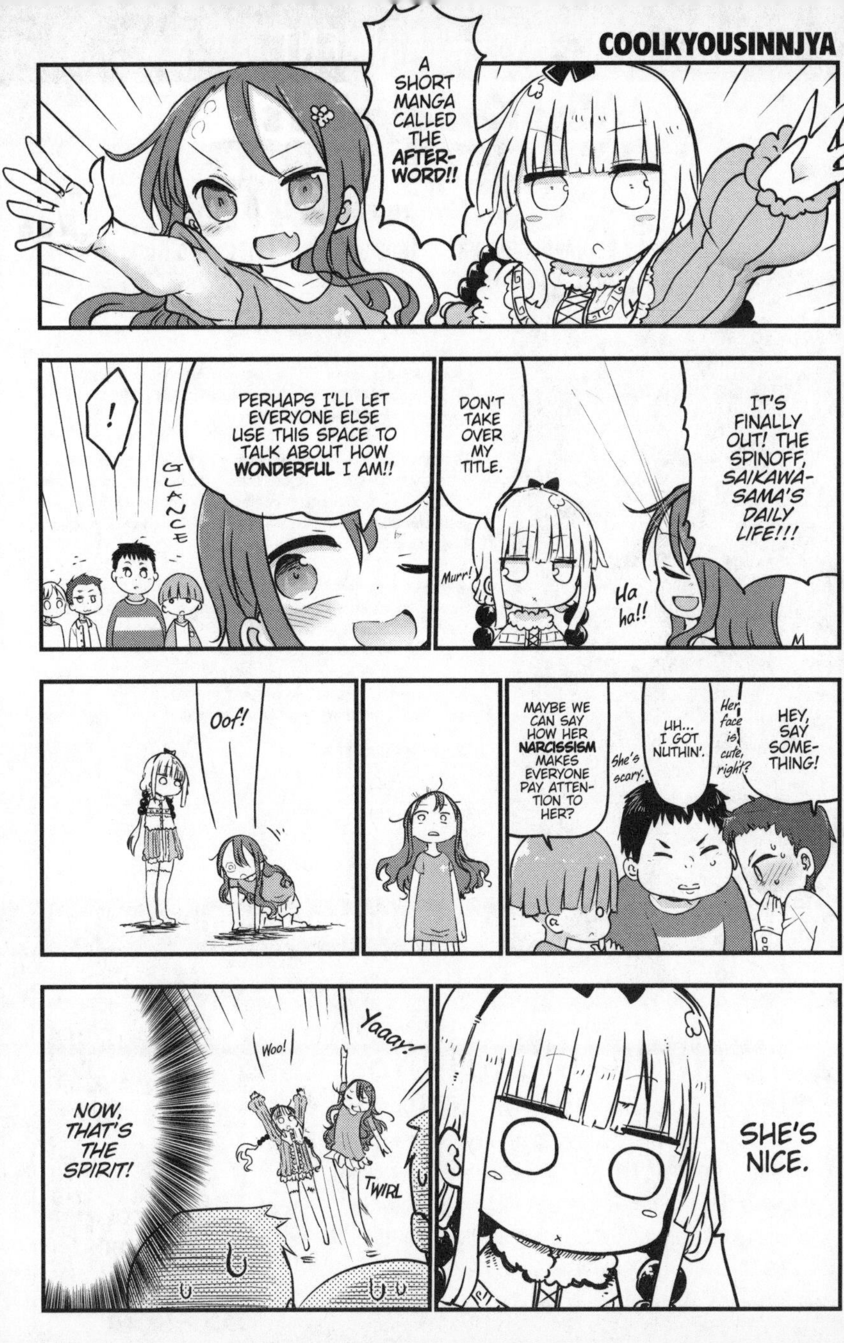
A SHORT MANGA CALLED THE AFTERWORD!!
IT'S FINALLY OUT! THE SPINOFF, SAIKAWA-SAMA'S DAILY LIFE!!!
Ha ha!!
DON'T TAKE OVER MY TITLE.
Murr!
PERHAPS I'LL LET EVERYONE ELSE USE THIS SPACE TO TALK ABOUT HOW WONDERFUL I AM!!
GLANCE
!
HEY, SAY SOMETHING!
Her face is cute, right?
UH... I GOT NUTHIN'.
She's scary.
MAYBE WE CAN SAY HOW HER NARCISSISM MAKES EVERYONE PAY ATTENTION TO HER?
Oof!
SHE'S NICE.
Yaaay!
Woo!
NOW, THAT'S THE SPIRIT!
TWIRL

SEVEN SEAS ENTERTAINM

Miss Kobaya
Dragon maid
Kanna's Daily Life VOL. 1

original story by **coolkyousinnjya**   story and art by **Mitsuhiro Kimura**

TRANSLATION
Jenny McKeon

ADAPTATION
Shanti Whitesides

LETTERING
Jennifer Skarupa

LOGO DESIGN
KC Fabellon

COVER DESIGN
Nicky Lim

PROOFREADING
Julia Kinsman

ASSISTANT EDITOR
Jenn Grunigen

PRODUCTION ASSISTANT
CK Russell

PRODUCTION MANAGER
Lissa Pattillo

EDITOR-IN-CHIEF
Adam Arnold

PUBLISHER
Jason DeAngelis

MISS KOBAYASHI'S DRAGON MAID: KANNA'S DAILY LIFE VOL. 1
© coolkyousinnjya, Mitsuhiro Kimura 2016
All rights reserved.
First published in Japan in 2017 by Futabasha Publishers Ltd., Tokyo.
English version published by Seven Seas Entertainment, LLC.
Under license from Futabasha Publishers Ltd.

Seven Seas books may be purchased in bulk for promotional, educational, or
business use. Please contact your local bookseller or the Macmillan Corporate
and Premium Sales Department at 1-800-221-7945, extension 5442, or by
e-mail at MacmillanSpecialMarkets@macmillan.com.

Seven Seas and the Seven Seas logo are trademarks of
Seven Seas Entertainment, LLC. All rights reserved.

ISBN: 978-1-626927-51-3

Printed in Canada

First Printing: January 2018

10 9 8 7 6 5 4 3 2

FOLLOW US ONLINE: *www.sevenseasentertainment.com*

READING DIRECTIONS

This book reads from *right to left*, Japanese style.
If this is your first time reading manga, you start
reading from the top right panel on each page and
take it from there. If you get lost, just follow the
numbered diagram here. It may seem backwards at
first, but you'll get the hang of it! Have fun!!

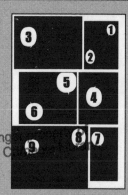